A History of Cooperstown

including

"THE CHRONICLES OF COOPERSTOWN"
By James Fenimore Cooper

"THE HISTORY OF COOPERSTOWN"
1839 - 1886
By Samuel M. Shaw

"THE HISTORY OF COOPERSTOWN"
1886 - 1929
By Walter R. Littell

——

1 9 2 9

PUBLISHERS' FOREWORD

This volume is presented to the public for the purpose of providing a complete and adequate historical record of the village of Cooperstown. It has been nearly half a century since any chronological record of the community life has been compiled and it is in the minds of the publishers that it will fill a present need as well as serving to preserve the record for coming generations and future historians.

To carry on the work so well begun by former historians no one better qualified than Mr. Littell could have been selected on account of his long period of observation of the passing events of the village in his connection with our local newspapers.

We have felt it more or less our duty to carry on this work because of the long time in which the Freeman's Journal has reflected the affairs of the village, now 121 years; and because the previous edition of the History was compiled by Samuel M. Shaw, its editor for fifty years.

It has been our aim to produce the volume in attractive and readable form. To add to its value we have caused an exhaustive index of the whole work to be inserted which will, we hope, be found of great service to many.

THE FREEMAN'S JOURNAL COMPANY
Rowan D. Spraker
Frank C. Carpenter

THE CHRONICLES OF COOPERSTOWN

By James Fenimore Cooper.

INTRODUCTION.

It is always desirable to possess authentic annals. The peculiar nature of American history, which commences in an enlightened age, renders that which is so desirable, in our case, practicable, and, with a view that posterity may know the leading facts connected with the origin and settlement of the village of Cooperstown, and that even the present generation may be set right in some important particulars concerning which erroneous notions now prevail, as well as possess a convenient book of reference, the following little work has been written.

This book has been compiled with care, by consulting authentic public records, private documents, more especially those in possession of the Cooper family, and living witnesses, whose memories and representations might be confided in. It is hoped no error has been admitted into its pages, and it is believed no essential mistake can be pointed out. Where the compilers have not found good reasons to credit their evidence, they have proceeded with caution, and made their statements with due reserve.

A work of this character can not have a very extensive interest, but it is thought it will have some with a county in which its subject composes the seat of justice; and by those whose fathers were active in converting the wilderness around about us, into its present picture of comfort and civilization, no records of this nature can be regarded with indifference.

The love of particular places, such as the spots in which we were born, or have passed our lives, contributes to sustain all the affections, and to render us better citizens and better men. This love is strengthened and increased by familiarity with events, and as time throws its interest around the past, reverence and recollections add their influence to that of the natural ties. With a view to aid these sentiments, also, have our little labors been conducted. If those who come after the compilers of the Chronicles of Cooperstown, should do as much in their generation, they who inhabit the place a century hence, will, beyond question, be ready to acknowledge that in one essential duty they were not forgotten by their predecessors.

In the early annals of this place there was a disposition, as in all new countries, to exaggerate its growth and various printed notices exist, by which its origin is stated to be several years too recent. These errors, as well as several connected with deaths, &c., that exist even in the church registers, and other official documents, have been carefully corrected in this book. In this respect, it is thought no more authentic accounts of the several subjects can be found.

CHAPTER I.

The site of the present village of Cooperstown, is said to have been a favorite place of resort with the adjacent savage tribes, from a remote period. The tradition which has handed down this circumstance, is rendered probable by the known abundance of the fish and game in its vicinity. The word *otsego,* is thought to be a compound which conveys the idea of a spot at which meetings of the Indians were held. There is a small rock near the outlet of the lake, called the Otsego rock, at which precise point the savages, according to an early tradition of the country, were accustomed to rendezvous.

In confirmation of these traditions, arrow heads, stone hatchets and other memorials of Indian usages, were found in great abundance by the first settlers, in the vicinity of the village.

It is probable that the place was more or less frequented by Indian traders, for a century previously to the commencement of the regular settlement of the township; but the earliest authentic account that exists of any attempt, by any civilized man, to establish himself at this point, refers to a much more recent period. On the 22d day of April, 1761, letters patent were granted to John Christopher Hartwick and others, for a considerable tract of land in this vicinity; and Mr. Hartwick, being under the impression that his grants extended to the shore of the lake, caused a clearing to be commenced not far from its outlet. Becoming satisfied that he had passed the boundaries of his estate, this gentleman soon relinquished his possession, and altogether abandoned the spot. This abortive attempt at settlement, took place about ten years before the commencement of the American war.

It appears by the documents in possession of the Cooper family, that Col. George Croghan, who was connected with the Indian department under the crown, obtained a conveyance from the Indians of 100,000 acres of land, lying north and adjacent to the before mentioned grant to Mr. Hartwick, and on the west side of the Susquehanna river, and of the Otsego lake, as early as the year 1768. On the 13th of December of the same year, Col. Croghan gave a mortgage under the Indian deed, to William Franklin, Esq., governor of the colony of New Jersey, to secure the payment of £3000; which money, as appears by the same documents, was obtained by Governor Franklin of certain persons in New Jersey, in the behalf of Col. Croghan, with a view to enable the latter to procure the regular title to the same lands, from the crown. This object was not effected until the 30th of November, 1769, when letters patent were issued by the colonial government, granting the same tract to George Croghan and ninety-nine other persons; there existing an order to prevent grants of more than a thousand acres at a time to single individuals.

On the 2d day of December, 1769, the ninety-nine other persons named as grantees in the patent, conveyed in three separate instruments their rights to George Croghan, in fee simple. These three conveyances, with the patent, still exist among the Cooper papers, and are unquestionably the first legal instruments conveying real estate in the township of Otsego.

On the 10th day of March, 1770, George Croghan gave a mortgage on that portion of the Otsego patent, as the aforesaid grant was then called, which has since been called Cooper's patent, for the further security of the payment of the said sum of £3000; both of which mortgages, with the accompanying bond, were regularly assigned to the persons already mentioned, as security for their advances. On the 23d day of March, 1773, judgment was obtained against George Croghan, in the supreme court of the colony of New York, upon the aforesaid bond.

All the securities above mentioned, became vested in William Cooper and Andrew Craig of the city of Burlington, in the state of New Jersey, by various deeds of assignment, now in possession of the descendants of the former, as early as May, 1785.

Mr. Cooper first visited lake Otsego in the autumn of 1785. He was accompanied by a party of surveyors, his object being to ascertain the precise boundaries of the land covered by his mortgage and judgment.

This party arrived by the way of Cherry Valley and Middlefield, and first obtained a view of the lake from the mountain which has since been called the Vision, in consequence of the beauty of the view it then afforded. Judge Cooper has been often heard to say, that on that occasion he was compelled to climb a sapling, in order to obtain this view, and while in the tree, he saw a deer descend to the lake and drink of its waters, near the Otsego rock. In January, 1786, Mr. Cooper took possession of the property that has since been known as Cooper's patent, under a deed given by the Sheriff of Montgomery county.

It ought to be mentioned, that in 1783, Washington, then on a journey of observation, with a view to explore the facilities for an inland communication by water, visited the foot of lake Otsego. We give the letter in which he speaks of this journey, entire, in the hope that the opinions of this great man may draw public attention more closely to the subject of improving our natural advantages:

PRINCETON, October 12, 1783.

MY DEAR CHEVALIER—I have not had the honor of a letter from you since the 4th of March last; but I will ascribe my disappointment to any cause sooner than to a decay of your friendship.

Having the appearances, and indeed the enjoyment of peace, without the final declaration of it, I, who am only waiting for the ceremonials, or till the British forces shall have taken their leave of New York, am held in an awkward and disagreeable situation, being anxiously desirous to quit the walks of public life, and under my own vine and my own fig-tree, to seek those enjoyments and that relaxation, which a mind that has been constantly upon the stretch for more than eight years, stands so much in want of.

I have fixed this epoch to the arrival of the definitive treaty, or to the evacuation of my country, by our newly acquired friends; in the meanwhile, at the request of Congress, I spend my time with them at this place, where they came in consequence of the riots at Philadelphia, of which, doubtless, you have been informed, for it is not a very recent transaction.

They have lately determined to fix the permanent residence of Congress, near the falls of Delaware; but where they will hold their sessions, till they can be properly established at that place, is yet undecided.

I have lately made a tour through the lakes George and Champlain as far as Crown point—then returning to Schenectady, I proceeded up the Mohawk river to Fort Schuyler (formerly Fort Stanwix), crossed over Wood creek, which empties into the Oneida Lake, and affords the water communication with lake Ontario; I then traversed the country to the head of the eastern branch of the Susquehanna, and viewed the lake Otsego, and the portage between that lake and the Mohawk river at Canajoharie.

Prompted by these actual observations, I could not help taking a more contemplative and extensive view of the vast inland navigation of these United States, from maps, and the information of others and could not but be struck with the immense diffusion and importance of it, and with the goodness of that Providence which has dealt her favors to us with so profuse a hand. Would to God we may have wisdom enough to make a good use of them. I shall not rest contented till I have explored the western part of this country, and traversed those lines (or a great part of them,) which have given bounds to a new empire; but when it may, if it ever should happen, I dare not say, as my first attention must be given to the deranged situation of my private concerns, which are not a little injured by almost nine years' absence, and total disregard of them.

With every wish for your health and happiness, and with the most sincere and affectionate regard.

I am, my dear Chevalier, your most obedient servant,

GEORGE WASHINGTON.

To the Marquis de Chastellux.

It should also be stated, that the present site of Cooperstown is connected with an event of some interest that occurred during the war of the revolution. An expedition having been commanded to proceed under the orders of Major General Sullivan, against the Indians who then dwelt in the vicinity of the Seneca lake, a brigade employed in the duty, under Brigadier General James Clinton (the father of the celebrated De Witt Clinton,) marched from Albany for that purpose. After ascending the Mohawk as far as Fort Plain, this brigade cut a road through the forest to the head of lake Otsego, whither it transported its boats. Traces of this road exist, and it is still known by the name of the Continental road. Embarking at the head of the lake, the troops descended to the outlet, where they encamped on the site of the present village. General Clinton's quarters are said to have been in a small building of hewn logs, which then stood in what are now the grounds of the Hall, and which it is thought was erected by Col. Croghan, as a place in which he might hold his negotiations with the Indians, as well as for the commencement of a settlement.

This building, which was about fifteen feet square and intended for a sort of block-house, was undoubtedly the first ever erected on this spot. It was subsequently used by some of the first settlers as a residence, and by Judge Cooper as a smoke house, and it was standing in 1797, if not a year later. It was then taken down and removed by Henry Pace Eaton, to his residence on the road to Pier's, where it was set up again as an out-house.

There were found the graves of two white men in the same grounds, which were believed to contain the bodies of deserters, who were shot during the time the troops were here encamped. These graves are supposed to be the first of any civilized man in the township of Otsego. All traces of them have now disappeared.

As soon as encamped, the troops of Gen. Clinton commenced the construction of a dam at the outlet, and when the water had risen to a sufficient height in the lake, the obstruction was removed, the current clearing the bed of the river of flood-wood. After a short delay for this purpose, the troops embarked and descended as far as the junction with the Tioga, where they were met by another brigade, commanded by General Sullivan in person.* On this occasion, the Susquehanna, below the dam, was said to be so much reduced that a man could jump across it.

Traces of the dam are still to be seen, and for many years they were very obvious.† At a later day, in digging the cellar of the house first occupied by Judge Cooper, a large iron swivel was discovered, which was said to have been buried by the troops, who found it useless for their service. This swivel was the only piece of artillery used for the purpose of salutes and merry-makings in the vicinity of Cooperstown, for ten or twelve years after the settlement of the place. It is well and affectionately remembered by the name of the Cricket, and was bursted lately in the same good cause of rejoicing on the 4th of July. At the time of its final disaster (for it had met with many vicissitudes by field and flood, having actually once been thrown into the lake,) it is said there was no very perceptible difference in size, between its touch-hole and its muzzle.

In addition to the foregoing statement, we are enabled to make the following brief history of the title to this tract of land, believing it may have interest with those who hold real estate within its limits. In this account, we include some matter foreign to the direct title, as explanatory of the whole.

On the 30th November, 1769, letters patent were issued, granting

---

*In the Gazetteer of New York, it is said: "The Indians upon the banks, witnessing the extraordinary rise of the river at midsummer, without any apparent cause, were struck with superstitious dread, and in the very outset were disheartened at the apparent interposition of the Great Spirit in favor of their foes."

†The last of the logs of that dam were removed on the 26th of October 1825, while the entire State of New York was more jubilant, perhaps, than ever before or since, and cannon, placed a few miles apart, from Buffalo to Albany, and thence to Sandy Hook, were proclaiming that Gov. Clinton had entered the first canal boat at Buffalo, and was on his way to New York. After the removal, the processsion were marched into the village, and were there addressed by Samuel Starkweather, Esq., during all of which proceedings a nine pounder upon the top of Mount Vision, at regular intervals, told the hills and valleys around that Cooperstown was rejoicing.

one hundred thousand acres of land to George Croghan and ninety-nine other persons as has been already stated.

December 2d, 1769, the ninety-nine other patentees conveyed, in three separate instruments, to George Croghan in fee.

On the 10th March, 1770, George Croghan mortgaged 40,000 acres of the above grant to William Franklin, as further security for the money borrowed to pay the fees, or the debt due the persons who were called the Burlington company. This mortgage included the present site of the village.

On the 12th March, 1770, George Croghan mortgaged 20,000 acres, being half of the above mentioned 40,000 acres, to Thomas Wharton, to secure another debt of £2,000.

On the 26th October, 1770, John Morton obtained a judgment of a large amount against George Croghan.

On the 22d March, 1773, judgment was obtained against George Croghan, for the debt due on his bond to William Franklin.

On the — April, 1775, George Croghan, William Franklin, Thomas Wharton and John Morton entered into an agreement, in writing, that the 40,000 acres of land should be sold under the two judgments, and that the proceeds of the sale should go, firstly, to pay the judgment held by William Franklin; secondly, to pay the mortgage held by Thomas Wharton; and, thirdly, to pay the judgment held by John Morton; or as much of each, according to the priority of the debts and securities, as there should be assets. This agreement was never complied with, in consequence of the war of the revolution.

On the 20th December, 1775, William Franklin and his wife assigned the mortgage of George Croghan, on the 40,000 acres, and all the securities connected with it to five of the original lenders of the money, for their several shares of the debt, the remaining three accepting lands elsewhere for their claims; the amount of the shares of these five assignees being £1,500, New Jersey currency, with interest from the date of the bond.

On the 3d April, 1780, George Croghan conveyed in fee, 25,477 acres of the above mentioned 40,000, including the site of Cooperstown, to Joseph Wharton, subject to the two mortgages, for the consideration of £9,553, Pennsylvania currency; Mr. Wharton being induced to accept this land for a debt of that great amount, in consequence of Mr. Croghan's being unable to pay him in any other manner.

On the 26th June, 1780, George Croghan conveyed, in fee, the remainder of the same tract, to Joseph Wharton, for the consideration of £100, this being all the land in the Otsego patent that he had not conveyed in fee, previously to granting the two mortgages, and of course all that was subject to them.

By several deeds poll, made between the years 1776 and 1785, all the rights of the original lenders of the aforesaid sum, with the interest on it from 1768, in the several bonds, in the judgment of 1773, and in the oldest mortgage, were vested in William Cooper and Andrew Craig of Burlington, New Jersey.

On the 14th January, 1786, all the lands of George Croghan that were subject to the judgment of 1773, and which lay in the Otsego patent, being in amount as near as might be, 29,350 acres, were conveyed by Samuel Clyde, Sheriff of Montgomery county, to William Cooper and Andrew Craig, as judgment purchasers, under the judgment aforesaid, for the sum of £2,700, leaving a balance of £1,139.8s. unpaid, and which has never been satisfied since.

On the 8th December, 1786, Joseph Wharton, for the consideration of $2,000, conveyed, in fee, all his right to the land in question, to William Cooper and Andrew Craig, then in actual possession of the same as judgment purchasers and mortgagees.

On the 12th November, 1787, Augustine Prevost and Susannah Prevost, for the consideration of $1,250, released their right to the equity of the redemption of the mortgage on the whole 40,000 acres, to William Cooper and Andrew Craig; the said Susannah Prevost being the natural daughter and devisee of George Croghan.

On the 16th January, 1788, William Cooper paid for quit rents on the said land, the further sum of £631.3s.

On the 26th October, 1799, William Cooper paid $7.35 for commutation of quit rents, on the village plot, containing then 112 acres of land.

The patent of 1769, signed Clarke; the deeds from the ninety-nine other patentees to George Croghan; the bond of Croghan to Franklin; that of Franklin to the Burlington company; the mortgage of Croghan to Franklin, with the assignment by latter to the unpaid members of the company; all the mesne conveyances of the same to William Cooper and Andrew Craig; the deeds of Croghan to Joseph Wharton, and the deed of Wharton to William Cooper and Andrew Craig; the release of Augustine and Susannah Prevost, and the certificates of payments of quit rents, together with several conveyances from Andrew Craig to William Cooper, exist still, among the papers of the Cooper family.

The deed of the Sheriff of Montgomery county to William Cooper and Andrew Craig has been lost; supposed never to have been returned from the county Clerk's office; but it is recorded at Johnstown, and an exemplified copy exists among the other papers.

There exists, among the same papers, a copy of a bill in chancery, of the date of 1786, at the complaint of William Cooper and Andrew Craig, setting forth that the parties to the agreement of 1775, refused to release to them according to the understood terms of that agreement, and that the said agreement was withheld from them to their injury, and praying relief in the premises. It is supposed that this suit was arranged by compromise, as the original agreement is now among the same papers.

A copy of the assignment of the mortgage on the entire tract, under the Indian grant, also, is to be found among the same papers.

As it may be a matter of curious history hereafter, we subjoin an account of what the 29,350 acres actually cost the proprietor under whom the country was settled:

Amount of judgment, Jan. 14, 1786, ...£3,839.08
Quit rent, Jan. 16, 1788, ... 631.03
Consideration money paid Joseph Wharton, ... 800.00
   do.   do.   Augustine and Susannah Prevost, ... 500.00

           £5,770.11
    or $14,426.37½

This sum, with the Sheriff's fees and other incidental expenses, would make the actual cost of the property about 50 cents the acre. Col. Croghan and his family received for the same, as follows:

Debt to Franklin £3,839.08
Debt to Joseph Wharton, ... 9,553.00
Paid his daughter, ... 500.00

Pennsylvania currency £13,892.08

This is considerably more than $35,000. If the mortgage to Thomas Wharton be included, and it is believed the debt is unpaid to this day, will amount to more than $40,000, without interest, which is probably five times as much as the property was worth on the day of George Croghan's death.

CHAPTER II.

FROM 1780 TO 1799.

In addition to the abortive attempt at a settlement by Mr. Hartwick, on the present site of the village, between the year 1761 and 1770, Col. Croghan, with his family, resided for a short time on this spot. Appended to one of the deeds of George Croghan to Joseph Wharton, is a map purporting to show the improvements of the latter, at the foot of lake Otsego, but it is supposed that this map was made for effect, as all accounts agree in stating that in 1785, the improvements were very insignificant, consisting of the remains of a few log fences, a clearing away of underbrush, with felled and girdled trees. The block-house mentioned was the only building standing, and the place had been abandoned for years.

Mr. Cooper commenced the settlement of his tract in the winter of 1786, many families coming in before the snow had melted. Deeds were given to Israel Guild and several others, who established themselves on spots that are now within the limits of the village, in the summer of that year. This was as farmers, however, rather than as villagers, it being the intention of Mr. Cooper, the proprietor who had the entire control of the property, and who so soon purchased the right of his associate that the connection of the latter with the place never was of any moment, to lay out the village plot in a line extending north and south, instead of in the direction it has actually taken.

In June, 1786, John Miller, now the oldest living inhabitant of the village, as regards residence, arrived at this place, accompanied by his father. They reached the banks of the river at the outlet, where Mr. Miller felled a large pine across the stream to answer the purposes of a bridge. The stump of this tree is still to be seen, within the grounds of Lakelands, and it is marked, in white paint, with the words Bridge tree. At that time most of the dam of Clinton was still remaining.

When Mr. Miller arrived, a widow of the name of Johnson, had the only resident family in the place. She lived in a log house, not far from the present stone dwelling of Mr. Pomeroy, though she was then building a frame house near the same spot. This frame building was sold by Mrs. Johnson to William Ellison, the well known surveyor, who removed it the same summer, to a position near the outlet, and on what are now the grounds of Edgewater. This was unquestionably the first framed and otherwise regularly constructed house in the village of Cooperstown, as the block-house was the first in logs. It was of respectable size, and of two stories, being intended for a tavern, to which purpose it was applied as soon as habitable. William Abbott arrived in the summer of 1786, and established himself on the farm that still bears his name, about half a mile south of the village. Other persons came and went, and many settlers remained permanently in different parts of the patent. Mr. Cooper was here, once or twice, in the course of the season, but he did not cause any building to be constructed. Mr. Miller remained, himself, but a short time. Many persons were here during the summer of 1786, among others James White, but it is believed none passed the winter within the village plot, but the families of William Ellison, Israel Guild and Mrs. Johnson. The latter soon after removed leaving no descendants in the place. Mr. Guild took possession of the block-house.

In the spring of 1787, more emigrants appeared. Early in the season Mr. Cooper arrived, accompanied by his wife, who came however as a mere traveler. They reached the head of the lake in a chaise, and descended to the foot in a canoe. Mrs. Cooper was so much alarmed with this passage that she disliked returning in a boat, and the chaise was brought to the place, in two canoes. In order that it might reach the eastern bank, and to serve the public generally, a bridge was built at the outlet, which was the first real bridge across the Susquehanna at this spot. This bridge was composed of log abutments, sleepers, and logs laid across the latter. A road had been cut through the forest, following the direction of the lake, and coming out along the bank of Lakelands, at this bridge. It was, however, so rude and difficult to pass, that when the chaise left the village, men accompanied it with ropes, to prevent it from upsetting.

During the summer of 1787, many more emigrants arrived, principally from Connecticut, and most of the land on the patent was taken up. Until this season negotiations were going on among the different creditors of Col. Croghan to redeem this property by paying the claims of Messrs. Cooper and Craig, and taking assignments of the bonds and mortgages; those gentlemen, though legally in possession of the estate, preferring to receive the amount of their debt to keeping the securities. Being persuaded, however, that the land was scarcely worth the money, the creditors, by this time, had abandoned the intention, and Mr. Cooper, towards the close of 1787, began seriously to think of establishing himself permanently in this part of the country. With this view he commenced extending his possessions in the adjacent patents, and either by arrangements with the different great landholders, or by actual purchases, he soon had the settlement of a large part of the present county more or less subject to his control. The effects were very visible, for there is scarcely an instance of a more rapid growth of a district, in any other part of a country so remarkable for advancement of this nature. When it is remembered that this extraordinary success was obtained in a region so difficult of access, one that is not easily tilled, and which has a severe climate, the energy and abilities that were employed, may be properly appreciated. The proprietor, however, was much favored by the salubrity of the air, the diseases usual to new countries having been scarcely known in this mountainous region.

During the summer of 1787, several small log tenements were constructed on the site of the village, and arrangements were made by Mr. Cooper to erect a building for his own use, the succeeding season. Still there was no great accession to the permanent population, which at this time did not amount to twenty souls. The circumstance that neither Mr. Ellison nor Mr. Guild had children, and that Mr. Miller was not yet married, contributed to lessen the number of the inhabitants.

Early in 1788, the house of Mr. Cooper was erected, it being the second regular dwelling in the place. This house stood on Second street, facing Fair street, commanding a full view of the lake, and of course immediately in front of the present Hall. It was of two stories, with two wings, and a back building was added in 1791. The siding was of wide boards, beaded, but not planed. A very good representation of this house is to be seen on the original map of this village, where it is marked Manor House. It was removed a short distance down the street in 1799, and was destroyed by fire in 1812.

In this year Mr. Cooper seems seriously to have set about the formation of a village, a plot being regularly laid out for that purpose. Agreeably to this plan, six streets were laid out in an east and west direction, and three that crossed them at right angles, in a north and south. The street along the margin of the lake was called Front street, and the others parallel to it were numbered from Second up to Sixth street. That next to the river was called Water street, and that at the opposite side of the plot, West street. The street between them, being divided into two parts by the grounds of Mr. Cooper, had two names, viz: Fair street and Main street. All these names are preserved, though Fifth street has never been opened, and one-half of Fourth street, and about one-third of Main street, are also enclosed.

The map, which is well made on parchment, like all similar documents of that period, has its base line on the west side of Water street, with its direction marked "North, 20° East." The map is dated "*9th Month 26th*, 1788," or "September 26th, 1788," and was made by William Ellison. It is now among the Cooper papers.

By a certificate of the redemption of the quit rents on "the town plat of Cooperstown," dated October 26, 1799, among the same papers, it would appear that the plat of the village as designed on this map, contains one hundred and twelve acres.

In the autumn of this year, Israel Guild erected a small frame building of a story and a half, on what is now Second street, about one hundred feet from the intersection with West street. Mr. Guild had purchased the farm that here adjoined the village plat; all the land west of that point being without the proprietor's plan for the town. This house was originally in a lot; it is still standing, being used as a bakery and a hatter's shop, and it unquestionably is now the oldest house in the place, the Manor House having been destroyed by fire, as mentioned, and that of Mr. Ellison having been pulled down when the late Mr. Isaac Cooper built at Edgewater, or in 1812. Mr. Guild, however, continued to live in the block-house until 1789. John Howard, tanner, came this year and prepared to commence his business, at the spot long known as the Tannery.

Although the settlement of Cooper's patent commenced early in 1786, the regular commencement of the village dates properly from 1788, for while the idea of a town is older, it was not systematically planned until this summer. It follows that this year (1838) completes the first half century of the existence of the place. The name of Cooperstown, it is true, appears in one or two papers as early even as 1786; but the place was indiscriminately known by this appellation, and that of the Foot of the Lake, until the year 1791, when it became the county town.

In 1789, Mr. Cooper finished his house and set up a frontier establishment. His eldest son, the late Richard Fenimore Cooper, Mr.
Charles Francis of Philadelphia, Mr. Richard R. Smith of New Jersey,
and several other gentlemen, were his occasional associates. The late
Hendrik Frey of Canajoharie, was a frequent visitor, and the traditions
of the festivities of the Manor House, during that and the succeeding
years, are still agreeable to the lovers of good cheer.

The lake abounded with the most delicious fish, and Shipman, the
Leatherstocking of the region, could at almost any time, furnish the
table with a saddle of venison. Among the laughable incidents that
accompanied the free manner of the living, so peculiar to a border life,
the following stories seem to be well authenticated.

In the course of the winter of 1789-90, during one of the periodical
visits of Col. Frey, a large lumber sleigh was fitted out, with four
horses, and the whole party sallied upon the lake for a morning drive.
An ex-officer of the French army, a Monsieur Ebbal, resided by himself
on the western bank of the lake. Perceiving the sleigh and four approaching his house, this gentleman, with the courtesy of his nation,
went forth upon the ice to greet the party, of whose character he was
not ignorant, by the style in which it appeared. Mr. Cooper invited his
French friend to join him, promising him plenty of game, with copious
libations of Madeira, by way of inducement. Though a good table
companion in general, no persuasion could prevail on the Frenchman to
accept the offer that day, until provoked by his obstinacy, the party laid
violent hands on him and brought him to the village by force. Monsieur
Ebbal took his captivity in good part, and was soon as buoyant and gay
as any of his companions. He habitually wore a long skirted surtout,
which at that time was almost a mark of a Frenchman, and this surtout
he pertinaciously refused to lay aside, even when he took his seat at
table. On the contrary he kept it buttoned to the very throat, as it
might be in defiance. The Christmas joke, a plentiful board, and heavy
potations, however, threw the guest off his guard. Warmed with the
wine and the blazing fire, he incautiously unbuttoned; when his delighted
companions discovered that the accidents of a frontier, the establishment
of a bachelor who kept no servant, and certain irregularities in washing
days, that were attendant on both circumstances, coupled with his
empressement to salute his friends had induced the gallant Frenchman
to come abroad without a shirt. He was uncased on the spot, amid the
roars of the *convives,* and incontinently put into linen. "Cooper was so
polite," added the mirth-loving Hendrik Frey, when he repeated this
story for the hundredth time, "that he supplied a shirt with ruffles at the
wristbands, which made Ebbal very happy for the rest of the night.
Mein Gott, how his hands did go, after he got the ruffles!"

These wags told Monsieur Ebbal, that if chased by a bear, the most
certain mode of escape, was to throw away his hat, or his coat, to induce
the animal to stop and smell at it, and then to profit by the occasion, and
climb a sapling that was too small to enable his enemy to fasten its claws
in it, in the way it is known to ascend a tree. The advice was well
enough, but the advised having actually an occasion to follow it the
succeeding autumn, scrambled up a sapling first, and began to throw

away his clothes afterwards. The bear, a she one with cubs, tore to pieces garment after garment, without quitting the spot, keeping poor Ebbal treed, throughout a cool autumnal night, almost as naked as he was when uncased at the celebrated Christmas banquet. It appears that the real name of this person was *L'Abbe de Raffcourt*.

During the winter of 1789-90, Mr. Cooper had a stock of goods brought into the village, Mr. R. R. Smith doing the duty of the merchant. This was the first store established in the place, and of great service to the settlers. Up to this period, the latter had been compelled to go to Canajoharie to make their purchases. Even later, they were obliged to go that distance to find a mill, not unfrequently carrying their grists on their shoulders. The distance, it will be remembered, is twenty-five miles.

October the 10th, 1790, Mr. Cooper first brought his family to Cooperstown, giving up his residence in New Jersey entirely. From this time, dates the steady and progressive growth of the village. There exists a document to show that in 1790, Cooperstown contained seven framed houses, three framed barns, and thirty-five inhabitants. It is supposed that this enumeration of the inhabitants was made previously to the arrival of the family of Mr. Cooper, as that family alone, with its inmates and domestics amounted to about fifteen persons. It is also supposed, that the houses, three or four in number, that stood without the old village plat, like that of Mr. Guild, the Tannery, &c., were not included. The house standing at the southeast corner of Second and Water streets, and which for the last forty years has belonged to the Ernst family, was erected this summer by Mr. Benjamin Griffin. It is now the second oldest house in the village.

February 16th, 1791, the county of Otsego was formed and Cooperstown was designated as the county town, Mr. Cooper being appointed the first Judge of the county court. A Court House was built at the southeast corner of West and Second streets. It was thirty feet square; the lower story, which contained four rooms, being used as a jail, and the whole of the upper story, as a court room. The lower story was built of squared logs, and the upper of framed work. The entrance to the court room was on the north front, two flights of steps on the exterior of the building, meeting at a platform before a door that opened into the air.

The jury rooms were in a tavern occupied by the jailer, that stood on the same lot, and which was erected the same year. The first sheriff was Richard R. Smith, who being altogether superior to entering into the lower duties of the office, appointed —— Stephens, jailer.

During this summer, the Red Lion tavern, which projected half way across Second street, was erected, as was also the house at the corner diagonally opposite, now owned by Judge Russell. The two houses that stand third and fourth from the corner of West street, on the south side of Second street, were also erected this year, as were several others. The first lawyer who came to reside in the village, was Mr. Abraham Ten Broeck of New Jersey, and the second was Mr. Jacob G. Fonda of Schenectady; both these gentlemen came in 1791.

Mr. Joseph Strong, a native of ·Orange county, came a. year or two later, and also Mr. Moss Kent, a brother of the celebrated Chancellor Kent. These four gentlemen were the first of their profession in Cooperstown. They all removed within the first twelve. years of their residence, though descendants of Mr. Strong, in the second and third generation, are still inhabitants of the place. Several stores were also set up in 1791, of which the principal was owned by Mr. Peter Ten Broeck.

The first physician also appeared in the spring of this year; his name being Powers. Doctor Fuller, so long and so favorably known, for a professional career that lasted forty-six years in the same place, arrived in June. In the course of the year, Dr. Powers was accused of mixing tartar emetic with the beverage of a ball given at the Red Lion. He was tried, convicted, put in the stocks and banished for the offence; this sentence, as a matter of course, terminated his career in this spot. A Dr. Farnsworth came a year or two later, and Dr. Gott about the same time; but for many years, nearly all the practice of the country was in the hands of Dr. Fuller, who is said to have been the medical attendant of more than two thousand births.

There exists no positive information of the increase of the village during the year 1791, but it was relatively great, for the times. At the end of the year, Cooperstown certainly contained twenty houses and stores, and probably a hundred inhabitants. As most of the emi· grants were young, their families were necessarily small, which accounts for the feeble number of the population. From this period, or for the ·last forty-six years, the place has been more gradual in its growth, the increase being steady and regular, and not subject to the sudden changes of more speculative neighborhoods.

The first child born actually in the village was Nathan Howard, a son of John Howard; and the first death was that of a son of Mr. Joseph Griffin, which took place October 11th, 1792. On the occasion of this death, a piece of ground was selected as a place of interment, near the junction of Water and Third streets, or where Christ Church now stands.

The first child born on the patent was a son of Bill Jarvis of Fly Creek. He was born in 1787, and was named after the proprietor, receiving fifty acres of land as a memorial of the circumstance.

William Abbott had a son born previously to the birth of Nathan Howard, but he did not reside immediately in the village, although forming a part of the village community. The boy was called Reuben, from the circumstance of his being the first born.

The first school was kept by Joshua Dewey, but it was not commenced until a year or two later.

CHAPTER III

FROM 1792 TO 1797

The village at the commencement of the year 1792, stood principally on Second street, with a house or two on Water street, one or two more on Front street, and a few on West street. The shops and taverns were collected in the vicinity of the four principal corners, where were also the Court House and Jail. It is evident to the geologist that water has once flowed over the site of the place, and originally many deep holes or hollows existed, which had the appearance of having been formed by powerful eddies or currents. Most of these holes have disappeared, by leveling and filling up, but a few are still to be seen, especially in the grounds of the Hall where they have been preserved as helping the ornamental walks, &c., &c.

Some of these inequalities, of course, existed in the streets, and many persons still remember the place when there were considerable ascents and descents in them. Opposite to the present bank there was, as recently as the commencement of this century, a little rise in the road, and in West street, at the point near that where the present inclination commences, was a short, sharp pitch down which vehicles had to descend with great care. Judge Cooper's barns, stables, &c., down to the year of 1798 certainly, if not to a later day, were in the rear of the stone store that now belongs to Mr. J. R. Worthington, and they stood many feet below the level of the streets. Nor did the stumps disappear altogether from even Second street, which is the principal avenue of the village, until the close of the century. The road to Fly Creek diverged from the Hartwick road near Howard's farm, and the narrow part of Second street continued enclosed as part of the farm of Mr. Guild, until about the year 1795.

Mr. James Averell was an early settler on the patent, having occupied the farm since known as the Howard farm, in 1787, but he exchanged with Mr. Howard this farm against the Tannery, and removed into the village, or rather into what is now the village, in the year 1792. Here, by his enterprise and industry, he raised the works in question into some of the most important of the sort that then existed in the newer part of the State. Mr. Averell soon became conspicuous for his habits of business, and subsequently was much connected with the increase of Cooperstown and its vicinity, in wealth and industry.

Between the years 1792 and 1797, Messrs. Wade, Stevens, Rensselaer Williams, Richard Williams, Norman Landon, Peter Ten Broeck and Le Quoy arrived and established themselves as merchants; Mr. R. R. Smith relinquishing business and going to Philadelphia, where he was soon a partner in an extensive wholesale house.

Mr. Wade was an Irishman by birth, and had served as a captain in the British army. He remained but a year or two, when he returned to New York. The present Major Wade of the United States army is his son. Mr. Stevens returned to Philadelphia also, in a few years; but the Messrs. Williams continued their connection with the place, down to the periods of their deaths: their collateral descendants and heirs still existing in Cooperstown. The Messrs. Ten Broeck returned to New Jersey, at the end of a few years. Mr. Landon died, and is interred in the old burying ground.

Mr. Le Quoy excited a good deal of interest during his stay in the place, as he was a man altogether superior to his occupation, which was little more than that of a country grocer; an interest that was much increased by the following circumstance.

Among the early settlers in Otsego county, was Mr. Lewis de Villers, a French gentleman of respectable extraction and good manners. Mr. de Villers was in Cooperstown about the year 1793, at a moment when a countryman, a Mr. Renouard, who afterwards established himself in the county, had recently reached the place. Mr. Renouard was a seaman and had the habit of using tobacco. Enquiring of Mr. de Villers where some of his favorite article might be purchased, Mr. de Villers directed him to the shop of Mr. Le Quoy, telling him he would help a countryman by making his purchase of that person. In a few minutes Mr. Renouard returned from the shop, much agitated and very pale. Mr. de Villers inquired if he were unwell. "In the name of God, Mr. de Villers who is the man who sold me this tobacco?" demanded Mr. Renouard. "Mr. Le Quoy, a countryman of ours." "Yes, Mr. Le Quoy de Mersereau." "I know nothing about the *de Mersereau*, he calls himself Mr. Le Quoy. Do you know anything of him?" "When I went to Martinique to be port captain of St. Pierre" answered Mr. Renouard, "this man was the civil governor of the island, and refused to confirm my appointment."

Subsequent inquiry confirmed this story, Mr. Le Quoy explaining that the influence of a lady had stood in the way of Mr. Renouard's preferment.

The history of Mr. Le Quoy has since been ascertained to be as follows; When governor of Martinique he had it in his power to do a friendly office to Mr. John Murray of New York, by liberating one of his ships, Mr. Murray being at the head of the old and highly respectable commercial house of John Murray & Sons, then one of the principal firms of the country. This act brought about an exchange of civilities between Mr. Murray and Mr. Le Quoy, which continued for a few years. When the French revolution drove Mr. Le Quoy from the island, he repaired to New York, and sought his friend Mr. Murray to whom he stated that he had a small sum of money, which he wished to invest in a country store, until his fortunes might revive. Between Judge Cooper and Mr. Murray there existed an intimacy, and the latter referred Mr. Le Quoy to the former. Under the advice of Judge Cooper, Mr. Le Quoy established himself in Cooperstown, where he remained more than a year. At the end of that time he made his peace with the new French government, and quitting his retreat, he was employed for some months in superintending the accounts of the different French consulates in this country. It is said that he soon after

returned to Martinique in his old capacity, an ddied the first season
of yellow fever.   When Mr. Fenimore Cooper was in France, the
Comte d'Hauterive, who had been French consul general in America,
at the period of Mr. Le Quoy's residence, spoke of the latter gentleman, and in part, corroborated this history of him.   The following
letter appears to have been written soon after he left Cooperstown,
and at the moment he commenced his consular duties:

PHILADELPHIA, 10TH, Oct., 1794.

DEAR SIR—I have experienced too much of your friendship to believe you will not hear of my fate with some degree of concern.   I am
to go to Charleston in S. C., about some business which will keep me
most all of the winter.   I hope for a more permanent employment than
what I have at present; if not, I know where to find peace, good business, good friends.   I shall always consider you among the number.

I wish you and all your family health and happiness, and I remain,
dear sir, your most humble servant   F. Z. Le Quoy.
Mons. W. Cooper, in Cooperstown, Otsego county.

Later letters show that Mr. Le Quoy did not quit this country until
1796.

January 27th, 1795, Mr. James Barber, tailor, died of the small pox.
This was the first adult who died a natural death in the village.   He
lived in the large old building which stands north of the dwelling of
Mr. Lawrence McNamee, and which was erected the year before.   But,
Mr. Jabez Wight, cabinet maker, was drowned while bathing, near the
outlet, August 14th, 1794.   This was the second death in the place:
The same year a child of Mr. Averell's was drowned, but not in the
lake.   All these persons were interred in Christ church burying ground,
where their headstones are still to be seen.

During the first ten years of the existence of the village, the people
depended entirely on chance for the little religious instruction they
received.   The emigrants to the place, more particularly, those who
had any property, were singularly divided as to religious faith, the
Presbyterians, though the most numerous sect, being the poorest.
Missionaries occasionally penetrated to this spot, and now and then a
traveling Baptist, or a Methodist, preached, in a tavern, a school house,
or a barn.   The first regular clergyman, who had any engagement to
officiate in Cooperstown, was the Rev. Mr. Mosely, who was employed
for six months.   This was in the year of 1795.   He was a Presbyterian,
and went away at the expiration of his engagement.

In the way of schools, the village did a little better.   It has been
said that Joshua Dewey kept the first school.   He was soon succeeded
by Oliver Cory, who conducted the common school of the place, with
commendable assiduity and great credit to himself, for many years.
Nearly all the permanent inhabitants of the village, who are between
the ages of forty and fifty-five, received their elementary instruction
from this respectable teacher.   Mr. Cory did not neglect religious instruction altogether, but every Saturday was devoted to this object.

His care in this respect, as well as his lessons on deportment, were attended with the most beneficial results, and it is to be regretted that they have not been imitated in our own time. He kept his school originally in the Court House, and then in the first regular school house ever built in the place. This school house was a small wooden building that stood on the lot that is now occupied by the dwelling of Mr. Elihu Phinney. Subsequently Mr. Cory held his school in the Academy.

Notwithstanding the apparent neglect on the subject of religion, which, in all probability, is to be referred more to the division in sentiment mentioned, than to any other cause, the people of Cooperstown showed great public spirit on the subject of establishing an Academy, a plan for which was started as early as 1795. We subjoin the following copy of a subscription paper for that purpose, in proof of what we say, and which is still in existence, viz:

"We the subscribers do severally undertake to contribute the sums opposite to our respective names, towards an academy in Cooperstown, for the county of Otsego. April 5th, 1795.

Huntington & Ingals,	25.00	James Gardner,	10.00
William Cooper,	$ 725.00	Nathan Davison,	5.00
William Abbot,	40.00	Joseph Griffin,	42.50
Elisha Fullam,	7.50	John Howard,	30.00
Jonas Perry,	2.50	William Cook,	25.00
Lemuel Jewel,	2.50	Benjamin Griffin,	25.00
Thomas Fuller,	40.00	Jacob Morris,	62.50
Samuel Tubbs,	12.50	Benjamin Gilbert,	30.00
Uriah Luce,	10.00	Griffin Crafts,	30.00
James Averell,	50.00	Nathaniel Gott,	12.50
Francis Henry,	5.00	William Ellison,	12.50
Jabez Hubbell,	5.00	Stephen Ingals,	5.00
Norman Landon,	45.00	Abner Dunham,	6.25
Timothy Sabin,	3.75	E. Phinney,	40.00
Barnet Whipple,	5.00	Lewis De Villers,	15.00
Bill Jarvis,	2.50	Robert Riddle,	7.50
Moses Kent,	25.00	Aaron Noble,	7.50
Peter Lambert,	7.50	Matthew Bennet,	7.50
Joseph Holt,	10.00	Isaac Stacy,	10.00
John Miller,	7.50	Joseph N. Jones,	5.00
James White,	15.00	Levi Wentworth,	6.25

Total $1,441.25

The odd cents are from the subscriptions having been in the old currency. This document shows several interesting facts. There forty-two names, which makes an average subscription of more than $33 to each name; and it may be doubted if anything like such an average could now be obtained for any public object whatever. Of these forty-two names, twenty-three were then residents of the village, and considering the public spirit that prevailed, it is fair to suppose that this comprised at least two-thirds of the heads of families that were then to be found in the place. It will probably be safe to say that Cooperstown contained in 1795, about thirty-five families, and quite as many houses. As the heads of families were generally young, an average of five persons to each family would be sufficiently high;

this would give a whole number of one hundred and seventy-five souls. If to these we add twenty-five for single persons, we get a total of two hundred for the population, which could not be far from the truth.

The Academy was raised September 18th, 1795. It was one of those tasteless buildings that afflict all new countries, and contained two school rooms below, a passage and the stairs; while the upper story was in a single room. Nothing superior to a common English education was ever taught in this house, all attempts at classical instruction failing. This must be ascribed to the general want of means in the population, at the time; the few who gave their children classical educations, usually sending them abroad for that purpose.

The Academy, containing at that time the largest room in the place, was as much used for other purposes as for those of education. Religious meetings were generally held there, as well as other large assemblages of the people. The school exhibitions of Mr. Cory, in which Brutus and Cassius figured in hats of the cuts of 1776, blue coats faced with red, of no cut at all, and matross swords, are still the subject of mirth with those who remember the prodigies. The court on great occasions was sometimes held in this building, and even balls were occasionally given in it; in short, it was a jack of all work, rather than of the particular work for which it was intended.

Notwithstanding the failure as respects a classical school, the year was memorable for the establishment of another species of instruction, that probably was more useful to this particular community, at that early day. On the 28th of February, 1795, Mr. Elihu Phinney, a native of Connecticut, arrived in Cooperstown bringing with him the materials for printing a newspaper; and on the 3rd day of April of the same year, the first number of the *Otsego Herald, or Western Advertiser,* a weekly paper, made its appearance. This was the second journal published in the State, west of Albany. We see by its title that, in 1795, it was considered a western print, whereas at the present day, Cooperstown is probably a hundred leagues east of the central point around which journals are now to be found.

By means of this print we are enabled to make the following curious statistical statement, by which the reader will obtain an insight into the actual condition of the western part of this State at that time. In 1794, Judge Cooper was elected Representative in Congress, from a district composed of the counties of Montgomery, Herkimer, Tioga, Ontario, Onondaga and Otsego, as they then existed. His opponent was Mr. Winn of Montgomery, and the following is the result of the canvass:

	COOPER.	WINN.
Montgomery,	304	970
Herkimer,	746	144
Tioga,	89	88
Ontario,	30	2
Onondaga,	95	6
Otsego,	1271	216
Total,	2535	1426

Here we see that the county of Ontario, at that time comprising so much of the State, gave but 32 votes, while Otsego gave 1487. The fact shows the great rapidity with which the latter county had been settled.

A brewery was established in 1794, by two Englishmen, of the names of Mulcock and Morgan, but it was in advance of the country, and after a short experiment it failed.

July 9th, 1795, a man named Porteus was flogged at the whipping post, for stealing some pieces of ribbon. This was the first of two instances of the same punishment on the same spot. The whipping post and stocks stood nearly opposite the jail door, in West street, but on the west side of the street. Porteus was *banished,* as well as flogged, the former punishment being used in Cooperstown. It is to be regretted that it has fallen into disuse.

By an article in the Otsego Herald of October 30th, it would seem that the year 1795 added much to the size of the place, no less than thirty buildings having been constructed that season. Many of these, however, were shops, offices and stores. Among others were the Brewery and Academy, already mentioned. The former stood near the present bridge, and is described as having been 83 feet in length, 25 feet wide, and 19 feet posts. The Academy was 65½ feet long, 32 wide, and 25 feet posts. The summit of the belfry was 70 feet from the ground.

On the evening of the 20th November, 1795, a building attached to the pottery of Mr. Joshua Starr, a respectable inhabitant of the village, was destroyed by fire. This is believed to be the first accident of the sort that ever occurred in Cooperstown.

The mills that still exist on the Susquehanna, were erected by Mr. William Ellison, as early as 1792.

It appears that the Rev. Elisha Mosely preached the first thanksgiving sermon in Cooperstown, on the 26th November, 1795, in the Court House. By the latter circumstance it would seem that the Academy, which indeed was only raised on the 18th September, had not been completed. It is also stated in the Otsego Herald, that in this year the village paid in excise, and through the inns and stores, &c., and by the duty on carriages, thirty-six pounds. The first carriage that was ever used in the place, was a phaeton of Judge Cooper's. This was in 1792. In 1795, he set up a chariot, which by the aid of four horses, was enabled to perform a journey from Cooperstown to Cherry Valley, between breakfast and supper.

The first road to communicate with the lower country, was that mentioned already as running along the eastern margin of the lake. Its course did not differ essentially from that of the present turnpike. A rude road existed previously to the revolution, from Cherry Valley, as far as the Ingals farm in Middlefield, and this road was brought round the end of the Vision and into the village, about the year 1791. It followed the present margin of the forest on the side of the mountain, until it reached the spot where Woodside now stands, when it traversed the present grounds of Lakelands, diagonally, to the outlet.

This end of the road was three times altered; first, by bringing it down to the river a little below the mills; secondly, by leading it more diagonally across the fields, and lastly, to its present route.

A state road was laid out between Albany and Cooperstown, in 1794. This road crossed the mountain, and descended the Vision by the line that is still used as a foot-path. A bridge was then first constructed, where the present bridge now stands.

In 1802, the second company of the Great Western turnpike brought the present turnpike road through the village. The labors of this company sensibly improved the surface of Second street, and may be set down as the commencement of the present handsome appearance of the principal streets. The lake turnpike was constructed in 1825. The State road was continued west by the people, in 1796, nearly on the line of the present turnpike, some aid being obtained from the State. The Hartwick and Pier's roads have been but little altered since 1786, though both have been straightened near the village.

In 1795, the township of Otsego, then much larger than at present, however, contained 2160 males above the age of 16, a prodigious increase for ten years. It had 491 electors under the laws of that period, viz: 368 £100 freeholders; 55 £20 freeholders; and 60 persons renting tenements at £2. It is said that in 1738, all the electors in the State west of Albany, the latter included, excepting, however, the manor of Rensselaer, were but 636. In 1795, the number in the same counties was 36,026. It probably now exceeds 200,000.

It is mentioned that lake Otsego was free from ice on the 1st of January, 1796. It did not close the present year (1838) until the 23rd January. March, 1796, was memorable for the flocks of pigeons that flew through this valley; elderly persons declaring that they saw more on a single morning than they had previously seen in all their lives.

At the close of the year 1796, Judge Cooper made his contracts for the construction of the Hall. This, it is believed, was the first building in the county, and, with the exception of the German settlements, almost the first private building in the State, west of Schenectady, that was not built of wood. By an instrument that is still in existence, William Sprague and Barnet Whipple contracted to do the carpenter's and joiner's work of this house, all the materials being found on the spot, for the sum of $1,350. The work was begun in the year 1796, but it got no higher than the foundation in 1797. In 1798, the walls were raised and the house was effectually enclosed. In June, 1799, the building was completed, and the family of the proprietor removed into it. It was, however, inhabited by some of the workmen in 1798.

The grounds of the old building, which was called the Manor House, and those of the Hall, were not identical. The former extended back no farther than to the site of the present building, whereas the latter, as is known, reached to Third street. At this time and for some years later, many pines were still standing in the fields south of Third street, and most of the spots that had been cleared were covered with a young second growth. Otsego Hall was, for many years, the largest private residence in the newer parts of the State and it is still much the most considerable structure in Cooperstown, a village that is so singularly well built. Some idea of the strength with which it was constructed may be gained from the fact, that in 1834, when the present owner commenced his repairs and improvements, the floor above the great hall, which is near twenty-five feet by fifty in surface was raised three feet, one corner at a time without injury even to the ceiling below. The joists were of oak, the planks of the best quality, and the fastenings of wrought iron spikes. The house was struck by lightning in 1802, on which occasion the first lightning rod in Cooperstown was erected.

The Free Masons opened a lodge in the village on the first Tuesday in March, 1796, and on the 27th December, they held a great religious festival in the Academy. They dined in the same place, and in the evening they had a ball.

The first library was opened in this village, March 11th, 1796, Capt. Timothy Barnes, librarian.

The year 1794 was memorable in the history of Cooperstown, for what is still called the Indian alarm. This alarm was false, having proceeded from the combined circumstances that a report prevailed of a considerable body of Indians having been seen lurking in the woods at no great distance, and that a party who had brought in some counterfeiters discharged their pistols at midnight. Scouts had been previously sent to ascertain the fact about the Indians, and this discharge of pistols was supposed to proceed from these scouts, in the wish to alarm the village. Many ludicrous accounts are given of the effect of the fright, one man in particular, secreting himself in a log abutment of the bridge that had then been recently constructed at the spot where the present bridge now stands. We learn in the fact, the infant condition of the country, as it was then possible to create an alarm on account of the Indians.

Up to this period the lake was full of fish, and hauls of hundreds of the delicious bass were made at a time, during the proper season. The trout also abounded, as did deer. The fisherman of the day was known as Admiral Hearsey, pronounced Hassy, a man who was unhappy unless in a boat or before a lime kiln. He was, perhaps, more thoroughly aquatic than his successor, the Commodore, who has now commanded the lake more than thirty years, but on the whole, less skillful. At that time pickerel, now so abundant, were seldom caught at all.

In 1794, there was a large flat boat on the lake, called the ship Jay, on board of which Admiral Hassy first hoisted his flag. His sails were boards, and his speed more than doubtful.

The old road along the east bank of the lake was abandoned about this time; those who went to Springfield going by way of Pier's; and those who went to Albany, or to the Mohawk, by the way of Cherry Valley.

A journey taken by Judge Cooper in 1795, of which the memorials still exist, will give an idea of the means of communication that were then in the country. He left Cooperstown soon after breakfast, with his wife and two children, in the old-fashioned chariot already mentioned, and drawn by four horses. At Middlefield Center the party stopped, bated and dined. It reached Cherry Valley a little before sunset, where it passed the night. Left Cherry Valley next morning after an early breakfast, and stopped to dine with Mr. Christopher Yates; thence to the house of Hendrik Frey, at Canajoharie, to supper and to sleep. Quitting Mr. Frey's after a late breakfast, or at ten o'clock, it reached an inn for the night, about ten miles from Schenectady. The next morning, making an early start, it reached Gilbert's in Schenectady, to a late breakfast, and succeeded in getting to Albany about sunset.

At this period lime-kilns and brick-kilns existed at the outlet, owing to which circumstance, and to the diggings of the different roads, the western bank has been much defaced, it having resembled the eastern a good deal, in its native state; though a small flat always existed a little below.

In 1707, the Rev. Thomas Ellison of Albany, and the Patroon, both regents of the university, visited the Cherry Valley academy, and then extended their journey to Cooperstown, where the former preached in the Court House. This was the first time service, according to the rites of the Protestant Episcopal church, was ever performed in the place.

CHAPTER IV.

In 1799, the Rev. John Frederick Ernst, a Lutheran clergyman, settled in Cooperstown, under a temporary arrangement with the inhabitants, to perform religious service. Perhaps Mr. Ernst, who was a native of Germany, was the only person of his own persuasion in the village, and the reason of this selection was connected with a hope of getting the benefit of a bequest made for the purpose of education and religious instruction, by the late Mr. Hartwick. This hope proved fallacious, and Mr. Ernst remained but two or three years in the place, though he purchased property in it, and his descendants in the fourth generation are now to be found among us. Mr. Ernst was the second regularly employed clergyman in Cooperstown, though, owing to his peculiar sect, he can hardly be said to have had a regular church.

The first law for establishing a post route from some convenient point on the line of post route between Albany and Canandaigua, "through Cherry Valley to the Court House in Cooperstown, in the county of Otsego," was passed on the 8th May, 1794. The post-office was first opened in the village June 1st, 1794, Joseph Griffin, postmaster. The mail arrived weekly for some years; it then came twice a week; then thrice; then daily; and several variations occurred even after this, the daily mail not having been permanently established, as at present, until the year 1821.

In 1799, the Rev. John McDonald of the Scotch Seceders, was arrested for debt in this village, bailed, and was placed on the limits. Mr. McDonald during his imprisonment preached regularly in the Court House, though he had no call, supporting himself by instructing a few classical scholars. He went away in 1800.

The Presbyterians and Congregationalists, in and about Cooperstown, formed themselves into a legal society on the 29th of December, 1798.* The spiritual organization of this church took place on the 16th of June, 1800, Isaac Lewis, moderator of the meeting. On the 1st day of October, 1800, the Rev. Isaac Lewis was installed the pastor of the aforesaid church and congregation. He was the first regularly and permanently settled clergyman in Cooperstown, and he officiated altogether in the Academy, as Mr. Ernst had done during his stay. His connection with this church was dissolved in 1805.

The Rev. William Neill was ordained and installed as the successor of Mr. Lewis in 1806. This connection was dissolved in 1809. In 1810, the Rev. John Chester was engaged for a few months to fill the pulpit of this church. On the 7th of February, 1811, the Rev. John Smith was ordained and installed as the successor of Mr. Neill. This

---

*It will be found by reference to Book B, County Clerk's office, that a legally convened meeting of inhabitants of this town was held at the house of Capt. Isaac Williams, Jan. 12, 1795, at which was organized "The First Religious Society in the town of Otsego." The organization of the society mentioned by Mr. Cooper is supposed to have been the outcome of this meeting.

connection continued until the year 1833. On the 26th day of November, 1834, the Rev. Alfred E. Campbell was installed as the successor of Mr. Smith. The departure of Mr. Smith, and the causes which induced it, being of a spiritual character, were connected with a separation of this congregation into two congregations, one of which held its religious worship in the Court House and in the great hall of the Hall, the latter building being at that time unoccupied by any person but a keeper. This division was healed on the occasion of the call of Mr. Campbell, who is still the pastor of the reunited congregations.

On the 10th day of September, 1800, Miss Cooper, the eldest daughter of Judge Cooper, a young lady in the 23rd year of her age, was killed by a fall from a horse. Her funeral sermon was preached by the Rev. Daniel Nash of the Protestant Episcopal church, and she was interred according to the rites of that church, which were now performed for the first time in this village.

This young lady, who had been educated in the schools of New York, and who, from having accompanied her father in his official visits to the seat of government, was perhaps as extensively and favorably known in the middle states as any female of her years, was universally regretted. She had improved her leisure by extensive reading, and was a model of the domestic virtues. During his visit to this country, M. de Talleyrand passed a few days in Cooperstown where he was an inmate of the family of Judge Cooper. The Otsego Herald of October 2, 1795, contains the following acrostic on Miss Cooper, then in her eighteenth year, which tradition, ascribes to the celebrated *diplomat*. We give it as a literary curiosity, rather than as a very faultless specimen of poetry, although it is quite respectable in the latter point of view:

> Aimable philosophe au printemps de son age,
> Ni les temps, ni les lieux n'alterent son esprit;
> Ne cedant qu'a ses gouts simple et sans etalage,
> Au milieu des deserts, elle lit, pense, ecrit.
> Cultivez, belle Anna, votre gout pour l'etude;
> On ne saurait ici mieux employer son temps;
> Otsego n'est pas gai—mais, tout est habitude;
> Paris vous deplairait fort au premier moment;
> Et qui jouit de soi dans une solitude,
> Rentrant au monde, et sur d'en faire l'ornement.

Miss Cooper was killed in the public highway, about a mile from the residence of General Morris, in the town of Butternuts, where a monument has stood these thirty-seven years to commemorate the sad event. She is interred in the burying ground of her family, under a slab that, singularly enough, while it is inscribed by some feeling lines, written by her father, does not even contain her name.

Mr. Nash, since so well known in his own church, for his apostolic simplicity, under the name of Father Nash, was then a missionary in the county. From this time he began to extend his services to Cooperstown, and on the first day of January, 1811, a church was legally organized, under the title of Christ Church, Cooperstown.

This was the second regularly established congregation in the place. On the same day, the Rev. Daniel Nash was chosen rector of Christ church, which office, through the delicacy of the clergyman who succeeded him in his duties, he informally held down to the period of his death in 1836. In 1818, Mr. Frederick T. Tiffany was engaged by Christ Church as a lay reader. This gentleman was admitted to deacon's orders in 1820, in St. John's church, New York, and to priest's orders in Christ church, Cooperstown, in 1828, by the Right Reverend Bishop Hobart, and his connection has continued with the church down to the present moment.

In 1822, the Rev. Dr. Orderson, a clergyman from Barbadoes, West Indies, officiated occasionally in the church for several months. Whilst here, the honorary degree of D. D. was conferred upon him by the faculty of Union college.

The Methodist persuasion has had service, from time to time, for more than forty years in the village, occasionally with regularity, and at intervals, with long intermissions. From the discipline and system of this church, it is impossible for us to give any accurate account of the different clergymen employed.

The Universalists organized their society on the 26th April, 1831, under the name of the Second Universalist Society of Otsego, another existing in the township. At this moment, this congregation possesses about eighty members. The Rev. Job Potter was the first pastor, having been installed in 1831. He was succeeded by the Rev. O. Whiston in July, 1836.

The Baptist church was organized the 21st January, 1834; Rev. Lewis Raymond who still officiates, being the first pastor. This sect has occasionally had service in the village for near forty years also, the baptismn near Otsego rock being of frequent occurrence about the commencement of the century.

The first edifice constructed for religious worship in the village of Cooperstown was erected by the Presbyterians, on the east side of West street, between Third and Fourth streets, in 1805. It is of wood, being 64 feet long by 50 feet in width, having a tower and cupola ninety feet high. In 1835, this building was extensively altered and repaired, and it continues to be the place of worship of its congregation. This denomination purchased the house that stands on the southeast corner of Third and West streets for a parsonage, in 1838, for the sum of $1,600.

In 1807, the Episcopalians erected a brick building 54 feet long and 40 feet wide, as their place of worship. It was consecrated by the Right Reverend Bishop Moore, on the eighth day of July, 1810.— This building stands on the west side of Water street, also between Third and Fourth streets, and in a line with the house first named. This denomination built a rectory on the southwest corner of Water and Third streets, or adjoining the churchyard, in 1832. The latter building cost about $1,200, exclusively of the lot.

The Methodists erected a wooden building with a tower, having no spire or cupola, on the west side of Chestnut street, in 1817. It has never been painted, and the service in it is still very irregular.

In 1833, the Universalists erected a wooden building on the northeast corner of Third and West streets, with a tower and pinnacles. It is 50 feet long and 38 wide, and stands on the site of the old Academy, the latter building having been destroyed by fire on the 31st day of March, 1809. This church with the lot, cost about $3,000.

The Baptists erected a church in 1835-6. It is 54 feet by 40, and has a dome 60 feet high. The house and lot cost about $3,000.

These five buildings are all that have ever been erected for the purposes of public worship, in the village, and they are all now standing.

CHAPTER V.

Between the years 1795 and 1803 the growth of Cooperstown was gradual but steady. A document exists to show that in January of the latter year, the village contained seventy-five dwelling houses, thirty-four barns, and three hundred and forty-nine inhabitants. No account exists of the number of stores and shops, which probably would have raised the total of the buildings, exclusively of barns, &c., to about one hundred. The families were not yet large, as this account gives less than five souls to each dwelling house.

Apple hill was early selected by Richard Fenimore Cooper, Esquire, as the site for a house, and during the summer of 1800, he caused the present building to be erected. This was the second house in the place that was erected off the line of the streets, or which had the character of a villa.

John Miller erected a house in bricks, in the summer of 1802, also. It stands on his farm, but within the present limits of the village, and is the second building in the place that was not constructed of wood.

In 1804, Judge Cooper caused a stone dwelling to be constructed on the southwest corner of Water and Second streets, for his daughter, who was then married to Mr. George Pomeroy, a native of Massachusetts, who had become a resident of the place in the year 1801. This was the first stone building in the village.

Between the years 1795 and 1802, John Russell, Elijah H. Metcalf and Robert Campbell, Esquires, also became residents of Cooperstown, in which place they have since held conspicuous social or political stations. All three of these gentlemen married in the village, and their descendants in the second and third generations, now form a portion of its population. Judge Metcalf died in 1821, but the other two are still living. Mr. Russell was the second member of congress ever elected from the place, and Mr. Metcalf was in the legislature of the State two terms.

In 1801, a man dressed in a sailor's jacket, without stockings or neckcloth, but cleanly and otherwise of respectable appearance, and who seemed to be between forty and fifty, presented himself to Judge Cooper, with a request to know whether a small piece of low meadow land, that lies between Fenimore and the village, was to be sold. The answer was in the affirmative, but the applicant was informed that, on account of its position, the price would be relatively high, amounting to a considerable sum. The stranger requested that a deed might immediately be made of it, and he counted down the money in gold, giving his name as Esaias Hausman. Mr. Hausman left the Hall the owner of the lot in question, which has ever since been known as the Hausman lot. The habits, attainments and character of this man soon attracted attention. He spoke five or six of the living languages, and had a tolerable knowledge of the classics. He lived entirely alone, in a small house he had caused to be built on his purchase, and in the rudest manner. Occasionally he would disappear, and his absences sometimes extended to months. He frequently spoke of his past life, though it is not known that he ever gave any connected or explicit history of his origin, or of the events that led him to America. According to his own accounts of his adventures, he had served in the imperial army, and he was once heard to say that the death of Robespierre alone saved him from the block. Casual remarks of this nature increased curiosity, when Hausman became more reserved, and he soon ceased to touch at all on the events of his past life. Sometime about the year 1805, he had been absent for several months, when it was discovered that he was teaching Hebrew to the President of one of the eastern colleges. This occupation did not last long, however, for he was soon back again in his hut on the lake shore. In this manner this singular man passed many years, apparently undetermined in his purposes, rude and even coarse in many of his habits, but always courteous and intelligent. He died in Herkimer in 1812, and without making any particular revelations concerning himself or his family. As he died intestate, his property escheated, the lot on the shore of the lake being sold by the public. It is said that a considerable sum in gold was found in a purse that he wore between his shoulder blades.

Nothing further was ever known of Esaias Hausman. He was certainly shrewd and observant, and his acquisitions, which were a little exaggerated, probably, by vulgar report, were of that kind which denotes in Europe, a respectable education. He had not the appearance or manners of a Polish gentleman, for he called himself a Pole, and the most probable conjecture concerning him, a conjecture that we believe is sustained by some of his own remarks, made him a Jew. The name is German, but the people of that persuasion often assume new appellations.

The estate, which is bounded by the Susquehanna and lake Otsego, on the west, belonged to Henry Bowers, Esquire. On the death of this gentleman, it descended to his only son, John M. Bowers, Esquire. At a very early period, the land immediately around the outlet, and of course opposite to Cooperstown, was cleared and a farm house erected. On his marriage, however, Mr. Bowers determined to reside on his property, and to build at this spot. He came into the village in 1803, accordingly, where he resided, for a short time, and commenced the construction of the present house at Lakelands. This building was erected in 1804, and its proprietor took possession of it in 1805. Since that time it has continued to be the residence of the gentleman who caused the house to be built. This place is not within the limits of Cooperstown, or even in the township of Otsego, but standing within musket shot of the former, its inhabitants properly belong to our community.

In 1797, the Masons erected a hall on the northeast corner of Front and West streets, which is still standing.

The population of Cooperstown underwent essential changes, between the years 1800 and 1806. All the lawyers originally settled in the village, without an exception, had removed, and their places had been supplied by a new set. The same alterations also occurred among the merchants, who have frequently changed since the settlement of the country. Of the latter, Mr. Lawrence McNamee, who opened a store in the village in 1802, is the only one who has continued in the same occupation, and in the same place, down to the present time.

The only bookstore in the village, or that has ever been in the village, that of the Messrs. Phinney, has been continued since 1795, also, in the same family.

Between the years 1800, and 1810, the growth of the village, without being rapid, was regular and respectable. Many places, that, a few years previously, were much inferior to it in size and wealth, now began to surpass it, but its own population gradually grew easier in their circumstances, and, as a matter of course, enlarged their manner of living. Still, the people depended chiefly on the trade of the few adjoining towns, on the presence of the county buildings, and on such of the more ordinary manufactures as found consumers in the vicinity.

On the 22d December, 1809, died William Cooper, Esquire, the original proprietor, after whom the village was named. Judge Cooper was in his fifty-sixth year at the time of his death, and his connection with the place had continued near twenty-four years. For nineteen, he had been a regular inhabitant of the village. He died in Albany and was interred in the burying ground of his family in Christ church yard. To the enterprise, energy and capacity of this gentleman, the county of Otsego is more indebted for its rapid settlement, than to those of any other person.

A law was passed in 1806, for the erection of a new court house and jail for the county of Otsego. The commissioners appointed for that purpose selected the spot a little remote from the center of the village, on the south side of the turnpike, and west of Chestnut street. Here a building was constructed in 1806-7. It is 56 feet long and 50 feet wide, and has been used ever since for the public service. It is of bricks, and the court room is capacious and convenient. The jail is in the lower story, and is crowded and inconvenient. The jailer has also rooms in the building.

A fire-proof County Clerk's office was constructed near the court house in 1814.

The removal of the court house to the extreme western limits of the place, has had no sensible effect on the direction taken by the village in its growth, but a very few houses having been since erected in that quarter of the town. The old court house, jail and tavern, on the east corner of Second and West streets, were torn down in 1810, and a range of brick stores was erected on the lot in 1811.

In the year 1803, a market house was erected in the center of Fair street, about half way between Front and Second streets. The attempt to induce the butchers and the people of the surrounding country to use it, however, failed, and the building was removed into West street, and converted into a school house, in 1809, or soon after the destruction of the Academy by fire.

On the third day of April, 1807, a law was passed authorizing the inhabitants of the village of Cooperstown, to elect trustees, under an act of incorporation, which styled the place The Village of Otsego. This change of name arose from party politics, and the majority of the inhabitants of the village being opposed to the measure, elected trustees, who rendered the law a dead letter, by declining to do any thing under its provisions.

June 12th, 1812, a new act was passed, incorporating the place, by the name of The Village of Cooperstown under which law, the people proceeded immediately to organize the local government. By the act of incorporation, as since amended, the people elect annually five trustees, who choose their own president. The people also elect a clerk and treasurer, three assessors, a pathmaster, and constable. The board of trustees possesses powers to pass by-laws for the security of the village, in cases of fire; to prevent obstructions in the streets, or other nuisances; for regulating the streets; for lighting the same; erecting public pounds and for making wharves, docks, &c., &c. No taxes, however, exceeding four hundred dollars in total amount shall be laid in any one year. The village charter was amended April 30, 1829, the limits of the corporation being considerably extended. By the plan of Judge Cooper, the village plat originally contained one hundred and twelve acres, as has been stated, whereas the present boundaries probably include more than four hundred acres, though not more than a third of this surface can be said to be actually occupied by the streets and dwellings.

In 1812, at the time of the incorporation of the place, Cooperstown contained 133 houses, &c., 57 barns and 686 inhabitants. January, 1816, there were 183 houses, offices, shops, 68 barns, 826 inhabitants.

A small fire engine was purchased by the village, in 1812, and a second was presented to it by the heirs of Judge Cooper, in 1815.

The business of Cooperstown became enlarged in consequence of the establishment of manufactories, in its vicinity. This enterprise was commenced in 1809, by the erection of the Union cotton manufactory, on the Oaks; since that time, many other similar works have been constructed in the neighborhood. In the village itself, works of various kinds have been gradually established, increasing the wealth and adding to the industry of the place.

After the erection of the range of stores on the old court house lot, a better style of buildings was introduced for similar purposes. Since that time, most of the stores, and many of the principal shops, have been constructed in brick or stone.

The late Isaac Cooper, Esq., commenced the house called Edgewater, in 1810, and removed into it in 1814. This building, which is 66 feet long, by 45 in width, is one of the best in the place.

The residence of Mr. Henry Phinney, on Chestnut street, was commenced in 1813, and completed in 1816. This is also one of the principal dwellings in the village.

Richard Fenimore Cooper, Esq., died in Albany, in March, 1813, and was brought to this place for interment. This gentleman, when a youth, accompanied his father to Otsego, and was one of the oldest inhabitants of the village. His son and grandchildren still exist in the place.

In 1808, a second newspaper, William Andrews, editor, was established under the name of the *Impartial Observer*. This print soon passed into the hands of John H. Prentiss, Esq., and its name was changed to that of *Cooperstown Federalist*. At a still later day the title of this paper was changed to that of the *Freeman's Journal*, under which appellation it is still known. With the exception of a short interval, the same editor and proprietor has been at the head of the establishment, for about twenty-nine years.

A paper called the *Watch Tower*, was set up in opposition to the *Cooperstown Federalist*, in 1814, Israel W. Clark, editor. In May, 1817, this paper was transferred to Edward B. Crandal, who remained its editor until its discontinuance, in 1831.

The *Tocsin* was established in 1829, but took the name of the *Otsego Republican* in 1831, under which title it still exists.

In July, 1813, died Elihu Phinney, Esq., aged fifty-eight. The arrival of this gentleman in the village has already been mentioned. Mr. Phinney was one of the judges of the county court for several years, and continued to control the *Otsego Herald* to the period of his death. The paper was published by his sons H. & E. Phinney until the year 1821, when it was discontinued, after an existence of 26 years.

In 1814, the children of Augustine and Susannah Prevost, who had purchased the judgment of John Morton, against their grandfather, George Croghan, which was the oldest judgment on record, attempted to revive the same by *scire facias* against all the terre-tenants on Cooper's patent. This measure of course made all the freeholders in the village parties in the suit. The executors of Judge Cooper, however, managed the defence. The proceedings connected with this lawsuit, lasted several years, when they were discontinued in consequence of the statute of limitations. As the heirs of Susannah Prevost, who was the devisee of George Croghan, held assets to more than the amount of the judgment, in consequence of a failure of title through informality, under one of the judgment sales against their ancestor, there can be no doubt that had the issue been tried on its merits, the defendants would have prevailed, without having recourse to the agreement of 1775, according to which, the lands were to have been sold, firstly to satisfy the judgment of Gov. Franklin, or that under which the terre-tenants held, secondly, to pay the mortgage of Thomas Wharton, and lastly, to satisfy this very judgment, which it was now attempted to revive, after a lapse of forty years.

On two several occasions, officers of the federal government established recruiting parties in this village. The first was in 1779, during the *quasi* war with France; Lieut. Joseph C. Cooper, who succeeded in enlisting about thirty men in the county, commanding the party. The second occasion occurred during the war of 1812, when a considerable detachment of riflemen was recruited in the vicinity, and collected in the village, under Capt. Grosvenor.

In the way of irregular troops, there have been several volunteer corps in Cooperstown, though none of any permanency, with the exception of the artillery. The first artillery company was established in 1798. William Abbot, captain, Samuel Huntington, first lieutenant, and George Walker, second. The pieces of this company entirely supplanted the Cricket, and since that time the villagers have never been without regular brass guns for their parades and festivals.

A volunteer company of horse was established in 1794, Captain Benjamin Griffin, commandant. Many persons now living, can recollect a celebrated sham fight between this cavalry and a party of men disguised as Indians. The charges of the horse, on that occasion, are described as having been infinitely severe. At that time, the log fences, a good deal decayed, inclosed a great portion of the two principal blocks of the place, and the manner in which the cavalry got over them and through them, probably caused as much surprise to themselves as to the spectators. In this part of the field especially, the Indians are said to have discovered much the greatest address, although both parties, as usual, claimed the victory.

The first regular organization of the militia, in this part of the country, appears to have taken place in the year 1798, although detached companies existed previously. Jacob Morris, Esq., of Butternuts was the first brigadier-general appointed, and Francis Henry, Esq , the first colonel of the regiment which included the village. John Howard was the first captain of the ordinary militia company of the beat. Capt. Howard was unfortunately drowned in the Susquehanna the next year, in making a noble effort to save a person who had got beneath some floodwood, and he was succeeded by William Sprague.

For a long time after the commencement of the village, Cooperstown suffered but little from fires; several small buildings, it is true, were burned at different times, but the first considerable conflagration occurred on the night of the 30th of March, 1809, when the printing office of H. & E. Phinney took fire. The flames were communicated to a new dwelling house belonging to William Dowse, Esq., and both were consumed. These buildings stood on West street. The next day the Academy was also destroyed in the same way, and no attempt has ever been made to rebuild it.

A dwelling house and store, standing on Second street, and occupied by Joseph Wilkinson, were destroyed by fire, March 17, 1814.

A long range of storehouses belonging to the estate of Judge Cooper, also standing on Second street, was burned down in the winter of 1813. A part of this range was composed of the old Manor House, which had been converted into a storehouse.

The next considerable conflagration occurred on the night of the 27th of April, 1818, when a fire broke out in the hatter's shop of Ralph Worthington, and it was not subdued until it had consumed all the buildings on the north side of Second street, between the west corner of Fair street and the alley called Beaver alley, making six buildings altogether. This is much the most considerable fire that ever occurred within the limits of the village.

But the summer of 1823, was a serious time for the inhabitants of the village of Cooperstown. A succession of fires took place, under circumstances that scarce leave a doubt that they were mostly, if not entirely, the acts of an incendiary. The Tannery was consumed on the night of the 12th July. On a thorough examination of the facts, it was generally believed it had been set on fire. A stone house, which had been erected at Fenimore, by J. Fenimore Cooper, Esq., between the years 1814 and 1817, was the next consumed. This place which, like Lakelands, stands without the village limits, properly belongs to the village community, and the principal dwelling was of considerable size and of a good finish, having all the conveniences of a country residence. The house was not completed nor inhabited, though it contained all the wood work and a large amount of valuable lumber. As it stood quite alone in the center of an extensive lawn, there can be but little doubt that it was set on fire. This house was destroyed to the naked walls.

Several barns which stood in the most compact parts of the village soon followed. Fortunately the injury, in few of these cases, extended beyond the buildings which first took fire. The incendiary, or incendiaries, were never satisfactorily discovered, though plausible conjectures have been made.

Since the recent alterations and repairs of the Hall have been going on, a window has been opened and a place has been discovered where tinder, oiled cotton, burnt matches and other combustibles were lying together, leaving little doubt that one if not more attempts were made to destroy that building also, and probably about the same time.

There are other instances in which there is reason to suppose that incendiaries had been at work in the village, one of which is a recent case of fire in the court house. This building was discovered to be on fire about four o'clock on the morning of the 24th of May, 1837, but the flames were subdued before they had done much injury. One of the prisoners in the jail was suspected of having set the building on fire, though the charge could not be substantiated.

Of late, scarcely a year passes without one or more fires, which usually proceed from defective or badly secured stove pipes, but no structure of any importance has been consumed. Indeed, it is the subject of surprise that no considerable dwelling house has ever been destroyed by fire within the village of Cooperstown, with the exception of that of Mr. Dowse and of one or two of secondary value and size, which were burned in the great fire of 1818. Almost every other building that has been burned, has been either a shop, barn, or store.

Cisterns for the collection of water have been sunk in the streets; hooks and ladders, fire buckets and hose are provided, and considering the size of the place, the provisions against fire are respectable. The firemen have usually been found active and bold, and cases have often occurred in which they have saved large portions of the village.

CHAPTER VI.

The size of Cooperstown received considerable accessions between the years 1805 and 1820. Several young lawyers established themselves in the place among whom were William Dowse, George Morell, Samuel Starkweather, Joseph S. Lyman, Eben B. Morehouse, H. Flagg, and A. L. Jordan, Esquires. Mr. Morell removed to Michigan in 1832, and is at present one of the Judges of the Supreme Court of that state. Mr. Lyman was elected to Congress in 1818, but died during his term of service. Mr. Dowse was also elected a Member of Congress at a still earlier day, but never took his seat having died previously to the meeting of that body. Messrs. Jordan and Flagg removed from the village after a few years' residence. Mr. Flagg died in one of the southern states, shortly after he left here.

The village has given the following Members to the Congress of the United States, to wit, William Cooper, who was first elected in 1794; John Russell, Esq., who was elected in 1804; John M. Bowers, Esq., who sat part of a session in 1813-14, but lost his seat in consequence of a decision of the House; William Dowse, Esq., elected in 1812, and died as already mentioned; Joseph S. Lyman, Esq., elected in 1818, and died in 1821; and John H. Prentiss, Esq., who is the sitting member.

The county of Otsego has for several years composed a Congressional District by itself, and of eleven Members chosen at different periods from the county, six have been residents of Cooperstown.

Several other gentlemen became residents of the place during the period already mentioned, and continued to increase and improve its society; among these were Messrs. Edmeston, Atchison, Augustine Prevost, and G. W. Prevost. A singular fatality attended the first three of these gentlemen. Col. Prevost was lost in the well known shipwreck of the Albion packet. Mr. Edmeston was drowned while bathing, and Mr. Atchison fell by his own hand during an access of fever. Neither of these melancholy events occurred in the village.

Five deaths by drowning, in the lake, have occurred among the inhabitants of the village since the settlement of the place.

The village was much improved by the fire of 1818; stone and brick buildings having been principally erected in the place of those destroyed.

The first public house in Cooperstown, as has been said already, was kept by William Ellison, on Water street, near the outlet. But the first public house of any note, was the old Red Lion, kept by Joseph Griffin, on the projecting corner of West and Second streets. This building, which at different times has been much enlarged, repaired and improved, has continued to be one of the principal inns of the place for forty-six years. The old sign, which was painted by an amateur artist, R. R. Smith, Esq., the first sheriff of the county, stood for many years, but to the great regret of the older inhabitants of the place, it has been made to disappear before some of the more ambitious improvements of the day, the house being now called the Eagle Tavern.

The second public house of any consequence, was the Blue Anchor, kept by William Cook, on the corner diagonally opposite to the Red Lion; this house was in much request for many years among all the genteeler portion of the travelers. Its host was a man of singular humors, great heartiness of character, and perfect integrity. He had been the steward of an English East-Indiaman, and enjoyed an enviable reputation in the village for his skill in mixing punch and flip. On holidays, a stranger would have been ápt to mistake him for one of the magnates of the land, as he invariably appeared in a drab coat of the style of 1776, with buttons as large as dollars, breeches, striped stockings, buckles that covered half his foot, and a cocked hat large enough to extinguish him. The landlord of the Blue Anchor was a general favorite, his laugh and his pious oaths having become historical.

There were many other taverns in the place, the most considerable of which was Washington Hall. It stood on the north side of Second street, one door from the corner of Fair street. This house at one period was in more request than any other in the place, but not until the functions of the popular landlord of the Blue Anchor had ceased.

In 1832, the house adjoining the old Washington Hall was removed, and a spacious inn was erected on its site; this is at the eastern corner of Second and Fair streets, and the inn is known by the name of Union Hall.

A tavern was kept by Daniel Olendorf, on the northeast corner of Second and Chestnut streets for several years. This house was probably in more demand than any other that has been kept in the village, but it was discontinued in the early part of the present year, though it is still in request as a boarding house. The Eagle Tavern and Union Hall are now the two principal inns of the place, the first being the stage house.

According to the census of 1820, the population of the village had increased to 1,000, and in 1825 it was reduced to 857, while in 1830 it was 1,115. By the census of 1835, it was found to be 1,190. The growth of the village has been in some degree retarded by the mania for western emigration and there was a period at the commencement of the century, when Judge Cooper made large drafts on this village and the surrounding country, for settlers on his other estates. The law abolishing imprisonment for debt, has also had a tendency to lessen the population of this village, in common with those of all the small county towns in the interior.

Notwithstanding the apparent stagnation in the place, Cooperstown has actually been greatly improved within the last fifteen years. Several houses have been erected in brick or stone, of respectable dimensions and of genteel finish: among these that of Mr. Elihu Phinney on West street, that of Mr. William Nichols on Fair street, that of Mr. Ellery Cory, also on West street, and that of Mr. John Hannay, on Second street, are among the most considerable. The last three are of stone.

A law was passed on the 8th day of April, 1830, incorporating a bank, by the title of the Otsego County Bank, and a stone bankinghouse was erected on the south side of Second street, nearly opposite to Fair street, in 1831. This bank has a capital of one hundred thousand dollars, and Robert Campbell and Henry Scott, Esquires both old and respectable inhabitants of the village, have been its president and cashier, since the formation of the institution. This incorporation has been well managed, and as it has been found very serviceable to the community, while it has escaped the imputations that rest on so many similiar establishments in other places, it is in favor with all the intelligent part of the population.

Few of the very early heads of families in the village now remain; many of those even, who came in about the close of the last or the beginning of the present century, are already dead, and several of those who accompanied their parents as children, have followed them to the grave. Isaac Cooper, Esq., the second son of the proprietor, who for many years was an active inhabitant of the village, and who contributed little less than his father, to its improvement and embellishment, died on the 1st of January, 1818. His two brothers, William and Samuel survived him but a short time.

Thomas Shankland, Esq., died 21st August, 1823, and his wife Rachel, 21st October, 1826. He was the owner of the mills south of the village at the time of his death.

James Averell, Esq., whose activity in business has been already mentioned, died as lately as December, 1836. His wife having preceded him to the grave about two years.

Dr. Thomas Fuller, whose practice in the village commenced in 1791, died on the 11th July, 1837.

Mr. Joshua Starr, another of the old inhabitants, died the 17th February, 1838, and his wife on the 5th May, 1837.

Mr. Ralph Worthington and Mr. John Frederick Ernst, both respectable residents for a long time, died early, the first on the 9th September, 1828, and the second, on the 29th November, 1830.

Descendants of all these families exist in the second and third, and in some cases, in the fourth generations.

The families longest resident in Cooperstown, are the following, the date of the connection with the place being put opposite to the name of each, viz.: Cooper, 1785-1790; Miller, 1786; Averell, 1786-1788; White, 1788; Baldwin, 1790; Fuller, 1791; Starr, 1792; Griffin, 1792; Ingalls, 1793; Graves, 1793; Phinney, 1795; Russell, 1796; Ernst, 1799; Metcalf, 1799; Bowden, 1799; Pomeroy, 1801; Campbell, 1802; Worthington, 1802; McNamee, 1802; Olendorf, 1802; Foote, 1804; Scott, 1805; Prentiss, 1808, &c., &c., &c. ·To these may be added several families that have long been settled in the adjoining country, and of which some of the members now reside in the village. Among the latter, we find the names of Fitch, 1790-1814; Clark, 1796-1812; Jarvis, 1786-1832; Stowel, 1792-1822; Doubleday, 1794-1821; Luce, 1788-1830. The family of Bowers may also be enumerated, though not within the village limits, coming in 1803. Of the above mentioned names, Messrs. Miller, White, Baldwin, Russell, Griffin, Bowden, Campbell, Pomeroy, Foote, McNamee, Scott, Olendorf, and Prentiss the original head of each family are still living, as is also Mr. Bowers.

John Miller is now, and indeed, for a long time has been, the oldest living settler. His children own the property which he first cleared from the forest. James White, a carpenter, well known for his industry and hard application to his work, is the next oldest settler, and Joseph Baldwin, cooper, is the third; the fourth male is James Fenimore

Cooper, Esquire. This gentleman was born in 1789, and in 1790, was brought an infant, a year old, into the village, with the family of Judge Cooper, of which he was the youngest child. His sister, Mrs. Pomeroy, is the longest resident among the females, neither of those already named as older inhabitants, her own father excepted, having been married at the time of the arrival of her family. The next oldest female resident, we believe to be the wife of Joseph Baldwin.

Of descendants, there have been four generations of the Cooper family in the place, from father to son. This is the only instance, we believe, in which the fourth generation has yet been reached in the same name, though it has been several times done through females. The grand-children of the older settlers are in active life, however, in very many instances.

The following names belong to families that may now be considered as old inhabitants, though their residence is of comparatively recent date, viz: E. Cory, Gregory, Nichols, G. A. Starkweather, Waterman, Paul, Perkins, Tracey, Wilson, Spafard, Lewis, Besancon, H. Cory, Cooley and Davis.

Some of the members of these families are now among the most respectable and useful inhabitants of the place.

In 1825, Samuel, Nelson, Esquire, the judge of the circuit court, married the only daughter of Judge Russell, and became an inhabitant of Cooperstown. Judge Nelson resided some time at Apple hill, but in 1829 he purchased Fenimore, and enlarging the farm-house, he converted it into a spacious and convenient dwelling. The walls of the ruins left by the fire of 1823 were removed in 1826, and no traces of that situation now remain, but its foundations. Judge Nelson was promoted to the bench of the Supreme Court in 1833, and in 1836, he became its chief justice.

John A. Dix, Esquire, the present Secretary of State, purchased Apple Hill of the heirs of R. Fenimore Cooper, Esq., in 1828, but sold it to Levi C. Turner, Esq., at his removal to Albany, on his being appointed Adjutant-General. Mr. Turner is married to the daughter of Robert Campbell, Esq., and is the present owner of that beautiful situation.

In 1829, Eben B. Morehouse, Esquire, purchased a few acres of Mr. Bowers, on the side of the Vision, at the point where the old state road made its first turn to ascend the mountain, and caused a handsome dwelling in stone to be constructed. This place, which has received the appropriate name of Woodside, has been extensively embellished, and as it enjoys the advantage of possessing a beautiful pine grove, it is generally esteemed one of the most desirable residences of the neighborhood. In 1836, Mr. Morehouse sold Woodside to Samuel Wootton Beall, Esquire, a native of Maryland, who had married into the family of Cooper.

After the death of the late Isaac Cooper, Esquire, the house at Edgewater was sold. An abortive attempt was made to get up a female school, and this house was altered, in order to meet such an object. This project failed, and in 1834, the property was sold to Theodore Keese, Esquire, of New York, by whom it has been repaired, and the grounds restored to their original beauty, and indeed improved. Mr. Keese uses Edgewater as a summer residence, having married into the family of Pomeroy.

The Hall having passed into the hands of J. Fenimore Cooper, Esquire, that gentleman, shortly after his return from Europe, or in 1834, had it extensively repaired, and a good deal altered. The roof had rotted, and it was replaced by a new one on the old inclination, but the walls of the building were raised four feet. On these were placed battlements and heavy cornices in brick, that add altogether eight feet to the elevation of the building. The distance between the rows of the windows was increased three feet, by filling in the lower ends of the upper windows, and by placing new stools, the necessary height having been obtained above. Much ornamental brick work has been added, and the effect has been altogether advantageous. All the floors of the second story have also been raised, giving to the principal rooms a better height than they formerly possessed, while those above have been improved the same way, by the addition to the general height of the building. Appropriate entrances have been made on both fronts, that are better suited to the style of architecture and to the climate than the ancient stoops, and two low towers have been added to the east end, which contribute greatly to the comfort of the house, as a residence. The improvements and alterations are still proceeding slowly, and this dwelling, which for ten or twelve years was nearly deserted, promises to be one of the best country houses in the state again. The grounds have also been enlarged and altered, the present possessor aiming at what is called an English garden. During the life of Judge Cooper, these grounds contained about three acres, but they are now enlarged to near five.

Great improvements have been made in the streets of late years, which have been accurately graded, and in some instances the sidewalks have been flagged. The carriage ways are smooth, in general, and we believe no stump now remains in any of the public avenues. There is a deficiency in the supply of water, however, Cooperstown being less abundantly furnished with this great necessary in 1838 than it was forty years ago; for at that time, log aqueducts were led under ground, from the western mountain into the village. Wells are numerous, though the water is usually hard, and unsuited to domestic purposes; luckily there are several excellent springs within the circle of the houses, and from these the inhabitants obtain most of their supplies. A law was passed in 1827, to incorporate a company to supply the place with water, and it is to be hoped that the day is not distant when its very desirable objects will be carried into effect.

CHAPTER VII.

Having now given the simple and brief annals of the place, from the time when the site of Cooperstown was a wilderness, down to the present moment, we shall close our labors, with a more general account of its actual condition, trusting that posterity will not permit any period to extend beyond the memory of man, without adding to that which has been here given, in order that there may always exist authentic local annals, for the information and uses of those most interested.

The village of Cooperstown stands in the 44th° of north latitude, and as near as can be ascertained from maps, in the 76th° of longitude, west from Greenwich. It contains within the corporate limits, according to an enumeration that has been made expressly for this work, the following buildings, viz.:

Dwelling Houses	169	Churches	5
Stores	20	Bank	1
Shops	42	Court House	1
Offices	14	Engine House	1
Total			253

To these buildings may be added between sixty and eighty barns, carriage houses, stables and minor constructions, that stand in the rear of the lots. The buildings of Lakelands, Woodside, and Fenimore, all of which places, though quite near the village, stand without its legal limits, are also omitted in this enumeration. If these latter, and some ten or twelve dwelling-houses that stand between Fenimore and Cooperstown, be included, the total number of buildings of all sorts, would not be far from three hundred and fifty.

The population does not probably vary much from 1,300 souls at the present moment.

Cooperstown is better built than common, for a village of its size. Of the dwelling-houses, there are a good many of stone or brick, as there are also stores and shops. In the whole, near forty of the buildings are of one or the other of these materials. Many of the dwellings, besides those particularly named, are genteely finished, and would be considered respectable habitations even in the larger towns.

The village is beautifully placed at the southern end of the lake, being bounded on one side by its shores, and on another by its outlet, the Susquehanna. The banks of both these waters are sufficiently elevated, varying from twenty to forty feet. Apple hill probably stands sixty or seventy feet above the river, which it almost overhangs. There is an irregular descent from the rear of the town towards the banks of the lake, and which has been brought to a regular grading in some of the streets running north and south. The place is clean, the situation is dry, and altogether it is one of the healthiest residences in the State.

Lake Otsego is a sheet of limpid water, extending, in a direction from N. N. East to S. S. West, about nine miles, and varying in width from about three-quarters of a mile to a mile and a half. It has many bays and points, and as the first are graceful and sweeping, and the last low and wooded, they contribute largely to its beauty. The water is cool and deep, and the fish are consequently firm and sweet. The two ends of the lake, without being shallow, deepen their water gradually, but there are places on its eastern side in particular, where a large ship might float with her yards in the forest. The greatest ascertained depth is at a place about two miles from the village, where bottom has been got with a line of one hundred and fifty feet. There are probable spots of a still greater depth. The fish of the Otsego have a deserved reputation, and, at particular seasons, are taken in great abundance. Among those that are edible may be mentioned the following, viz.: the lake fish, or salmon trout, the bass, eels, perch, sun-fish, pickerel, cat-fish, or bull-pouts, and suckers. The river has the white fish, and many of the small neighboring streams are richly supplied with common trout. The trout is little, if any, inferior to the salmon, and has been caught as large as from twenty to thirty pounds; those that weigh from eight to twelve pounds are not uncommon. The bass, or Otsego bass, is also a delicious fish, resembling the white fish of the great lakes. The pickerels and the eels are both excellent of their kind, and very abundant in their seasons.

The shores of the Otsego are generally high, though greatly varied. On the eastern side, extends a range of steep mountains, that varies in height from four to six hundred feet, and which is principally in forest, though here and there a farm relieves its acclivities. The road along this side of the lake is peculiarly pleasant, and traveled persons call it one of the most strikingly picturesque roads within their knowledge. The western shore of the lake is also high, though more cultivated. As the whole country possesses much wood, the farms, viewed across the water, on this side of the lake, resemble English park scenery. Some of the glimpses of the settlement, which has obtained the name of Piers from the circumstance that several farmers of that family originally purchased lands there, are singularly beautiful, even as seen from the village.

Immediately opposite to the village, on the eastern side of the valley, (for the Susquehanna winds its way for near four hundred miles through a succession of charming valleys,) the range of mountain terminates, heaving itself up into an isolated hummock, however, before it melts away into the plain. This rise is called the Vision, and its summit is much frequented for its views which are unrivaled in this part of the country. The ascent is easy, by means of roads and paths, and when there, the spectator gets a bird's-eye view of the village, which appears to lie directly beneath him, of the valley, and of the lake. The latter, in particular, is singularly lovely, displaying all the graceful curvatures of its western shores, while the landscape behind them, embracing Piers, and the hills beyond, is one of the richest and most pleasing rural pictures that can be offered to the eye. Nothing is wanting but ruined castles and recollections, to raise it to the level of the scenery of the Rhine, or, indeed, to that of the minor Swiss views.

Prospect rock, which lies on the same range with the Vision, also offers a good view of the village and the valley, though it does not command as extensive an horizon as the first.

The mountains south of Cooperstown form a background of great beauty, and it is seldom that a more graceful and waving outline of forest is met with any where. The Black hills in particular, are exceedingly fine, and are supposed to be nearly a thousand feet above the level of the lake.

As the valley of Cooperstown is about twelve hundred feet above tide, it will readily be conceived that the summers are cool and the air invigorating. These facts are very apparent to those who come from the low counties during the warm months. Even with the thermometer at eighty, as sometimes happens, there is a sensible difference between the oppress'on produced by the heat here, and by that produced by the same heat at a less elevation. The lake, also, has the effect to produce a circulation of air, it being seldom that' there is not a breeze either up or down this beautiful sheet of water.

The banks of the lake abound with eligible situations for country houses. On its western side, there is scarcely a quarter of a mile without one and we feel persuaded that nothing but a good road to the Mohawk is wanting to bring this spot into so much favor as shall line the shores of the Otsego with villas. As the roads now are, it requires but twenty hours to go to New York, and by the improvements that are in progress there is reason to expect this time will ere long be shortened to ten or twelve hours. When that day shall arrive, we predict that Cooperstown, during five months of the year, will become a place of favorite resort for those who wish a retreat from the dust and heat of the larger towns.

The society of this place is already of a higher order than that of most villages of its size. In this respect, Cooperstown has always been remarkable, more liberal tastes and a better style of living having prevailed in the place from its commencement than is usually to be found in new countries. At different periods, many families and individuals accustomed to the best society of the country have dwelt here, and they have imparted to the place the habits and tone of their own condition in life. So far from gaining by a closer connection with the commercial towns therefore, in this respect, there is reason to think that the village might not be better off than it is at present.

Lying as it does off the great routes, the village of Cooperstown is less known than it deserves to be. Few persons visit it without acknowledging the beauties of its natural scenery and the general neatness and decency of the place itself. The floating population, it is true, has brought in some of that rudeness and troublesome interference which characterizes the migrating and looser portion of the American people; but a feeling has been awakened among the old inhabitants that is beginning to repel this innovation, and we already, in this class, see signs of a return to the ancient deportment, which was singularly re-

spectable, having been equally free from servile meanness and obtru-
sive vulgarity. One or two instances of audacious assumptions of a
knowledge of facts and of a right to dictate, on the part of strangers,
have recently met with rebukes that will probably teach others caution,
if they do not teach them modesty. On the whole, the feeling of the
community is sound, and is little disposed to tolerate this interference
with the privileges of those who have acquired rights by time and a
long connection with the place.

It has been said, both directly and indirectly, that the village of
Cooperstown is well built; unlike most such places, its best houses are
private residences, and not taverns. The Hall and Edgewater are both
American country houses of the first class. The house of Mr. Henry
Phinney, which is sometimes called the Locusts, is a very pretty pavilion of considerable size, and the building is well finished and in good
style; all three are of brick. Woodside is also a substantial and respectable dwelling, in stone. Lakelands is not a very large house, but it is
well placed, and is finished more like a villa than any other building
around it. Apple hill has a house of no great beauty, but the situation
is much the best within the limits of the village. The present house at
Fenimore is respectable, though with very little pretensions to architecture; but the whole of the grounds are delightful, and the site of the
old building is one of the most beautiful in the State, for a residence
of that character. In addition to these places, which, from possessing
select grounds, are the most conspicuous, there are a dozen other dwellings that have more or less advantages, and some of which are also
well placed. Even many of the buildings that stand directly on the
principal streets are above the ordinary level, and the general impression made on the observer is that of respectability and good taste.
Many of the houses have gardens, though the original plan prevented
the introduction of court yards, of which there are but eight or ten that
deserve the name in the place.

The present condition of Cooperstown is sufficiently prosperous,
without being in that state of feverish excitement that has afflicted so
many other small towns. The trade is not great, but it is steady and
profitable. The village contains six dry goods stores, all of which are
on a respectable scale; four groceries; two druggists; hatters, watch-
makers and jewelers, tinmen, and the customary number of more common* mechanics, such as tailors, shoemakers, blacksmiths, &c., &c.,
some of which establishments are on a scale larger than common.

Distinctly within the recollection of many now living, or some
forty years ago, there were not probably half a dozen pianofortes, if as
many, in the State, west of Schenectady. There was one in the Hall,
which was certainly the only one in the county of Otsego at that time.
There are now two manufactories of the instrument in the village, both
of which also make organs, and no less than thirty-five private houses
in which pianos are to be found. Three of the churches have organs.

---

*Mr. Cooper, by the term "common," here means of course, *general*, i. e., mechanics
generally found in all places.

Lessons in music are given by three different competent persons, and a good taste in this delightful art is fast obtaining.

There are two boarding schools for females in Cooperstown, though no good classical school for boys has ever existed in the place. The proximity to the Hartwick Academy, distant only five miles, is supposed to retard the accomplishment of so desirable an object. Nevertheless, a higher order of instruction is gradually coming into use, particularly among the females, and as Cooperstown has always possessed good models, it is hoped the attainments and principles which render the sex so attractive and useful, as well as respectable, will take deep root in the community. As they improve their minds and tastes, the young of that sex, on whose example so much depends, will obtain new sources of happiness, which, while they create a disrelish for the less refined amusements, will give them a still higher standard of attainments, juster notions of their own dignity, and an increasing dislike for those familiar and unladylike pursuits that are too apt to form the aim of a mere village belle. The term village belle, however, is inapplicable to the state of society that already exists in this little community, and we regard, with satisfaction, the signs of a more general advancement than formerly, in the accomplishments that mark an improved association, the possession of which is so certain, when carried beyond their elements, to bring with it its own regard.

Cooperstown has two weekly newspapers, the *Freeman's Journal* and the *Otsego Republican,* the former of which has always been esteemed for a respectable literary taste. In politics, as a matter of course, these papers are opposed to each other.

There are nine practitioners in the law, at present residing in the village, viz: Messrs. Campbell, Crippen, Morehouse, Cooper, Bowne, Walworth, Lathrop, Starkweather and Turner. William H. Averell, Esquire, is also in the profession, but he does not practice. Of these gentlemen, Messrs. Averell and Cooper are natives of the place; Messrs. Campbell and Crippen of the county.

The principal mercantile firms are those of H. B. & G. W. Ernst, L. McNamee, E. D. Richardson & Co., J. Stowell, John Russell & Co., and H. Lathrop & Co. Most of these gentlemen are natives of the village, or of the country immediately around it. Mr. McNamee is a European by birth, but he has resided in Cooperstown, as a merchant, thirty-six years.

There are four practising physicians at present, viz: Doctors Spafard, Curtis, Johnson and Harper.

The printing establishment of Messrs. H. & E. Phinney is one of the most extensive manufactories in the village, if not the most extensive. It ordinarily employs about forty hands, of both sexes, and consumes annually 3,000 reams of paper. It has five presses in almost constant use. Large Bibles and school books are chiefly produced. Of the former, this house publishes 8,000 copies annually. It also publishes 60,000 volumes of other books, chiefly school books, and 200,000 almanacs, toy books, &c.

The tannery is still kept up, and it produces a considerable amount of leather, annually. Iron castings are also made in the village. The manufactory of Messrs. E. & H. Cory, in cabinet ware, pails, &c., &c., is on a respectable scale. The manufactory of hats, by J. R. Worthington, an establishment that has passed into the second generation of the same family, is also considerable; Ralph Worthington carried on the business in 1802. Mr. Stephen Gregory has long had a respectable shoe store and manufactory, that is still kept up. The industry of the place, however, as a whole, is directed more toward supplying the wants of the surrounding country, than to exportation. In this sense, the business is considerable, and is gradually increasing, with the growing wealth of the county.

Although Cooperstown, which has now had an existence of half a century, may not have produced any very eminent men, it has had a fair proportion of respectable citizens. Several young artists and mechanics, that were born here, have risen to some notoriety in their several callings, and the clergy and the members of the bar, have generally maintained respectable stations in their respective professions.

Cooperstown for the last twenty years has been rather remarkable for its female population. Perhaps no place of its size can boast of a finer collection of young women than this village, the salubrity of the climate appearing to favor the development of their forms and constitutions. The beauty, indeed, of the sex in this village, has been celebrated in verse even, and we think quite justly.

As the growth and improvement of Cooperstown have been steady, and, with very trifling exceptions, regularly progressive, they may be expected to continue in the same ratio, for a long time to come. We shall have no mushroom city, but there is little doubt that in the course of time, as the population of the country fills up, this spot will contain a provincial town of importance. The beauty of its situation, the lake, the purity of the air, and the other advantages already pointed out, seem destined to make it more peculiarly a place of resort, for those who live less for active life than for its elegance and ease. It is highly probable that, half a century hence, the shores of the lake will be lined with country residences, when the village will be the center of their supplies of every kind. Were an effort made, even now, by the erection of proper lodging houses, the establishment of reading rooms and libraries, and the embellishment of a few of the favorable spots, in the way of public promenades and walks, it strikes us that it would be quite easy to bring the place into request, as one of resort for the inhabitants of the large towns during the warm months. The mode adopted in the smaller European towns, would be the most suitable for commencing such an experiment. If a few persons with narrow incomes, and who possessed proper buildings, were to fit up rooms, as parlors and bed rooms, a set in each house, furnish the breakfasts and tea, and, if required, the dinner, persons of fortune would be induced to frequent the place, would pay liberal prices, and the village in a few years, would reap the benefit of a large expenditure. The system of common boarding houses will not for a long time draw to Cooperstown company in sufficient numbers to remunerate; or company even of the right quality; but half a dozen furnished lodgings, on a respectable scale, we think would lay the foundation of a system that might prove to be exceedingly serviceable to the interests of the place. There is everything that is wanted for such an object, and, as society produces society, a few years would bring an accession of this important requisite, that would be certain to sustain itself.

To conclude, Cooperstown is evidently destined to occupy some such place among the towns of New York, as is now filled by the villages and towns on the shores of the lakes of Westmoreland, in England, and by the several *bourgs* on those of the different waters of Switzerland. The period of this consummation may be advanced, or it may be retarded by events; though nothing will be so likely to hasten it, as to provide the means of comfortable private lodgings. As it is, scarcely a summer passes that families do not reluctantly go from this beautiful spot, to others less favored by nature, and with an inferior society, in consequence of their being unable to obtain the required accommodations. Still every thing shows a direction towards this great end, among which may be mentioned the increasing taste for boating, for music, the languages, and other amusements and accomplishments of the sort, that bespeak an improving civilization.

THE CHRONICLES—CONTINUED

By S. M. Shaw.

CHAPTER VIII.

FROM 1838 TO 1851.

During this period of thirteen years, Cooperstown witnessed comparatively few marked improvements or changes, and little, or no increase in population—the removal of the Phinneys' printing business and bindery to Buffalo, after the destruction of their establishment by fire in 1849, causing the change of residence of a number of families, some of whose members had found employment therein. The social life of the village was quiet and pleasant—more truly enjoyable, some of the old residents think, than it has been since the time when the "general lake party," some seasons repeated, was the one grand feature of the summer season, and the "select ball" that of the winter. The village newspapers of that period paid very little attention to local matters, and hence can be drawn upon for but few items of interest. But we are enabled to record the following:

1839.—E. Beach, C. E., was employed to survey a route for a railroad from Cooperstown to intersect the proposed Catskill and Canajoharie railroad, at a point near the latter village. He made a report at a public meeting held here January 30th, of this year, over which James Stowell presided. It proposed the construction of a road on the east side of the lake; estimated cost for a road 29 miles long, $301,160. A meeting was held February 14th, at which a committee was appointed to apply to the legislature for a charter. That was the last of the enterprise, so far as Cooperstown was concerned. The people of Canajoharie were more interested, and we have heard it stated that a small piece of the proposed road was graded near that village.

On the last Sunday in May, Coroner Isaac Lewis of this village was called to Springfield, to hold an inquest on the bodies of five persons who were drowned in Lake Summit. They attempted to cross that pond in a leaky boat, which sunk with them.

A County Educational Society, whose object it was to improve the public schools of Otsego, with Hon. Samuel Nelson as president, existed in 1839. Mr. Cooper presided at the meeting held here which organized the Society. Horace Lathrop, Esq., was secretary.

In September, President Martin Van Buren visited Cooperstown, and received quite an ovation. He was accompanied hither from Fort Plain by Judge Nelson and Col. Prentiss. He was met, about a mile out of the village, by a large cavalcade of men of both political parties. On his arrival he was formally welcomed by Judge Morehouse, and he made a brief response from the piazza of the Eagle Hotel. He remained from Saturday till Monday, and then went to Cherry Valley. During his visit he was called upon by a great many party and personal friends.

1840.—On the 27th of June, a Mr. Ballard and Mr. Minor were rowing on the lake, when accidently the boat was upset, and Ballard was drowned. Minor was rescued, although nearly exhausted, and revived after a short time.

Gov. Seward made the 4th of July oration at Cherry Valley this year. On the evening of that day, Dr. Russell, Wm. Nichols and Geo. W. Ernst of this village, as a committee, waited upon and brought him to Cooperstown. The next day was Sunday, and the Governor attended the Episcopal and Presbyterian churches. On Monday a lake party was given at the Point, in his honor, which was largely attended by the villagers and people of the surrounding country. L. J. Walworth, Esq., made an address of welcome to Governor Seward, who replied at length. The party that came down the lake, on the old scow, stopped in front of the Echo, and several persons tried their voices to show off the wonderfully clear reverberation that would be given. "Joe Tom," who had been "chief cook" on the occasion, and who was now at one of the long oars, was asked to try the echo. "Hurrah for Governor Steward!" "You got it to a t, Joe!" exclaimed the Governor.

Party politics ran very high in Cooperstown this year, and many meetings were held in and near the village. The village had long been noted for its many prominent and active politicians.

The County Jail, which succeeded the old log structure, was burned Dec. 17. Strong efforts were then made by other towns to change the location; but they failed, and in January, 1841, the sum of $10,-000 was appropriated by the Supervisors for a Court House, Jail and Sheriff's residence. They were completed in October of that year.

Three of what Mr. Cooper would style "very respectable" residences, all of wood, were put up this year, and all in the same general style: one by Mr. G. W. Ernst on Water street; one by Mr. Levi Wood at the southern terminus of West street, and one by Mr. Benj. F. Kipp on the same street, on the sight of his present brick building.

1841.—On the 23d of Feb., a little son of Mr. Alonzo Woodward of this village, in attempting to jump upon a sleigh, missed his hold and fell under one of the runners, which passed over his body before the horses could be stopped. The child expired in about 15 minutes.

The residence of Mr. William Nichols took fire in the attic, May 18th, and very narrowly escaped destruction. It was materially damaged.

At the Circuit Court held the week beginning Sept. 13th, occurred the trial of the libel suit brought by J. Fenimore Cooper against Park Benjamin, editor of the New World, in which the defendant was mulcted in $375 damages. At the Montgomery Circuit Court held the following month Mr. Cooper received $400 against Mr. Thurlow Weed, in a similar trial for libel. S. S. Bowne, Esq., and Richard Cooper, Esq., were attorneys for Mr. Cooper in this and several other similar suits.

1842.—At the Circuit Court held in Cooperstown during April of this year, Mr. Cooper received judgments against two other editors, and in September of the same year a verdict of $200 was rendered for the plaintiff, in a libel suit instituted by Mr. Cooper against the Albany Evening Journal.

On November 8, Searle's Tavern, situated where the Central Hotel now stands, very narrowly escaped destruction by fire, the roof being burnt off and the third story much injured.

In December, the Rev. F. T. Tiffany, rector of Christ Church of this village, was elected to the place of Chaplain of the House of Representatives— an honor which gave much pleasure to his many friends here.

1843.—Unusual, and to a great extent successful efforts, were made in this town during this year to enforce the temperance laws. The "Washingtonian" movement was then in full blast. At the annual meeting of the County Medical Society, held in July, 65 members were present and a resolution was passed adopting the Washingtonian pledge. The movement was one of great popularity, and it accomplished much good.

Governor Bouck, who had been in attendance at a meeting of the Board of Trustees of Hartwick Seminary, of which he was a member, stopped over night in Cooperstown at the Eagle Hotel.

Doct. John Russell, long a resident of this village, the father of Mrs. Judge Nelson, died the 2d of August in the 71st year of his age. He had been much in public life, including Member of Congress and County Clerk. He was a large land-owner in the village, and a public-spirited citizen. His wife was a Miss Williams, whose near relatives were closely identified with large business interests in and near Cooperstown. Dr. Russell resided in the house which stood on the corner of Main and Pioneer streets, where is now the store of H. M. Hooker & Co. Judge Nelson afterward occupied this dwelling, and about 1835 put up the brick building adjoining, now owned and occupied by the Murphy Sisters. Mrs. Frederick T. Starkweather, a grand-daughter of Dr. Russell and youngest daughter of Judge Nelson, is now, with her children, a resident of Cooperstown.

A large convention of Town Superintendents of Public Schools was held here in September, which was also attended by others feeling an interest in the cause of public education, and a noted address was made by James Henry, Esq., of Herkimer, which was afterwards published.

1844.—Another "Presidential year," and the local papers taken up almost exclusively with politics.

Commodore Omar Boden, spoken of by Mr. Cooper as coming here in 1798, died in May, aged 78 years.

Only a few buildings were erected on the corporation during the past two or three years.

1845.—As early as January of this year, a Hop Growers' Association was formed here, with J. W. Tunnicliff as president, and Geo. W. Ernst as secretary. It did not accomplish any thing of apparent benefit to the growers.

In this year, and again in 1847, additions were made to the water supply for the village, after which the company represented their total expenditures at about $8,000. The water all came from two large springs.

1846.—A County Temperance Society was formed here, with Col. John H. Prentiss as President. It was soon carried into politics, and did not long retain its organization.

Levi Clearwater was tried September 14th, for the killing of Nathan Tiffany, of Milford, on May 12, of this year, while under the influence of liquor. He was defended by ex-Gov. Seward, and the verdict was manslaughter in the 3d degree, with a sentence of four years in Auburn State Prison.

1847.—On the 4th of March a large meeting assembled at the Court House to organize measures for the relief of the suffering people of Ireland. Robert Campbell, Esq., presided, and an address was made by James Fenimore-Cooper. The effort to raise substantial assistance was quite successful.

On the 15th day of March, a dwelling house on Fair street, owned by Judge Nelson, and occupied by E. S. Coffin and S. McK. Thompson, took fire and was consumed, together with a large portion of the furniture of the tenants. The total loss was about $1,500.

1848.—During a large part of this "Presidential" year, the local papers were mainly filled up with discussions of the three-cornered political contest, and were very personal and bitter in their remarks.

In the spring there were several cases of small-pox reported on the corporation, which did considerable damage to the business of the place. Only two deaths occurred from that much-dreaded disease.

In April of this year, Judge Morehouse held his first Circuit in Cooperstown, and established his reputation at home as an able jurist.

1849.—Twice, during this winter, was the large establishment of H. & E. Phinney—embracing printing office, bindery and bookstore—set on fire. The first attempt was in February, on the main, four-story, brick building, on West (now Pioneer) street, in which was most of the machinery and stock. All were burned—except what property was on the first floor, most of which was removed. Other buildings were endangered, and some times on fire, but only that in which the fire originated was consumed. The loss to the Messrs. Phinney was upwards to $25,000. They also suffered large damage from derangement to their business. A second building near, in which they also had paper and other material, was not destroyed. Four weeks later, occurred the second and finishing incendiary fire, which destroyed the other building used by this firm in their business. It was discovered about 5 o'clock in the morning, and was probably set a few hours earlier. The loss was about $10,000; the insurance only one-half that amount. A large number of persons in the employ of the Messrs. Phinney, were obliged to leave the village after this disaster, from a lack of employment, and thus it was a serious affair in respect to the interests of the place, as the business was removed to Buffalo.

The original of the following paper, in the handwriting of Col. J. H. Prentiss, was handed us by Mr. George W. Ernst, while on a visit to Cooperstown, the day on which the preceding paragraph was put in type, and we give it as of interest in this connection. All but three of the subscribers were living here when the editor of this book came to Cooperstown, in the fall of 1851; and all but eleven of them are now deceased:

Whereas, several incendiary letters have been addressed to the Messrs. Phinney, within the past two years, threatening the destruction of their buildings and property, received through the drop in the Post-office; and whereas, on the morning of the 3d inst. their brick building was destroyed by fire, through which they suffered great loss, and the property of several other of our citizens was damaged and seriously endangered; and since that date, another of those incendiary letters have been received as aforesaid, in which the burning of the building is avowed and other depredations, threatened, in case the Messrs. Phinney do not do a certain act; therefore, the undersigned deem it proper that the Trustees of the village of Cooperstown should offer a suitable reward for the detection and judicial punishment of such offender or offenders, and to that end authorize them so to do, and as an indemnification for such proceeding on their part, agree to pay to them upon such detection and conviction, the several sums set opposite their names hereto signed. Dated February 21, 1849.

Calvin Graves,	$ 25.00	L. McNamee,	$ 20.00
W. H. Averell,	50.00	J. L. Fox,	5.00
J. R. Worthington,	25.00	H. C. Fish,	5.00
Henry Scott,	25.00	Schuyler Crippen,	5.00
Theodore Keese,	25.00	E. S. Coffin,	10.00
H. & E. Phinney,	200.00	C. Thiny,	5.00
Jno. H. Prentiss,	25.00	R. Waterman,	25.00
Robert Davis,	25.00	E. P. Byram,	5.00
E. & H. Cory,	25.00	Chas. McLean,	5.00
G. W. Ernst,	25.00	H. F. Clark,	5.00
Stephen Gregory,	20.00	Russell Warren,	10.00
J. H. Nellis & Co.,	15.00	P. E. Johnson,	10.00
S. Doubleday,	10.00	P. G. Tanner,	5.00
Richard Cooley,	10.00	S. A. Bailey,	10.00
James Stowel,	25.00	H. Hollister,	5.00
W. A. Comstock,	5.00	W. C. Keyes,	5.00
Alex. H. Clark,	30.00	Levi Wood,	10.00
Chandler Root,	20.00	Levi J. Pierce,	25.00
Henry J. Bowers,	25.00	S. W. Root,	10.00
Z. Willoughby,	10.00	L. & D. Ball,	10.00
Stillman & Wood,	5.00	J. Fenimore Cooper,	25.00
R. A. Lesley,	5.00	Geo. A. Starkweather,	20.00
Beadle & Bailey,	5.00	S. Nelson,	50.00
William Lewis,	25.00		

During this year Mr. George W. Ernst constructed the stone block of two stores on Main street, one of which he occupied as a dry goods merchant until 1862. He was appointed the first U. S. Internal

Revenue Collector for this District by President Lincoln. He is still living—at present a resident of Maryland, where he is closing up his business preparatory to returning to his old home in Cooperstown, his native place. Robert Russell is the present owner of this stone block.

Judge Morehouse died suddenly December 16. His death was severely felt, both in his profession and the social circle in which he was prominent. He had been recently chosen Judge of the Supreme Court. The Bar of Otsego county met on the 17th, and drew up resolutions of respect. He was one of the most genial, pleasant, witty gentlemen, who ever graced the society of Cooperstown.

1850.—On the morning of January 31, the dry goods and grocery store of Mr. James Cockett was seriously damaged by fire, being saved, with the adjacent buildings, only by the strenuous efforts of the firemen and citizens. The loss was covered by insurance.

During this year the Messrs. Phinney erected their building, now known as the "Phinney block." The firm occupied the first floor, the second was rented, and the third was engaged for an Odd Fellows' Hall—now occupied by the Masons as a lodge room.

In July, Capt. Boden launched the "Leatherstocking," a pleasure boat capable of carrying about 75 persons.

The most noted village improvement made this year, was the building of Mr. Joshua H. Story's large stone store, designed to be the best then in the county. In it, up to the time of Mr. Story's death, in 1871, was transacted the largest dry goods trade in Otsego county. Mr. Story was a business man of great enterprise and energy, and at the time of his death, a large real estate owner.

This year closed with a great excitement in Cooperstown, growing out of the robbing of the Otsego County Bank, on the night of December 28, by burglars, of about $30,000—within two or three thousand dollars of the surplus of the bank. As the news spread over the county, the excitement increased. In the September following, Abijah Leonard was tried and convicted of the burglary; he undoubtedly had accomplices; some thought he was not here personally at the robbery, but made the tools and directed the movements. One of his brothers was here once or twice, just preceding the robbery, and stopped at the hotel opposite.

In this year the Empire House passed into the hands of Gen. Brown, who retained it till 1866. It enjoyed a just popularity under his excellent management.

CHAPTER IX.

FROM 1851 TO 1861.

This decade marked several noticeable improvements and evidences of enterprise in Cooperstown—the commencement of a new and prosperous era; of a steady increase in population.

1851.—The first regular "local department" appeared in the Freeman's Journal in August, when its present Editor assumed control of that paper. One of the first topics introduced was the practicability of establishing a large "Summer Hotel" at this place.

In the month of August Mr. H. C. Hepburn came here to consult citizens in regard to forming a telegraph company, to construct a line to Fort Plain. He met with a reception so favorable to his proposed enterprise, that the necessary stock was subscribed, and the work commenced the following month. It was completed the first week in November, and Mr. H. S. Babcock—who for many years held the office of Justice of the Peace—became the first operator. It at that time cost fifty cents to send a message of ten words to New York; the present charge is 25 cents.

It was the custom of Judge Nelson, of the U. S. Supreme Court, to occasionally hold a term of the Circuit in this village during his summer vacation, to accommodate those attorneys and parties who might be interested in some important suit. This always brought to Cooperstown a number of the most distinguished lawyers in the country. He held court in August of this year, and the array of eminent talent present was very large. The same thing occurred in succeeding years.

The yacht "Flying Cloud," owned by Capt. Boden, was launched on Otsego lake July 30, and long remained a favorite with those who enjoyed a sail on these waters.

At that time contemplating the purchase of a country seat in some pleasant village, Gov. Marcy came here in August of this year, with his wife and daughter, especially to view the Woodside property, then for sale, and owned by Mrs. Judge Morehouse. He was pleased with it, and with the idea of locating here; but Mrs. Marcy said the long stage-ride of 26 miles was rather too great a tax, and the Governor deferred to her views in the matter. A large picnic was given at the Point, by Judge Nelson and other prominent citizens, in honor of Gov. Marcy and his family. Crumwell's band furnished the music—and the leader, a colored man named John Crumwell, is still living and playing at dancing parties in this and neighboring counties.

For the first eight days in September, the mercury ranged from 88 to 94 degrees. The winter of 1851-'52 was a very cold one.

1852.—Cooperstown, still leading in newspaper enterprise, saw the erection of its first steam power press, for the Journal, in January—

the only one then in this, or either of the seven adjoining counties, with the exception of Oneida. Now there are twelve such newspaper presses running in this county, and probably over forty in the district mentioned.

In February of this year, a public meeting in aid of the Albany & Susquehanna Railroad was held in this village, Wm. H. Averell, Esq., presiding, on which occasion Cooperstown made a very liberal subscription to this enterprise, amounting to several thousand dollars.

Dr. Horace Lathrop opened an office in Cooperstown, in March, and he is now the oldest resident physician of the place.

In July, G. W. Ryckman, Jr., bought the "Hall," the old Cooper residence, and two lots near, with a view of fitting it up as a summer hotel. Early the next year a large corps of workmen was employed to remodel and enlarge this building, and in July it was opened to the public. Its career as a hotel was very short, however, as in October of the same year it was destroyed by fire, probably the work of an incendiary. It carried an insurance of $32,500, and some of the companies interested resisted payment, but finally comprised by paying about two-thirds of their risks.

This year also witnessed the erection of the Clerk's and Surrogate's office, a brick building which stood near the old Court House. It was taken down when the present Court House was built, in 1880.

As late as this year many men were engaged in making boots and shoes in this village, as we read that 25 journeymen shoemakers were on a strike for higher wages, in August. Now, 1886, not a pair of boots, and seldom a pair of shoes, is made on this corporation. The few journeymen remaining—at the head of whom stands the veteran Sam'l W. Bingham—being wholly employed in mending.

1853.—A suggestion appears in the Journal, in January of this year, that inasmuch as the Albany and Susquehanna Railroad is likely to be constructed, a branch should be built from Cooperstown to connect with it. The first steps were taken ten years later.

In the same month the suggestion of building a large Seminary of learning in Cooperstown was first made, the outcome of which was that in the following December a public meeting was held, to take steps to establish such an institution at this place. A committee of ten was appointed to take the matter in charge. Further meetings were held during the winter to push along the enterprise, and subscription books were opened in January. The village—outside the Methodist denomination—was asked to subscribe $15,000. On the 28th of March, 1854, the following committee was appointed to attend the Otsego Methodist Association, for the purpose of hearing propositions from that body: F. A. Lee, G. A. Starkweather, W. H. Averell, Robert Davis, J. M. Peak, L. C. Turner, S. M. Shaw—all of whom except the last named have since died. The committee, at a subsequent meeting, reported that an arrangement had been made with that body of Christians to take control of the Seminary—they to raise at least $15,000, and outsiders $20,000. The work went on, and 21 Trustees were chosen on the 11th April. The Board organized as follows: Elihu Phinney,

Sen. President, G. A. Starkweather, Vice President, S. M. Shaw, Secretary, F. A. Lee, Treasurer. The contract for the building was let to L. M. Bolles, June 1. The following gentlemen comprised the first Board of Trustees: Elihu Phinney, George A. Starkweather, George W. Ernst, Cutler Fields, S. M. Shaw, A. E. Daniels, Lyman Smith, Calvin Graves, F. A. Lee, Ellery Cory, Levi C. Turner, Robert Davis, Robert H. Weeks, J. G. Bush, Rev. Charles Blakeslee and Rev. Isaac Parks of Cooperstown, Caleb Clark of Middlefield, John Young of Springfield, John Cook of Westford, F. H. Bissell of Hartwick, Joseph Russell of Milford.

In July of the following year the main building was raised, and in November occurred the dedication, Bishop Simpson making the principal address. The same week witnessed its opening with a full corps of teachers and nearly as many pupils as it could accommodate. In a short time, the school overflowed with boarders—of whom there were nearly 300—and many found board in private families in the village. The first principal was Rev. Mr. McKown. He retired from the position in 1855. Rev. P. D. Hammond was his successor as principal in August of the same year. In June, 1856, the building was leased for five years by Messrs. Hammond and Pomeroy. In February, 1857, Rev. C. R. Pomeroy became sole principal. At this time the debt on the seminary was about $23,000. It was closed in the following spring, and remained so until September, 1859, when it was purchased by Mr. R. C. Flack, assisted by a loan of $5,000 from the citizens of Cooperstown, without interest, as long as he keeps the school in operation. It was reopened by Mr. Flack, November 11, 1859.

The Methodist Church of this county was shown to be prosperous, by a report of 32 churches, 11 parsonages, 24 traveling and local preachers, and 3,059 members.

This year reports the organization of the "Bank of Cooperstown," in January. Mr. Frederick A. Lee was the originator of this enterprise, and was the first Cashier of the bank. Mr. Calvin Graves was its first President, and Mr. Theodore Keese its first Vice-President. All the original directors of this bank are dead.

During this year extensive repairs were made on Christ Church, and the building was enlarged.

1854.—On the 21st of March an anti-Nebraska meeting was held at the Court House, presided over by Judge Hammond of Cherry Valley.

The Fourth of July was celebrated at the Point, and Mr. Andrew Barber, editor of the Republican, delivered the oration.

At the Annual County Fair held in the village in October of this year, Dr. E. P. Byram delivered the address. The Doctor is still a resident of Cooperstown.

As a greater precaution against fire, additional hydrants were placed in the streets by the village Trustees, in November.

A praiseworthy movement, during the winter of this year, was a course of free lectures given by some of the town's literati. They were largely attended, and were of much interest. The same thing was done in succeeding years.

On the night of October 14, the house of Mr. Holder Cory was entered by a burglar, who stabbed Mr. C. in the left breast, but the knife struck a bone, and the wound was not a serious one.

On the 12th December, there was held in the Presbyterian church of this village, the first Musical Convention, lasting four days and closing with a concert, ever held in this place; it was the second one ever held in this section of the State—the first one having occurred two months earlier at Gilbertsville. Both were held mainly through the efforts of Mr. Alfred P. Hayden, formerly of Middlefield. Prof. Wm. B. Bradbury of New York, was the conductor on both occasions.

1855.—The establishment of the "Worthington Bank," by Mr. J. R. Worthington, with a capital of $50,000, was announced in January.

During this year Mr. Levi C. Turner was a regular contributor to the Journal, over the signature of "Otsego." He was an easy, fluent writer, who had seen much of the world.

In May, one of the best stage routes in the Union was established between Cooperstown and Fort Plain, by A. A. Kendall & Co., who had recently bought this line. For several years it did a large business.

The distillery of Mr. William Brooks, near this village, was destroyed by fire in June, and the business was then closed.

The death of Andrew M. Barber, editor of the Otsego Republican, occurred, after an illness of some weeks, in the latter part of August. He was a man of pleasant, genial temperament, and had drawn about him a large circle of friends in the community and county. He left a widow, but no children. The Republican office then passed into the hands of Mr. George W. Ernst, as chairman of the Whig County Committee, and it was consolidated with the Democrat, owned by Mr. Hendricks. Mr. L. C. Turner was employed as its editor, until Mr. Wood went into the concern.

A noteworthy circumstance was the fall of six to eight inches of snow in early October, causing serious damage to fruit trees, etc. A man, in a state of partial intoxication, was frozen to death in the northern part of the town. He had been in attendance at the county fair, and was on his way home.

The example of the previous winter was followed by a similiar course of lectures, by home talent, F. A. Lee's being the initial effort of the season, followed by Dr. Lathrop, Rev. Mr. McHarg, G. Pomeroy Keese, Levi C. Turner, S. M. Shaw, and others.

In December a farmers' convention was held here, in which sixteen towns were represented, the object being the re-organization of the County Agricultural Society. H. Roseboom was appointed chairman, and F. M. Rotch of Morris was elected the first President, of the Society.

1856.—On the 10th of January, the stores with dwellings above, of G. M. Grant and N. W. Cole, on Pioneer street, were destroyed by fire. Mr. Kipp's residence was also injured.

In April and the following month, the Empire House was enlarged and improved by Gen. Brown; a third story was added.

The travel had so increased that in May, Kendall & Co. put on a noon line of stages, to run on the east side of the Lake.

In June, Hon. Joseph L. White purchased Woodside, of Mrs. Morehouse, and took up his residence there.

Mainly through the efforts of Mr. F. A. Lee, ground was purchased, and "Lakewood Cemetery Association" formed. The grounds were dedicated in the presence of a large concourse of people, in September of '57. It has proved of great and lasting benefit.

In August, Jerome B. Wood, Esq., purchased one-half interest in the Democrat and Republican, and became co-editor with J. I. Hendryx. He was a very pleasant and scholarly gentleman, but active politics were distasteful to him.

In the early fall, Mr. Edward Clark of New York purchased the "Apple Hill" property, on which, a few years later, he erected the most elegant and costly mansion, by far, in this section of the State; also a magnificent stone bath-house, stables, green-houses, &c. ·

As a new thing for this locality, the Democràts held a "barbecue" here, in September—an ox being roasted whole, in the grove then standing above the Court House.

In September, after a painful illness of two and a half years, which confined her to her bed and lounge, Mrs. S. M. Shaw was taken to her parents' house in Albany, where she remained for six years, under the care of leading physicians of that city. She was conveyed to Fort Plain on a spring couch made for that purpose, and which was the next morning placed in a special coach kindly put at our disposal by the Superintendent of the Central railroad—all under supervision of her kind medical attendant, Dr. H. Lathrop, who accompanied the party to Albany.

1857.—January 22 made about the coldest mark on record, the mercury going down to 32 below zero.

Much damage was done to trees and buildings, in April of this year, when snow fell to a depth of twenty to thirty-six inches, on the 14th, and about five feet in three days. A great many barns and sheds, and a few dwellings, were broken down by the weight of the snow.

On the night of December 28, all the prisoners confined in the county jail made their escape; quite an easy matter, owing to the general discreditable dilapidation of that building. It was presented by the grand jury as a nuisance, the following month.

1858.—Alonzo Bowen was drowned by breaking through the ice in the Lake, January 13th.

The upper part of the dwelling of widow Zenas Chapman, was destroyed by fire on the noon of March 12; and by the gratuitous labor of the kind-hearted villagers, a new roof was placed on the cottage before night of the same day.

In April, a small steamboat was placed on the Lake, but being found rather an unsatisfactory craft, its trips were discontinued after a few cruises.

The appointment of R. R. Nelson, Esq. to the U. S. District Judgeship of Minnesota, and the confirmation of this appointment by the Senate, occurred in May.

In May, the old Spanish shillings, sixpences and quarters disappeared, as those silver coins were then tabooed, and refused as a circulating medium, both here and elsewhere.

J. B. Wood, Esq., severed his connection with the Republican, in June, retiring from journalism to resume the practice of his profession—the law.

The hat and fur business, commenced about sixty years before by Ralph Worthington, and which, since his death, in 1828, had been continued by his son, John R. Worthington, was discontinued in the latter part of this year, and the stock in trade was advertised to be sold at cost.

Good old Judge Kinne, the friend of every man, had his hotel room entered one night in September, and his valuable gold watch and some money stolen.

1859.—Lieut. Orren Chapman, who had served an apprenticeship in the Journal office, and afterwards graduated from West Point Academy, died in St. Louis on the 6th of January. He left relatives in this village.

In June, Patrick McNamara, on trial for the murder of his wife, at Richfield, was found guilty of manslaughter in the first degree, and was sentenced to imprisonment for life.

The store of E. & H. Cory was broken into, and the safe robbed of $30, on the night of August 5.

The "Burgess block" of stores, situated about where the Postoffice now stands, was completed in the fall, the third story being set apart for a public hall—then the only one in the village. It would seat about 200 people comfortably.

The well-known "postrider," Jared Gardner, who had carried the village papers to certain southwestern towns for about 14 years, relinquished the route in November, when he was 79 years old.

1860.—The early part of this year recorded the completion of the Cooper monument, in Lakewood Cemetery, by the addition of the graceful statuette of Leatherstocking, which crowns the shaft. This monument was erected as a tribute to his memory, by friends and admirers of the great novelist, and has been the object of many pilgrimages by those attracted by the name and fame of Cooper, as well as by its graceful proportions. A special article on it will appear elsewhere in this book.

A great array of legal talent sojourned in the village during the arguing of the Sewing Machine cases before Judges Nelson and Smalley, in the month of June. In August the Judge decided in favor of the Wilson feed patent.

Dr. F. U. Johnston of New York, purchased the farm of 160 acres belonging to Elisha Doubleday, in September, and made his residence here for several years, until his purchase of the house on River street, which is still in his possession.   Cooperstown lost one of her best citizens on his removal to Westchester county a few years since.

The Univeralist society remodeled their house of worship, and placed a bell in the tower, in the fall of this year.

A friendly political discussion was held at the Court House, October 19th, the antagonists in this "war of words" being Hon. Joseph L. White and Levi C. Turner, Esq.   The former took the Democratic, and the latter the Whig side, in the debate.

An interesting murder trial was in progress in December of this year, a Mrs. McCraney of Oneonta being accused of the murder of her step-daughter.   She was acquitted of the charge, her defense being conducted by L. L. Bundy and L. S. Chatfield; District Attorney Countryman was assisted (a very little) by Attorney-General Myers.

CHAPTER X.

FROM 1861 TO 1871.

This period was perhaps the most important in the history of this country, as it witnessed the rise, progress and close of the great Civil War. Men here, as elsewhere, saw the cloud gathering with feelings of mingled sorrow, apprehension and alarm; they were divided in opinion as to the causes which led to the war; and party feeling, before actual hostilities commenced, very naturally strongly held sway over the minds of men who were active in political life. But all this changed when Fort Sumter was fired upon—our community was united as one man in patriotic feeling for the Union. Few places of its size did more to sustain its cause. In this decade, also, occurred the most decided advance in growth and prosperity ever witnessed by Cooperstown. The coming here, about that period, of such wealthy men as Edward Clark, Henry F. Phinney, George L. Bowne, and Jedediah P. Sill, and the intelligent use they made of ample capital and well-directed enterprise, together with what was done in the same line by some of the older residents of the village, told most favorably on the growth and prosperity of Cooperstown. The Cooperstown railroad was built and opened for travel; a steamer was placed on the lake; the Union School and new Catholic church were built; the Susquehanna at the outlet was spanned by a new iron bridge that cost upwards of $12,000; a "Village Improvement Society" was organized, which did much good work; scores of new, and many of them costly and elegant, dwellings, and stores and public buildings, were erected. We narrate the progress of events more in detail:

1861.—Extensive improvements were made, during the month of February, on the Presbyterian church edifice, and those begun a few months previous on the Universalist church, completed during the same month.

Col. John H. Prentiss appeared for the last time in public life in February of this year, when he went to a State Convention held at Albany to consider the state of the nation, as one of the four delegates appointed to represent this Assembly District. His health began to fail in the spring, and he died June 26. Thus passed away another of the men of rank of Cooperstown. He represented this District two terms in Congress, and was for 41 years editor of the Freeman's Journal. He was President of the Second National Bank at the time of his death.

Mr. E. S. Coffin was appointed Postmaster of this village in March.

During the spring, many Union Meetings, for the purpose of sustaining the loyal cause, were held throughout the entire county, and were addressed by active Democrats and Republicans, eliciting great interest and enthusiasm.

In May there was a subscription circulated for aid in forming a military company, to which there was a generous response.

In the latter part of May, the ladies of Cooperstown generously volunteered to furnish 1,000 "Havelocks" for soldiers in service near Washington. This was followed by other similar work on their behalf.

The streets of Cooperstown, which had hitherto been illuminated only by the "dim religious light" which a few oil lamps afforded, very gladly welcomed the introduction of gas, for which a petition had been in circulation in June of this year.

The benevolence of our citizens was again exhibited in August, by a subscription of $300 in aid of sick and wounded soldiers.

In the latter part of this month, forty volunteers left Cooperstown to join the van-guard rifle regiment.

A great outrage was perpetrated here in September, in the arrest of Mr. George L. Bowne, a native of this town, who resided in Florida at the outbreak of the war, and who had voted against secession in the legislature of that State. Moved by some representations made by an enemy—or by some person seeking to make money out of the affair—the authorities at Washington sent an officer here to arrest Mr. Bowne and convey him to Fort Lafayette. The affair created great excitement and much hard feeling. Mr. Bowne, who was in rather poor health at the time, was released after a confinement of two weeks. He built the "iron-clad" block, in which this book was printed, and put up the building on Lake street now owned by Mr. E. F. Beadle.

1862.—For the first time in a number of years, there was a general celebration of Washington's birthday, and the Rev. S. T. Livermore read the notable Farewell Address.

On the night of the 10th of April occurred a great conflagration, that destroyed at least one-third of the business portion of Cooperstown. The alarm was sounded at half-past 10 o'clock, and the unequal battle with the flames lasted till near daylight. The fire originated in the cabinet shop of E. Edwards, near the Cory store building, and it swept away all the stores and shops on that side of Main street, except the latter, from W. G. Smith's east to Pioneer street; by desperate efforts it was prevented from crossing the latter street, though the buildings on the two opposite corners were several time on fire. It then crossed Main street, destroyed three hotels and other buildings, and extended up the west side of Pioneer street as far as Mr. Phinney's house. Fortunately there was no strong wind blowing at the time, indeed it was perfectly quiet till 2 o'clock in the morning or a much greater damage would have been inflicted on the village. We never saw firemen work with more hearty zeal or intelligence than were displayed on this occasion; and men and women aided in passing buckets of water, and in removing and caring for furniture and goods. The following is a list of the number of buildings burned, the number of occupants, value and insurance:

Owners	Buildings	No. Occupants	Value	Insurance
L. J. Walworth	2	3	$3,000	......
H. Groat	3	1	2,000	$1,000
D. Peck	3	1	2,000	1,000
Kipp & Grant	2	2	2,500	......
J. H. Burgess	3	5	4,000	3,000
Wm. Lewis	6	1	7,000	2,000
W. Van Booskirk	1	1	1,200	......
W. C. Keyes	6	3	4,000	......
Mrs. Carr	2	1	2,000	......
Z. Willoughby	1	..	150	......
A. Robinson	1	2	1,000	800
L. Brown	3	3	1,200	......
E. & H. Cory	2	1	1,500	......
J. F. Scott & Co.	2	1	2,500	1,000
J. J. Short	2	2	1,700	......
E. & H. Cory	3	1	500	......
J. Wood	3	1	1,500	......
Bingham & Jarvis	3	2	4,000	2,000
H. Hollister	2	2	2,200	......
S. Nelson	3	2	5,000	2,500
H. N. Robinson	1	5	1,800	1,200
McNamee's estate	3	..	500	......
Other property, damaged about	.	..	1,500	......
Total	57	40	$52,750	$14,500

Some of the parties interested, placed their losses somewhat higher than the above. On the other hand, most of those lots made vacant by the fire, were thus largely increased in value.

The losses on personal property at this fire were given at the time as follows:

E. & H. Cory	$5,000	A. Robinson	$ 350
Edward Edwards	2,300	Daniel Peck	500
H. Holister	300	John J. Short	1,500
G. M. Grant & Co.	1,200	Geo. Jarvis	200
J. G. Cooke	1,200	Mrs. Sherman	150
W. C. Keyes	1,200	John Wood	500
Mrs. Carr	1,000	Loomis Brown	300
Harmon Groat	500	W. G. S. Hall	1,300
Lewis Bundy	200	Wm. Lewis	3,000
Bingham & Jarvis	3,500	John Burgess	300
H. N. Robinson	800	B. F. Kipp	800
C. R. Burch	100	Others, tenants	1,300

Total $27,500

Messrs. A. Robinson, H. N. Robinson, Peck, Burch, were fully insured, and Bingham & Jarvis for $1,500.

Total direct loss by this conflagration, about $80,250, insurance $17,750. The incidental loss was also considerable.

On the Monday night following this conflagration, a fire caught in the barn of the Otsego Hotel, corner of Main and Fair streets, and that entire property, and the dwelling house and barn of Mr. William K. Bingham, were destroyed. The total loss was about $10,000; insurance $4,000. The hotel was owned by H. B. Ernst. For a time this second fire cast an additional gloom over the village. Now, only one hotel, the Empire House, was left standing in Cooperstown.

What was at first very naturally regarded as a public calamity, in which individuals suffered considerable loss—though only a few of them were unable easily to bear it—in the end proved of great and lasting benefit to the place. It afforded an opportunity to make Main street of uniform width throughout its entire length—a great and very desirable improvement. The expense was largely met by private subscription. And then followed the erection of the Central Hotel, the "Iron Clad" and other fine brick and stone buildings on Main street, the Clinton House and Mr. Kipp's large brick house on Pioneer street, the Nelson block of stores, corner of Main and Chestnut streets, and other improvements. Cooperstown "arose from her ashes" a new and far more beautiful town—and still the improvements are gradually going on, as store after store follows the Bundy block on the old "Eagle Hotel lot."

On the 25th of April, a public meeting was held in the Court House, at which steps were taken to collect funds to aid those few persons who had been impoverished by the recent fires.

The buildings burned were located as follows: L. J. Walworth's dwelling, on a lot now embraced in the grounds of Elihu Phinney; Harmon Groat's building, once occupied as a piano factory, on lot now occupied by F. Carroll's paint shop; Daniel Peck's hotel, on the present Clinton House grounds; B. F. Kipp's dwelling, next north; J. H. Burgess, north of alley between him and Kipp, three shops and Hall above, on ground once occupied by Stephen Gregory's old shoe manufactory and a small residence; the Eagle Hotel on the corner, now occupied, together with a portion of the Burgess lot, by the Bundy block; a wooden building owned by Wm. Van Buskirk, and occupied by W. G. S. Hall as a saloon, next west of the Eagle hotel, now occupied by brick stores; W. C. Keyes' hotel, once known as the Isaac Fitch hotel, on which the Central hotel now stands; Carr's hotel, once called the Widow Fitch hotel, now partly occupied by the Bowen block and the vacant lot east; the present Carr's hotel stands partly on the Esek Bradford card factory lot, and partly on the Judge Foote lot, whose residence forms a part of that house. On the north side of Main street, A. Robinson's "town pump grocery," rebuilt; Loomis Brown's building, occupied as a bakery, and residence above, not rebuilt; E. & H. Cory's shop, occupied by E. Edwards, part of lot vacant, partly occupied by W. E. Cory's store; J. F. Scott & Co., store, stood next east; John J. Short, store and residence, next east; E. & H. Cory's shop, barns and sheds, in rear of stone building now owned by A. J. Wikoff; John Wood, market and dwelling stood on same ground now occupied by him; Bingham & Jarvis and H. Hollister, two stores, now occupied by "iron clad" building; S. Nelson, two stores, occupied by Grant & Co. and Joseph G. Cooke, next adjoining on the east; H. N. Robinson, stores occupied by self and C. R. Burch, corner Main and Pioneer streets.

The buildings which were erected on the burnt district within about a year after the fire, were as follows: Double brick building, corner of Main and Pioneer streets, by H. N. Robinson, afterwards purchased by J. H. Story, now owned by his sister, Mrs. Wm. E. Taylor of Binghamton; two brick buildings adjoining on the west, by the late Judge Nelson, and still owned by his estate; the large and elegant brick building, with iron front, two stores, offices and public Hall, with brick bakery in rear, by George L. Bowne, now owned by Asahel A. Jarvis; a handsome stone building, dwelling and market, by John Wood, and still occupied by him; a double frame building, with brick front, for two stores and dwelling, by John J. Short, who still occupies the dwelling part; a brick building by John F. Scott, who still occupies the upper stories in his hop and wool business; a brick store by E. & H. Cory, who were succeeded by the present occupant, Wm. E. Cory; a frame building, called the "town pump grocery," by A. Robinson, which has several times changed hands, and was recently purchased and remodeled by the present occupant, Harmon Groat. On the south side of Main street, the Central Hotel and Carr's Hotel—the former wholly new, the latter in part a dwelling owned by Mrs. Carr which escaped the flames. The "Bowen block," two stores and offices, was put up by the law firm of Countryman & Bowen, in 1875-'76. In 1880 the Bundy Brothers put up their double brick building, bank, store and postoffice on a part of the old Eagle Hotel lot; G. M. Grant & Co. put up their building adjoining, the year following; then in '82 J. Warren Lamb & Co. put up a similar building adjoining; followed by George L. White by his brick furniture store the next year. Two additional similar buildings adjoining on the west, are to be erected in the spring of 1886—one by Charles E. Moore as a grocery store, and one by Wm. H. Michaels as a market and dwelling. South of the postoffice, on Pioneer street, Benj. F. Kipp put up a large brick dwelling in 1862, and Daniel Peck built the Clinton House, hotel, in 1867, and it was opened for business in the fall.

On the 16th of May, a small dwelling house on Bay street owned by Winchester Childs was destroyed by fire. His loss was partly made up by the donations of a few liberal-hearted citizens.

In the month of July the Catholic Society of this village purchased ground for a cemetery on the hill west of the village, now owned by them. The consecration of the same, took place with imposing ceremonies on the first of August.

On the 28th of July, a large war meeting was held at the Court House, over which Judge Campbell of Cherry Valley presided. Addresses were made by Hezekiah Sturges, Esq., and Judge Graves of Herkimer.

In this year the government was making calls for large numbers of troops. The first meeting held for the purpose of voting a town bounty to Volunteers was held in the Court House, on the 8th of August, and $25 was voted. On the 29th of the same month the bounty was increased to $100.

On the 12th of September, Carr's Hotel was reopened for business, having in a large degree been rebuilt since the fire.

Silver change had become so scarce at this time, that the Worthington bank issued a large amount of small fractional notes. These were counterfeited at a later day, and the genuine were called in. Soon after this the government issued fractional notes, as low as three cents. So many persons had engaged in this business that the government wholly interdicted it.

Dr. Lathrop and E. M. Harris, Esq., were appointed commissioners for examining the men subject to draft into the military service of the government. They were kept very busy at this work through the month of October.

In November, Edwin M. Harris, Esq., was appointed County Judge, to fill the vacancy occasioned by the resignation of Hon. Levi C. Turner, who had accepted a position at Washington, under Judge Advocate-General Holt. Mr. Turner died in Washington, while holding this office, March 14, 1867, aged 61 years.

1863.—A new firm announced this spring, that of Cockett & Murdock—Mr. Harvey Marvin, late with the former, having died.

On the 1st of April, Judge Nelson started the "up-street" movement, then so much discussed among business men, by breaking ground for his brick block of two stores, corner of Main and Chestnut streets.

A great laugh was raised in the village one day in April, when it was made known that a couple of desperate fellows in the old county jail had made their escape, after locking in the Sheriff and Dr. Thos. B. Smith, physician to the jail!

The residence on Chestnut street, occupied by Rev. G. T. Wright, was destroyed by fire on the night of April 27—Mr. Wright losing considerable personal property.

Here, as elsewhere, the 30th of April was a gloomy day, being generally observed as a day of National Fasting and Prayer.

On the 1st of May, after the passage of the Albany and Susquehanna Railroad bill, which was finally approved by the Governor, (Horatio Seymour,) a public meeting was held in this village to consider the matter of building a branch road, to connect with it. On this occasion L. J. Walworth presided, and W. H. Bunn was secretary. The meeting was addressed by Engineer Edgerton, S. M. Shaw, and L. J. Walworth; a committee was appointed, with L. I. Burditt as chairman, to take further action. In February, 1865, another meeting organized a company, which elected the following gentlemen a first Board of Directors: L. I. Burditt, Wm. M. Clinton, Rufus Steere, J. P. Sill, G. W. Ernst, J. F. Scott, Calvin Graves, J. W. Shipman, Geo. L. Bowne, Wm. Brooks, J. H. Story, Ellery Cory, and Dorr Russell; $250,000 was subscribed and ten per cent of that amount paid in. In May of the same year the following officers were chosen at a meeting of the Directors: Luther I. Burditt, president; Joshua H. Story, vice president; George A. Starkweather, secretary; John F. Scott, treasurer. Surveying was commenced in November.

The 50th anniversary of the Otsego County Bible Society, of which Mr. F. A. Lee was then president, was held in the Presbyterian church, on the 16th of June.

On the 21st of August, 1863, Cooperstown was visited by a distinguished party of gentlemen, led by Secretary Seward, and including the following Foreign Ministers: Lord Lyons of England, Baron Gerolt of Prussia, M. Molina of Nicaragua, M. Tassara of Spain, Baron Strœckel of Russia, M. Mercier of France, together with the representatives of Italy, Sweden, and Chili, and several Secretaries and attaches of the different legations. They were handsomely entertained by different prominent citizens of the place, and they were entertained together at one of the Points on the Lake. On leaving they expressed themselves as very favorably impressed.

In August of this year there was great excitement here and elsewhere, over the draft for this District, which took place in Norwich. Otsego county was called upon to furnish 985 men for the army. And then, too, there was an "income tax" to pay, for the first time, in the fall.

E. & H. Cory were among those who built new stores this year, and they changed from the old stone store, which had escaped the flames, and which they had occupied for 34 years.

To help the unfortunate ones "out of the draft," the bounty offered by the town of Otsego, for Volunteers was increased to $600 in December—when notice was given that the quota of the county, under the next draft, would be 693 men.

1864.—In the latter part of January the Catholic society added about $400 to their church fund, the net proceeds of a successful festival held at that time.

The three Banks of the village decided in the early part of the year to adopt the "National" system.

Washington's Birthday was the occasion of a benevolent action on the part of some of our farmers, in generously donating wood to certain poor widows of this place.

The announcement of a new telegraph line to Herkimer, via Richfield, was made on the 1st of March. It has lately passed under the control of the great Western Union.

The patriotic and enterprising ladies of Cooperstown netted $557 from a fair held under their auspices, for the benefit of the soldiers, in July.

On the 4th of August, a National Fast was observed by a Union Service, the Rev. W. N. Newell of the Presbyterian church preaching the sermon.

In September the army quota of the town of Otsego was filled, and no drafted men were sent. The bounty had been raised to $1,025, for the war; and in December the town bounty was increased to $800 for "three years' men."

Gov. Seymour, who was the Democratic Presidential candidate this year, addressed a political mass-meeting in this village, in Oct.

1865.—Lieut. Morris Foote returned to his home in Cooperstown, in January, having happily made his escape from a rebel prison. His brother, Frank Foote lost a leg in the battle of the Wilderness, and was for a long time thought to have been killed.

In February, G. A. Starkweather, Esq., after a residence of about nine years in Milwaukee, returned to Cooperstown, his former residence, and resumed the practice of the law.

Cooperstown Seminary was purchased in February by Wm. M. Clinton, who repaired the building with a large outlay, and in the month following, Mr. R. C. Flack retired from his management of the institution, of about five years' duration. Prof. George Kerr, a most successful instructor, assuming charge as principal on the opening of the spring term in April, with a greatly improved and newly furnished building, and a large attendance of scholars. Mr. Clinton sunk a large sum of money in this venture.

In April occurred an impromptu celebration of the "Capture of Richmond," the program consisting simply of the usual demonstrations of victory—ringing of bells, firing of guns, and blazing bonfires. A little later in the month, the rejoicing at the surrender of Gen. Lee was manifested by a similar celebration. There was great joy manifested.

In the latter part of the month, Cooperstown was shrouded in gloom at the melancholy death of President Lincoln. Appropriate religious services were held on the 21st, in Bowne Hall, and a funeral oration delivered by Rev. C. K. McHarg.

The first day of June was observed as an occasion of humilation and mourning on account of the assassination of the President. A union service was held in the Presbyterian church.

The patriotism of our citizens was evinced by quite an elaborate celebration of the 89th anniversary of American Independence, there being a procession, oration, etc., during the day, and a fine display of fireworks in the evening. Wm. H. Averell, Esq., was President of the Day; Geo. W. Ernst, Marshal; Hon. Geo. H. Andrews, Orator; Rev. C. K. McHarg, Reader; Rev. E. R. Sawyer, Chaplain.

A building in the rear of the Seminary, used as laundry and washhouse, was burned in the latter part of September; the loss was about $3,500.

The "Pioneer Boat Club," organized in September, comprised about twenty-five such "young fellows" as Dr. Lathrop, D. A. Avery, B. F. Murdock, Rev. C. K. McHarg, S. G. Browning, Rev. E. R. Sawyer, F. G. Lee, S. M. Shaw, Dr. Blodgett, S. A. Bowen, Capt. P. P. Cooper, W. H. Ruggles, G. P. Keese, E. Phinney, John Worthington, and others. Most of them became very expert, the following summer, in "catching crabs" in their costly and elegant six-oared cedar boa

—which was not put into water after the second season and was finally sold for about what the oars cost!

1866.—The purchase of the Phœnix Factory by Mr. John F. Scott was announced in January. He expended about $75,000 in improvements on this property, which he fitted up as a woolen manufactory; but the venture proved unfortunate.

Another free lecture course was in progress during the winter months of this year.

Several deaths from that terrible disease "spotted fever," occurred here during the spring.

Principally through the efforts of Miss Susan F. Cooper, a "Thanksgiving Hospital" was established, or rather efforts were begun for its establishment, by the people of the village, among whom a subscription list was circulated, in July.

On the last day of July, a sad accident was recorded, the drowning in Otsego Lake of a young son of the Rev. Dr. Alfred B. Beach of New York, then a visitor here.

St. Mary's Catholic society of Cooperstown broke ground for their new brick edifice in October.

The report of the Supervisor of the town of Otsego, in November, showed that this town had paid for bounties, during the late war, $184,068.75—about one-half of which fell upon this village.

The "Young Men's Association of Cooperstown" organized, with E. Phinney president. One thousand dollars were subscribed and expended; a fine room rented and handsomely furnished; a library established, magazines and newspapers obtained. But the "young men," as a body, took very little interest in the society, we are compelled to record, and it languished and finally died, at the end of a few years.

1867.—The reading rooms of the Young Men's Association were opened on the first of February.

Rev. Dr. Kerr, after a successful principalship of two years, retired from his connection with the Seminary, and Mr. Clinton leased the building to his brother-in-law, Rev. Orren Perkins, who opened the spring term, in March, and continued it as a school for about two years, when its career as such closed. Dr. Kerr died here on the 13th of that month.

Quite a notable tea party was that held at the residence of Capt. Cooper in March of this year, on which occasion the united ages of the ten ladies present were 703 years—the eldest, 82, the youngest, 60; and their descendants numbered 182 persons. The following were the ladies present: Mrs. Pope, Mrs. Wm. Wilson, Mrs. Calvin Graves, Mrs. Field, Mrs. Luther Blodgett, Mrs. Levi H. Pierce, Mrs. Martha Murdock, Mrs. S. Van Sice, Mrs. Richard Cooley, Mrs. Sam'l W. Bingham.

On the last day of May, a meeting was held to discuss the condition of the bridge over the Susquehanna, and the desirability of building a new and substantial one, the cost of which was estimated at about $12,000. The project was carried to a successful result.

The corner stone of St. Mary's Catholic church, ground for which had been broken about nine months previous, was laid with imposing ceremonies in June. Its dedication occurred in December, Bishop Conroy preaching the sermon.

Carelessness with fire-arms was then not so common a cause of serious accident, it seems, as at the present time but one instance is recorded in August of this year, when a young German man-servant employed in one of the families of the village, with great recklessness pointed a gun, not supposing it loaded, at a female servant, and discharg-ing it, killed her instantly. The fellow got off without the punishment which many thought he deserved.

A fair was held in August, for the benefit of the proposed "Thanksgiving Hospital," the gross receipts of which were $940. This successful venture led to the dedication of the Hospital in November of the same year.

Three Mile Point was the scene of a merry-making on the 30th of August, when an old-fashioned lake party assembled there, attended by several of the "Old Guard," such as Messrs. Nichols, Averell, Crippen and Starkweather, and on this as on all similar occasions, the veteran "Joe Tom" was general caterer. Very few such parties have been held there since that time.

The "Clinton House" was completed and opened for business by Daniel Peck, in September. In this he had been aided by J. H. Story and Calvin Graves.

The 15th of October was observed as "General Training Day" at Cooperstown, Cols. Dunbar and Hubbard being in command, and the two regiments were reviewed by Major General Burnside of the State militia and staff. That ended the "training days" in Cooperstown. In the ranks were a large number of men who had participated in the Civil War.

Several attempts at burglary were made in October of this year, one successful raid being made on the dwelling of I. K. Williams, whose house was entered on the night of Oct. 26th, robbed of $54, a silver watch and several other articles.

Ex-Gov. Seymour visited Cooperstown in October, and after a serenade by the Boston Brass Band, he made an address from the piazza of the Empire House. A large number of the villagers called on him to pay their respects.

At a district school meeting held in November, it was resolved that legal steps should be taken for disposing of the two little old wooden buildings and sites then belonging to School District No. 1, town of Otsego, and the proceeds devoted toward the erection of a new brick school building; and that the sum of $6,000 additional should be raised for the same purpose.

A slight shock of earthquake was experienced in Cooperstown and vicinity, on the 18th of December. It was very sensibly felt by a number of people in the village.

1868.—The 1st of January, the Freeman's Journal appeared enlarged to a nine-column paper. The Republican enlarged to the same size soon after. Neither of these papers has ever adopted the practice, now so common among country newspapers, of using stereotype plates got up for their use in the cities—giving cheaper and poorer reading.

On the 14th of February, a second school meeting was held, at which it was determined to purchase a lot of ground on Susquehanna avenue, and proceed with the erection of a new District School House, in the spring. It was resolved, also, that a tax levy of $5,000 should be made and the old lots sold at auction. On the 4th of July, work had so far progressed that the corner stone was laid, on which occasion Rev. C. K. McHarg made an appropriate address. The building was finished and the school opened in October of the following year, with an attendance of over 200 pupils. The cost of building and lot was about $14,000. It was an improvement that was not accomplished without strong opposition; but from the start the school was such a success, that very few indeed regretted its cost. Mr. H. G. Howe was the first principal; Miss Gaylord, preceptress; Miss Ball, assistant. Thomas Clark was chairman of the building committee under whose supervision the school house was erected.

Work was actually begun, in February, 1868, the contract for building the Cooperstown R. R. having been let to James Keenholtz. In February of the next year, the depot was located, and Mr. J. F. Scott succeeded Mr. Burditt as president of the company, and in July 1869, the road was opened for business, the event being celebrated by the usual demonstrations of joy, firing of cannon and ringing of bells. The old "Colliersville stage" retired from service, making its farewell trip the day of the opening of the railroad. The town of Otsego bonded in the sum of $150,000, the town of Middlefield in the sum of $50,000, and individuals subscribed $58,405, to aid in the construction of this railroad.

The entrance of March this year was in the traditional lion-like manner, the mercury standing at 22 degrees below zero on the 1st.

The opening to patients of the Thanksgiving Hospital, occurred on the 1st of June.

The summer season of this year was the warmest in more than twenty years, the thermometer ranging for four consecutive days from 91 degrees to 96 degrees; such weather as prompted Sidney Smith to long "to take off his flesh, and sit in his bones."

The long-talked-of hotel on the "Otsego Hotel lot" was announced in August as soon to be built, causing much discussion in the newspapers as to the pros and cons of the project. This building, which financially swamped all the capital expended on it, now standing in its unfinished and slowly decaying state, is known as the "Skeleton Hotel," a very appropriate name. Its cost was about $57,000, and it was sold at auction to Mr. George Clarke for $9,000, on the collapse of the unfortunate enterprise. For several years past it has been used for storing hops. The "Otsego Lake Building Association" which constructed it, went into the hands of H. Sturges, Esq., as receiver, in May, 1872.

Our genial legal friend, Counselor George Brooks, paid a rather novel bet, lost on Horatio Seymour, by wheeling a barrel of flour from the Court House to the bridge over the Susquehanna, when, instead of making a hasty retreat, nothing abashed, he mounted the barrel and made a speech. It is thought that this experience cured him of his Democracy, as he has not since then acted with the party in which he was nurtured.

Simon Van Sice was a veteran and pensioner of the war of 1812, having served under Gen. Scott in two or three engagements. On the "golden wedding" anniversary of himself and wife, which occurred in November, they were kindly remembered by their many friends, one from Poughkeepsie sending a substantial gift of $50. Mrs. Van Sice is now the only person on this corporation drawing a pension for the services of her husband in "the second war of American independence."

1869.—Mr. Henry F. Phinney had returned to Cooperstown with a handsome fortune, with an increased love for his native village, and with great confidence in its future growth and prosperity, toward which he resolved to devote his time and money. He was a liberal subscriber to every good object and true charity. The Seminary property has passed into the possession of the Second National Bank, by which it was sold to Mr. Phinney in January, and in it he sunk not far from $65,000. The interior of the building was changed and improved, to fit it for the purposes of a summer hotel; the exterior and grounds were greatly improved; new outbuildings were erected, and new furniture added. When completed, the building was named the "Cooper House," and it was leased to Charles A. Watkins of Albany, who continued its landlord for two years. He was a popular young man, but he lacked capital, and mainly on that account was not successful in the business.

In January, S. M. Ballard, sold the Empire House to J. H. McDonald, of Delaware county, who sold it to Edward Clark and J. H. Story in the spring of 1871; they spent about $4,000 on it, named it the "St. James," leased it to D. L. Keyes, and it burned down in November, 1872. Loss on building about $14,000; on furniture, about $2,500.

In April, there was an unusually heavy fall of rain (2½ inches in one night) causing the creek running through the village to overflow, carrying away part of the culvert under Main street and doing a damage of about $1,000. Other localities were also damaged.

This was a year of great activity among builders and others in Cooperstown. During most of the summer and fall about one hundred carpenters, masons and painters were employed here. Mr. Edward Clark's stone mansion was erected, the first sash and blind factory —the capital for which was furnished by Mr. H. F. Phinney—the school house completed, the Seminary changed to a hotel, and a number of dwellings erected.

In September, Capt. D. B. Boden brought here by railroad a small steamboat, which it was stated had been used as a gunboat in southern waters during the war, carrying a single gun. It attracted no small attention as it was conveyed through Main street on trucks to the dock. It was enlarged and improved, named the "Mary Boden," and placed upon the lake the following summer. The "toot" of its whistle was not very loud, and one day Mr. J. P. Sill—who had been very active in aid of the Cooperstown railroad—joked the Captain on that fact, who replied: "You wait till I obtain the consent of this village to bond for about $50,000 for a steamer, and I will show you a steam whistle that will drown the sound of both the locomotive whistles!"

In September, the County Agricultural Society purchased of Spafard & Hooker the 26 acres of land now owned and occupied by the same near the corporation limits.

1870.—An old lady, named Bice, living in an old house opposite the Court House, called "Bull's Head," supposed to be very poor and needy, who had been aided many years by the town, died in January, and $300 in coin were found among her effects.

A fair, for the benefit of the Cemetery Gateway Fund, held in March, netted $250.

In March, the old jail was again "presented" by the Grand Jury, and the same month a bill was introduced in the legislature "to facilitate the construction of new county buildings at Cooperstown."

At the opening of the spring term of Union School, Mr. John G. Wight, was given the position of Principal—a place so long filled by him, with satisfaction to those most deeply interested in the welfare of the school.

In July, the village Trustees decided on extending Fair street through the "Cooper grounds," and Counselor Brooks was most active in the work. The way extended directly over the foundation walls of the "Hall."

This summer witnessed the presence of a large number of city visitors in Cooperstown—one of the best seasons the village has ever experienced.

A concert and sale for the benefit of the Thanksgiving Hospital netted about $400.

Early in September, a "Village Improvement Society" was organized in Cooperstown, for the general purpose of caring for the various points of interest, etc, in the vicinity. It did considerable good work.

The Baptist church of Cooperstown reopened for worship the 1st of September, after having been enlarged and greatly improved at a cost of about $4,000.

Mr. Keenholtz, the late contractor for building the C. and S. V. R. R., obtained a verdict against the company for $41,303—the full amount claimed by him as the balance due him. The case was appealed and a new trial granted.

During this year, there were 22 dwellings erected on the corporation, a number of which were put up by Mr. H. F. Phinney.

CHAPTER XI.

FROM 1871 TO 1881

Although this decade covered an extended season of general hard times throughout the county, Cooperstown experienced very little of its effects; even the individual cases were few among our citizens. The village grew and flourished, 1871 witnessing the erection of about 30 dwelling, including that of Fred. G. Lee on Lake street, afterwards purchased and doubled in size by Mrs. Jane R. Carter, and the completion of the large brick dwelling put on Main street by Mr. Joshua H. Story at a cost of about $20,000. A large steamer was put on the lake; the Fire Department was for the first time properly organized, and new apparatus bought; the Hotel Fenimore was built; a large addition made to the Union School building; a new Jail and Sheriff's residence, and then a Court House erected; the threatened bankruptcy of the Cooperstown railroad prevented; the Pioneer Mills erected at a cost of about $45,000; the Aqueduct Association enlarged its supply of water to meet the growing demands of the village; the census of 1880 showed a gratifying increase in the population of the place. In detail the record shows:

1871.—Mr. George Story, at an expense of several thousand dollars, added a new story to his brick block on Main street, adjoining his brother's new house—all now known as the Ballard House.

In January, the Village Improvement Society of Cooperstown took a lease of Three Mile Point, at a nominal rent, for 25 years, of Mr. Wm. Cooper of Baltimore, who owns that small but valuable piece of lake property.

In the same month Mr. J. R. Worthington sold the circulation of his bank to certain parties in Oneonta, who established the "First National" bank of that village, Mr. Worthington being one of its stock holders and directors. He also continued in business as a private banker in this village.

In the month of April, the old "Bull's Head" property, once kept as a hotel, was demolished by Mr. Phinney. In this hotel, Mr. Thurlow Weed was a boarder while working at his trade as a printer in this village, and there became engaged to be married to the daughter of Mr. Ostrander, then the proprietor, and a few years later they were married. Mr. Weed visited this village the following summer, when the editor of this book, who had known him for over twenty years, had a long conversation with him in regard to occurrences here while Mr. Weed was a resident.

Dr. Blodgett was appointed P. M. at Cooperstown on the first of May, and remained in office for nearly nine years.

As rather an unusual event, it may be mentioned, that there was a slight fall of snow here on the 7th day of May.

The Cooper House was this year leased to Coleman & Maxwell, who opened it on the 15th of June, and had a very successful season.

The new steamer "Natty Bumppo," owned principally by Messrs. A. H. Watkins and Elihu Phinney, had her trial trip on the 4th day of July. A few days later a set of colors was formally presented the boat by a few citizens of the village.

On the 3d August, Professor Maillefert gave an exhibition of the modus operandi of sub-marine blasting, on Lake Otsego, which was witnessed by a large number of highly interested spectators.

The Scotchmen of this village and surrounding country this year organized a society and held their first annual meeting at Three Mile Point. Addresses were made by Rev. Mr. McHarg, of this village, and Hon. Wm. W. Campbell of Cherry Valley. They had a genuine Scotch piper present, who furnished the music.

In October the people of this village showed their sympathy for the sufferers in the great Chicago fire, by contributing about $800 in money and many useful articles of clothing.

1872.—In January Mr. De Cordova opened a lecture course here with a humorous essay.

The firm of Newell & Pank took possession of the new sash and blind factory as lessees, and opened it for business on the 17th of January.

On the 7th of March the papers announced the death of Hon. Schuyler Crippen, then one of the oldest members of the Bar of Otsego county. He had sold his place on River street to Mr. H. M. Hooker, and was a boarder at Carr's Hotel.

On the night of the 11th of July, the steamer, "Natty Bumppo," which had just fairly commenced its season of running on the Lake, was destroyed by fire. There was a partial insurance, and the present steamer bearing that name was built, and launched in November.

THE RETIREMENT OF JUDGE NELSON—THE HONORS PAID HIM.

On the 28th of November Judge Samuel Nelson resigned his associate Justiceship of the U. S. Supreme Court. He might have been the Democratic candidate for President, at one time, had he consented to the use of his name before the national convention of that party. The Freeman's Journal of Dec. 5th, thus recorded an event which should have a place in this volume:

The Resignation of Judge Nelson as one of the Justices of the Supreme Court of the United States.

After a service of twenty-eight years on the Bench of the Supreme Court of the United States, and twenty-two years as a Judicial Officer of his native State, Judge Nelson on Thanksgiving day sent to the Secretary of State of the United States his resignation as one of the Justices of the Supreme Court, and it was accepted on the 1st inst. And thus closes a most remarkable and highly honorable career, covering a period of half a century. As to point of time and constant service, it is without precedent in this country or England, and we doubt if it has a parallel in the history of Jurisprudence. Lord Mansfield served 32 years and Lord Eldon 28 years, and they were longest on the Bench of Great

Britain; Chief Justice Marshall was 34 years on the Bench, Chief Justice Taney 30 years; Mr. Justice Story 34 years, and Chancellor Kent about 25 years—and of the distinguished Judges of this country they longest held judicial positions.

Judge Nelson was appointed Judge of the Sixth Circuit, which included Otsego county, in April 1823, which position he held until February 1831, when he was made Associate Justice of the Supreme Court of the State of New York, and on the resignation of Chief Justice Savage, in 1837, he took his place. In February 1845 he was elevated to the Bench of the Supreme Court of the United States, where he has won the highest honor as a Judge of strong common sense, broad views, the highest sense of honor, and a ready grasp of weighty topics. On questions in admiralty law and intricate patent suits, a writer in a leading Philadelphia paper recently remarked, especial deference was always paid to the opinions of Judge Nelson.

The Judge has with slight exception always enjoyed robust health, and has never been absent from duty at the State or U. S. Courts but one term, that of last year. At the closing session of the Grand High Commission in the spring of '71, which had lasted seventy days, and was not only of vast importance, but at times very laborious, Judge Nelson took a severe cold from sitting several hours in a room not sufficiently warmed, and after his return home was for several months confined to his house from its effects. From this he recovered, and for the past six months has enjoyed very comfortable health, while his mind has retained all of its wonted force and vigor.

There has been a strong desire on the part of many of his friends and admirers in the legal profession, that Judge Nelson should remain on the Bench a few months longer, that his half-century of service might be fully rounded out; it had even come to his knowledge indirectly—what we heard spoken of in Albany last spring, and quite recently—that it was in contemplation by leading members of the Bar in New York and other parts of the State to celebrate that event in a becoming manner, showing their high appreciation of him as a man and of his eminent services as a Judge but when it appeared evident to him that he could not go to Washington this winter and discharge the full duties of his office without running the risk of seriously jeopardizing his health—although still able to do all ordinary Chambers work—his strong sense of justice and duty impelled him to the course he has taken, feeling, as he unselfishly remarked, that with so much business pressing upon it, the Court needed the presence of an active working member in his place. Judge Nelson completed his Judicial labors the week of his resignation by deciding an important and final motion on the taxation of costs, amount claimed about $40,000, in a famous suit which had been in the courts during half the long time he has been on the bench—the "hook-headed spike case," Troy Iron and Nail factory (Burden & Co.) vs. Erastus Corning and others. The motion was heard last spring, and the examination of voluminous papers took time and involved considerable labor.

Judge Nelson reached the advanced age of 80 years on the 10th of last month, and his massive frame and strong mind and cheerful temperment, all give promise of the prolongation of a long and useful life. There is no question that we should have hailed him "Chief Justice" at the death of Judge Taney, had the Administration continued in Democratic hands.

Although the following letter from Secretary Fish is of a private character, it is so just, truly appreciative and well-deserved, that we have begged the privilege of publishing it—knowing full well that the public sentiment will be that the Secretary honors himself in honoring him to whom it is addressed, and that in speaking as warmly as he does he only expresses the feeling of the Judiciary, the Bar and the reading public wherever the venerable Judge is known:

WASHINGTON, November 30, 1872.

MY DEAR JUDGE:

I have just received your letter of the 28th, inclosing your resignation as an Associate Judge of the Supreme Court, and cannot allow the formality of an official asknowledgment to go without the expression of my personal regret that the time has come when you feel it your right to seek the repose to which an honored course entitles you, and that it falls to me to fill the paper which is to terminate your connection with the highest Court of the country, and to separate you from the administration of Justice, to which for half a century you have contributed an amount of patient labor, and of learning, and a purity, dignity and impartiality which have commanded the confidence, esteem and admiration of an entire nation, and the acknowledgment of Jurists in other lands.

Thanks, my dear Judge, for your congratulations on the result of the treaty, to whose negotiation you contributed so much learning and wisdom. It has had a "hard run" on both sides of the ocean, since it was launched on 8th May, 1871—but it seems likely, at last, to vindicate itself, and to find a quiet resting place in the security and confidence which it gives to two nations whose passions it has calmed.

May years of tranquil and happy life be yours, my dear Judge; and allow me to subscribe myself,

Very sincerely, your friend,
HAMILTON FISH.

HON. SAM'L. NELSON, Cooperstown, Otsego Co., N. Y.

On the 19th of January, 1873, a large meeting of the members of the Bar was held in the U. S. Court Room, New York, over which Charles O'Conor presided, to take suitable action on the resignation of Judge Nelson. Remarks were made by Messrs. O'Conor, Pierrepont, Clarence Seward, Evarts, and others, and a brief address to Judge Nelson was adopted. A committee of distinguished members of the Bar was appointed to present this address to Judge Nelson.

A similar meeting was held by the Bar of Washington, Dec. 13th, 1872, and a letter was adopted, signed by all of the leading Lawyers then in the city practicing in the Supreme Court of the U. S. and forwarded to Judge Nelson. The State Bar held a meeting in Albany in 1873, and adopted an address which was presented him by Chancellor John V. L. Pruyn in the fall of that year.

On the 13th day of February, 1873, the distinguished committee appointed by the New York meeting came here to present to Judge Nelson the address then adopted. The chairman, Judge Pierrepont, was detained at home and Mr. E. W. Stoughton took his place. His associates were seven leading members of the bar; and several U. S. Judges, and other gentlemen, were present by invitation. Judge Nelson was briefly addressed by Mr. Stoughton and Judge Woodruff, in feeling terms, and the address was then presented. In reply Judge Nelson said:

Gentlemen of the Committee—I cannot but feel extremely honored by this address of my brethren of the Bar on the occasion of my retirement from the Bench, not more from the friendly and complimentary opinions therein expressed than on account of the unusual and extraordinary mark of respect and affection with which it has been presented; and I am the more deeply impressed with this manifestation, from the consideration that the gentlemen of the Bar who have originated and promoted this honor, some of whom are before me, have been themselves not only eye-witnesses of the judicial administration which they so favorably commend, but in which many of them largely participated in their professional capacity.

It shall ever recur to the sessions of the United States Circuit Court held in the city of New York, extending over a period of more than a quarter of a century, with pride and pleasure. The calendar was large and many of the cases important, involving great labor and responsibility. As an evidence of the magnitude of the business for many years the Court was held three months in the Spring, and three in the Autumn of the year, and still left an unfinished calendar. But the gentlemen of the Bar concerned in the trials were intelligent, faithful to their clients and to the Court, whose learning and diligence in the preparation greatly relieved the Judge of his labors, and whose professional deportment and respect banished from the court room every disturbing element, leaving free the full and undivided exercise of the faculties of the Court and counsel in their inquiry after the truth and justice of the case. No one knows better than the presiding Judge how essential this state of feeling between the Bench and the Bar is, not only to the ease and pleasure of both, but to the sound and successful administration of the law.

I have said that the gentlemen of the Bar who have originated this unusual honor, have been eye-witnesses of the judicial service so highly commended. On the other hand I can say that I have witnessed their professional career from the beginning and until their present eminence, many of whom hold my license to practice, granted when Chief Justice of the Supreme Court of the State. The eminent chairman of the meeting, Mr. O'Conor, the eldest of them, is scarcely an exception. The first session of the Supreme Court of the State after my appointment as

Associate Justice was the May Term of 1831, held in the city of New York, more than forty-one years ago. He was then a young counselor, just rising in the profession. He held a good many briefs in cases before the Court from the young attorneys, and was struggling upwards, manfully and with youthful ardor, contending for the mastery against the aged and elder counselors at the Bar—Jay, Ogden, Colden, Munroe, the elder Slosson, Sherwood, Anthon, Duer and others, who then held almost a monopoly of the business before the Courts.

The prevailing impression had been and to a qualified extent was then among the junior members of the Bar, that the experienced seniors had the ear of the Court. This, according to tradition among them, had been undisguisedly so, and to a much larger extent, before the old and revered Supreme Court of the State. But even at·the time I speak of, this feeling in the Court, and which was perhaps not unnatural, had not entirely disappeared. It required, therefore, ability, courage and resolution on the part of the junior, to encounter this impression, which he must in some degree have felt in the trial of strength against the experienced and favored senior. In the country, where I have always resided, Talcott, a young counselor, remarkable for intellectual power and legal learning at his age, opened the way, under some discouragements in the trial and argument of causes before the circuits and in bank. Other juniors, taking courage from his example, followed. He was afterwards Attorney General of the State, the youngest counselor, I believe, ever appointed to that office in New York at the time, with perhaps the exception of Josiah Ogden Hoffman among the earliest of the Attorney Generals.

I was still young when advanced to the Bench of the State, and, as was perhaps natural, my sympathies inclined toward the younger members of the Bar struggling upward and onward in their profession, and as far as was fit and proper they had my favorable consideration and kindness.

I would do injustice to my feelings and convictions if I closed these few observations without making my acknowledgments to the Bar of the Second Circuit of my great indebtedness to them, for any judicial standing to which I may be entitled. Since my first advancement to the Bench, nearly half a century ago, I have had their uniform good will and friendship, have been instructed by their learning and encouraged by the expression of their favorable opinions. They have ever been not only ready but forward to economize and lighten the labors of the Court when the amount of business pressed the hardest, even at the expense of their own personal convenience. So uniform and habitual were these exhibitions of respect and friendship, that I felt when in Court and engaged in the administration of the law that I was surrounded, not in courtesy but in reality, by professional brothers, and that every error would be charitably considered and every act worthy of commendation would receive its full reward. The address of the Bar of New York on the termination of my judicial labors, and in approbation of them I look upon as the crowning reward, which will be a source of perpetual consolation in the decline of life, and so long as a kind Providence shall permit the speaker to linger here on earth in the enjoyment of faculties unimpaired.

These proceedings appeared in full in the Journal of Feb. 20, 1873, which closes them by saying: After the delivery of the reply, the Judge arose and received the congratulations of the Judges, the committee, and others present. An elegant and sumptuous entertainment, prepared by a noted caterer of Albany, followed. The committee and their friends were then treated to a sleigh-ride on the Lake; a portion of the evening was spent with Judge Nelson, and the next morning they returned home, well pleased with the discharge of a pleasant duty, and with their winter visit to Cooperstown. The affectionate regard with which in private conversation they spoke of "the old Chief," his qualities as a Judge, a lawyer, and a man, showed the sincerity with which they had entered into this public demonstration—and they may rest assured that all they said found a warm response in the hearts of the fellow citizens of Judge Nelson.

1873.—Joyful times among the merchants of Cooperstown at the opening of this year, when hops were selling at 55 cents a pound!

It is stated, on page 71, that the town of Otsego bonded to the extent of $150,000 in aid of the Cooperstown Railroad. To this sum the town afterwards added $50,000, making the total amount $200,000. The paid-up capital stock of the road is $308,405, of which the town of Otsego owns nearly two-thirds. Its railroad debt at the date of publication of this book, is $128,500.

In March, 100,000 young bass and 20,000 salmon trout were placed in the lake. The hatching had been superintended by Capt. P. P. Cooper.

The fire department of Cooperstown was re-organized in May, under the new law giving it a Chief Engineer with two Assistants—a movement which had been long advocated. The first chief was Marcus Field.

The corner stone of the Hotel Fenimore was laid on the 30th day of June.

On the 4th of July there was a grand celebration of the day in this village. Addresses were made by Rev. C. K. McHarg and Messrs. G. P. Keese and Edwin Countryman. A procession, including the Fort Plain Fire Department, paraded the streets, and in the evening an exhibition of fire works was given on the lake. As a remarkable fact, it did not rain.

In August, the Albany Zouave Cadets visited this village, and a grand ball was given at the Cooper House for their entertainment. While here they complimented Judge Nelson by a serenade.

The 18th of September, the Hon. John V. L. Pruyn of Albany presented to Judge Nelson an address from the Bench and Bar of this State, as a testimonial of their regard and appreciation. It was a quiet and informal affair.

On the morning of September 26, the village was startled at an early hour by the ringing of the Court House bell, the occasion of which was to apprise the citizens of the fact that the house of Edward Edwards, the cabinet maker, had been entered just before daylight by three burglars, who had robbed Mr. E. of $210 and a watch, shot him twice in the breast, and left him for dead. His daughter, who alone was in the house, gave the alarm, and the immediate neighbors went at once to her assistance. By that time, however, the men had escaped, and were never afterward caught, nor was any reliable clew to their identity ever obtained. Mr. Edwards died about three weeks later from the effects of his wounds, after enduring much suffering, and having been delirious most of the time. He was not able to give a very clear description of his assailants, and it remains to this day a mystery who they were.

The Board of Supervisors of this county having decided to appropriate $20,000 toward building a new Sheriff's residence and jail, on condition that the town of Otsego appropriate $5,000 additional toward the same object, Mr. Luther I. Burditt, then the Supervisor of this town, at once gave his check for that amount, trusting to his fellow-citizens interested to reimburse him. To do so, it was resolved to raise the money by subscription, although a special act had been passed authorizing its levy upon the town. All but about $600 was voluntarily pledged, and by comparatively few citizens. The begging was principally done by Fayette Hinds, D. L. Birge and S. M. Shaw. Every dollar subscribed was collected by Supervisor Hinds, who succeeded Mr. Burditt in office. He was a valuable worker in a good cause. Those who solicited subscriptions were constantly met with this remark: "We approve of the project, and would willingly pay our tax toward it, but object to paying the taxes of other people, many of them rich and giving but little, and others rich or able as ourselves and giving nothing"— and with that sentiment almost every subscriber will heartily sympathize, when he notices the omissions. Voluntary taxes for churches and charitable objects are all right—but in purely public matters like this, the money should be raised by a general tax. The following were the subscribers to the "jail fund":

Jedediah P. Sill	$500.00	J. R. Worthington	50.00
Edward Clark	500.00	Sam'l S. Edick	50.00
H. F. Phinney	250.00	Sturges & Countryman	50.00
W. C. Keyes	200.00	G. M. Grant & Co.	50.00
Samuel Nelson	150.00	Ellery Cory	50.00
Mrs. Jane R. A. Carter	100.00	Andrew Shaw	50.00
Lois A. Carr and others	100.00	Tyley & Hinman	40.00
Elihu Phinney	100.00	Wm. Brooks	30.00
Calvin Graves	100.00	R. Quaif	25.00
John Wood	100.00	George Brooks	25.00
Johnston & Field	100.00	F. A. Lee	25.00
H. M. Hooker & Co.	50.00	Griswold & White	25.00
L. I. Burditt	$100.00	Bowes & Jackson	25.00
Frederick G. Lee	100.00	Nelson Smith	25.00
A. A. Jarvis	100.00	C. K. McHarg	25.00
B. F. Murdock & Bro.	50.00	Beadle & Soule	25.00
R. Russell & Co.	50.00	Jarvis & Bliss	25.00
F. M. Robinson	50.00	E. M. Harris	25.00
O. R. Butler	50.00	Walter H. Bunn	25.00
Johnston Bro's.	50.00	Fayette Hinds	25.00
G. Pomeroy Keese	50.00	John F. Scott	25.00
D. A. Avery	50.00	P. H. Potter	25.00
W. H. Ruggles	50.00	Doubleday & Eldred	25.00
Geo. W. Ernst	50.00	M. & J. Austin & Co.	25.00
S. M. Shaw	50.00	B. J. Scofield	25.00
C. W. Smith	50.00	H. C. Fish	25.00
A. H. Watkins	50.00	Lynes & Van Horn	25.00
J. I. Hendryx & Son	50.00	Samuel A. Bowen	25.00

W. G. Smith	20.00	H. B. Walker	5.00
E. D. Shumway	20.00	D. E. Siver	5.00
C. Childs	20.00	Peter Sayles	5.00
H. Groat	15.00	J. D. Vanderwerken	5.00
Chas. R. Hartson	15.00	Orrin Benton	5.00
C. R. Burch	15.00	Peter Becker	5.00
Geo. Jarvis & Co.	15.00	John Pank	5.00
John B. Hooker	15.00	Frank Carroll	5.00
Sanford Casler	15.00	P. P. Cooper	5.00
McCabe Bro's.	15.00	H. L. Hinman	5.00
Smith & Spingler	15.00	W. T. Bassett	5.00
John L. McNamee	10.00	T. S. Blodgett	5.00
Jerome Fish	10.00	C. & L. Hinds	5.00
George B. Wellman	10.00	W. K. Warren	5.00
C. Z. Gregory	10.00	John Hinds	5.00
R. Spafard	10.00	Hills & Shumway	5.00
John Potts	10.00	S. Irvin Haynes	5.00
Rufus Wikoff	10.00	Hosea Chapel	3.00
Robt. Pearse	10.00	Albert Pierce	3.00
N. D. Gray	5.00	Wm. C. Persons	3.00
N. W. Cole	5.00	Buckingham Fitch	2.00
S. Harper	5.00	Charles Peck	2.00

The winter of 1873 gave us more than four months continuous sleighing. The ice remained in Otsego lake until the 4th of May, and the lake was again skimmed over on the morning of the 6th. No similar record had occurred for nearly 40 years, as shown by the record kept by Mr. G. P. Keese.

1874.—January 1.—Governor Dix appointed Edwin Countryman, Esq.; Justice of the Supreme Court to fill vacancy. He was not an applicant for the place.

A "mysterious stranger," who proved to be an imposter, spent several days in this village early in this year; he pretended to be deaf and dumb; intimated his desire to purchase real estate; had negotiations with bank officers and others; was evidently a "confidence operator;" his "box containing $40,000 in gold," did not reveal property of any value. The chief of police of the city of New York intimated that the fellow was not unknown to him by reputation. He was the sensation of the day, and evidently came here to victimize a bank. He gave the name of Wood, and claimed to have just arrived from England.

The ravages of an unusually severe storm, which visited this county in June, did much damage, destroying bridges and other property, to the estimated amount of $200,000. The rain-fall in this village was 2½ inches, and in and near Cooperstown considerable damage was sustained.

Hotel Fenimore was opened for business as a summer hotel, in June, and did a good business through the season. It was continued as such for several summers, at the risk and expense of Mr. Edward Clark, who was represented by his agent, Mr. Bunyan. In the aggregate, Mr. Clark was a loser to the extent of several thousand dollars. He gave the property to his son, Ambrose J. Clark, on whose death it again came into the possession of his father.

A fair in August, in aid of the "Orphan House of the Holy Saviour," resulted in placing $500 to the credit of that institution.

The Albany Institute held its 17th field meeting in this village on the 3d of October. Hon. J. V. L. Pruyn presided and gave a brief account of the organization and purpose of the Society; after which, papers were read and addresses were made by a number of gentlemen of the Institute and the village, and the society adjourned.

The first issue of the Otsego Republican, under the proprietorship of Russell & Davidson, who had bought the establishment of J. I. Hendryx & Son, appeared on the first of November.

Gen. Kilpatrick delivered his lecture on "Sherman's march to the sea" to a large audience, in December. Gen. K. was in command of Sherman's cavalry forces in that famous campaign, and his description of it was very graphic.

1875.—The Freeman's Journal office changed quarters, from "commerical row"—where it had been located for 60 years—to the "ironclad" building, the first week in February.

Hon. Edwin Countryman delivered a eulogy in Bowne Hall on the late Judge Nelson, in March. It was a very scholarly and able production.

Extensive repairs were commenced on the Methodist church, and completed at an expense of about $4,000. The reopening occurred in November, on which occasion Bishop Foster preached.

In October, the directors of the Cooperstown Railroad effected a settlement with the heirs of the late contractor Keenholtz, whose judgment against the company had been confirmed by the Courts.

The last week in December, an advertisement appeared in the Republican offering for sale—"by virtue of several executions issued out of the Supreme Court of this State," the real and personal property of this Railroad Co. This was an unexpected movement, which occasioned great surprise, in view of the fact that the general belief had been that the condition of the road was substantially sound, and that with prudent and careful management it could be extricated from its temporary embarrassment and be made a more valuable property. Time has justified that belief and proved that the course since adopted by the Directors was a wise and judicious one, and has resulted in verifying the more hopeful predictions then made as to the future of the road. In the following March, Mr. Andrew Shaw was elected president of the road, bonds to the amount of $40,000 were issued to meet the floating debt and to settle the Keenholtz claim, and from that time to the present, with slight interruption, the road has been slowly emerging from its debt.

1876.—The "Centennial Year" of the American Union was ushered in at Cooperstown by the firing of cannon, ringing of bells, bonfires, martial music, &c. A large crowd of people was on the streets until one or two o'clock a. m., waiting to hail the auspicious hour. The president of the village, and the supervisor of this town, was a native of Middlefield, James A. Lynes, Esq.

The work of demolishing the old jail building was accomplished in January.

In February, Judge Sturges received from Governor Tilden the appointment of Canal Appraiser, a position held by him upwards of three years.

The "Half Shire" bill was defeated in the Legislature, in April, and that ended a contest in which this village was deeply interested.

The firm of Bundy Bros. made their first business announcement in March.

The Ballard House was opened to the public in May, being the J. H. Story dwelling and the George Story brick block, on Main street.

The corner stone of the new building of H. M. Hooker & Co., Main and Pioneer streets, was laid with considerable ceremony, during the latter part of July. Remarks were made by citizens of the village, and the village band discoursed stirring music for the occasion.

"Kingfisher Tower," standing a little out from the shore, in lake Otsego, two miles north of Cooperstown, naturally attracts the attention of all visitors to these waters. It was constructed during this year, and in September the wealthy gentleman who caused it to be built at an expense of several thousand dollars, complied with the request of the editor of this volume, by penning the following article for the Journal, in which paper it was published:

"Point Judith," one of the most prominent, as it is one of the loveliest, of the many diminutive capes that jut out from the shores of our lake, presents to the discriminating lover of nature features of greater beauty and opportunities for embellishment scarcely afforded by any of the others. Appreciating this fact, Mr. Edward Clark, almost immediately after purchasing the property, caused to be erected the picturesque cottage in the manner of the Swiss chalets, (to be used as a rustic retreat, or more literally, a private picnicing house). Nestling among the trees it gave a suggestion of retirement and quiet, adding to the peaceful character of the spot it ornamented, while its varied detail and bright, though not gay, coloring harmonized with the infinite forms and colors of Nature's work. The design, however, was not complete until the erection of the structure just finished, which is to be known as "Kingfisher Tower." This consists of a miniature castle, after the style of the eleventh and twelfth centuries, standing upon the extremity of the Point and rising out of the water to a height of nearly sixty feet. It forms an objective point in the scene presented by the lake and surrounding hills; it adds solemnity to the landscape, seeming to stand guard over the vicinity, while it gives a character of antiquity to the lake, a charm by which we cannot help being impressed in such scenes. Some apprehension was felt lest a proper foundation could not be secured strong enough to resist the force of the ice in winter. This has been accomplished by driving a number of piles on which a grillage was formed of heavy timber, filled with concrete, and on this solid masonry was laid, several feet in height. The castle is about twenty feet square at the base, and at a height of five feet above the water is the main floor. Ten feet above this is the first platform, provided with ramparts and machicolated parapets. Above this stage the tower alone rises, eight feet square, crowned with a pyramidal roof pierced with a window on each side, the walls bearing at one angle a bartizan with conical roof. The walls of the structure are most solidly built of stone from the shores of the lake, the roofs covered with earthen tiles, the bright red color of which contrasts finely with the sober gray of the stone. The main windows are brilliant with stained glass, and each bears in the center a heraldic shield. A drawbridge connects the castle with the causeway running to the main land, while a portcullis can be lowered to close the entrance. The drawbridge, portcullis and doors are all of solid oak. Stairs lead to the highest platform of the tower, and from the numerous openings and loopholes with which the walls are pierced, a fine panoramic view of the lake and country can be obtained. The effect of the structure is that of a picture from mediæval times, and its value to the lake is very great. Mr. Clark has been led to erect it simply by a desire to beautify the lake and add an attraction which must be seen by all who traverse the lake or drive along its shores. They whose minds can rise above simple notions of utility to an appreciation of art joined to nature, will thank him for it. The original design for "Kingfisher Tower" was selected from several drawn by Henry J. Hardenburgh, Esq., architect, and the entire work upon it has been executed under his supervision.

The visits of tramps, during the entire winter, were disagreeably frequent throughout the county. A public meeting was held here to take measures to abate the nuisance, and action was also taken by the Board of Supervisors.

The first mile of steel rails on the Cooperstown railroad, was laid in December. They are now all steel.

1877.—A famous game of old-fashioned base ball was played here, in August—Judge Sturges heading the "Reds" and Judge Edick the "Blues"—16 on a side. The victory was with the "Blues." It called together a large concourse of people.

The first accident on the Cooperstown railroad, resulting in the loss of life, occurred October 3. A man named G. W. Hopkins, who had been an inmate of the County House, was seen walking on the track, and although the engineer immediately reversed the engine, the unfortunate man was struck by the pilot and instantly killed.

Cooperstown was visited by a grand excursion party from Oneonta, on the 17th October, in which more than 1,100 people participated. The Military Company, and the Fire Department of that village, were the more prominent features, and the day was pleasantly spent in target practice, a dress parade, &c., and closed with the presentation by our citizens of a number of elegant prizes to the best marksmen.

Cooperstown was slightly shaken by an earthquake, at two o'clock, A. M., November 4, lasting from six to eight seconds. It was rather the most notable event of this rather dull year.

1878.—The village was invaded by a small army of tramps, on the 20th of January, as was often the case during this period, and twelve of these recreants, were lodged in jail before night. Later in the year, another public meeting, called for the purpose of abating this tramp nuisance; was successful in its efforts—the tramps not liking the idea of being set to work breaking stone for a living.

On the night of February 15th, the sash and blind factory was destroyed by fire, the loss being about $18,000. About a month later, the Worthington Bank building and the stone store adjoining it were burned. The latter, it was generally believed, was of incendiary origin. There was a heavy insurance on dry goods being sold by a firm from the city who had a short lease of the building. Samuel Harper occupied the stone building as a furniture factory and store, and his stock was almost wholly destroyed.

Mr. Crittenden, the present proprietor of the Cooper House, took possession in May of this year, and made many striking improvements, preparatory to its opening to summer guests in June. He bought the building and furniture for about $17,000.

Myron A. Buel, the murderer of the young girl Catherine Mary Richards, at Plainfield Center, was brought to this village and lodged in jail, July 4. This young man, (not 21 years old at the time of the murder,) was tried and convicted the following winter, and executed in this village, November 14, 1879. The prosecution was by District Attorney Benedict and L. L. Bundy; the defense by James A. Lynes and S. S. Morgan. The execution was performed by the sheriff, Mr. James F. Clark.

The surviving members of the 121st Regiment held a reunion in this village in November. It was largely attended, and the "Boys in Blue" were well entertained.

The Court House building was condemned, by a committee appointed for its inspection, in December.

1879.—The lake was closed only 61 days this season, the shortest period in twenty years.

On the site of the old sash and blind factory, Mr. Clark, at an expense of about $45,000, erected the new Pioneer Flouring Mills, and Planing Mills, the former of which were leased to E. Delavan Hills & Co. for a term of years, and the latter run by Mr. Clark's Agent. These mills are located near the railroad depot, and are connected with the railroad by a side track and turn-table; are equipped with the best and most approved machinery manufactured. The power for propelling this machinery is furnished by two large boilers, a 150-horse-power Watts, Campbell & Co. engine, located in a brick building adjoining the mills. They were completed in March, and operations began in the following month.

The Fly Creek "Fantasticals" made a sudden descent upon Cooperstown on the 14th of August and caused much amusement by their ludicrous appearance and deportment while parading the streets.

The Board of Supervisors met in extra session in June, to consider the matter of building a new Court House, and decided that a new building was a necessity and that immediate action must be taken to erect one. The committee on finance was authorized to issue county bonds in aid of that purpose. The Old Court House having been declared unfit and unsafe for further use, the Sheriff was instructed to rent suitable quarters for the holding of Court, and accordingly secured Bowne Hall, a very commodious and comfortable room for such purpose.

A public meeting was held at Bowne Hall in July, to discuss the new Court House matter, and a committee appointed to take such action as might be desirable and necessary in support of that project; and during the regular session of the Board of Supervisors, held in November, final arrangements were made for the erection of this much-needed and handsome building.

The town of Otsego was placed in a peculiarly embarrassing position by the requirement made by the Board of Supervisors, that it make a special contribution toward the grounds and building of $10,000. How to raise so large an amount was a matter of much discussion. It was conceded that it could not be raised by voluntary subscription; and finally --by a very broad and liberal construction of the statute quoted below-- it was agreed to raise it by tax. The town records, and newspapers of that date, record the following:

"A special town meeting was held, pursuant to call, at the Clinton House, December 2, 1879. Called to order by the Town Clerk, and the following resolution was submitted by S. M. Shaw: 'Resolved, That the Supervisor of the town of Otsego, in behalf of said town, be and he is hereby authorized to apply to the Board of Supervisors of Otsego Co. for power and authority to purchase a site for a Town Hall and to purchase or erect a building for such Hall, as provided by subdivision 20, of section 1, of chapter 482 of the laws of 1875, and to borrow on the credit of said town the sum of $10,000.' Nine hundred and seventy-two votes were cast, of which 654 were in favor of the resolution, and 328 opposed to it."

A leading member of the Bar and an ex-County Judge remarked at the time: "This is about the broadest and most liberal construction I have ever known given to a statute law—but it seems to be the only way to raise the required amount, to dispose of a troublesome matter, and to settle once more the question of county town, and I think we shall have to acquiesce." The town of Oneonta was before the Board of Supervisors at the time with a proposition to put up the county buildings at its own expense. By a vote of two to one in numbers, representing not less than four-fifths the taxable property of the town, the tax-payers thereof had voted, and nearly all of them afterward cheerfully paid, this tax— which they all thought should not have been made necessary by the action of the Board of Supervisors.

In November, the Cooperstown Aqueduct Association purchased the old Gregory Mill property, thus getting control of the "water power" for running their pumps, and decided to reconstruct the entire water works, by building—on the site of the old grist mill—a new brick pump house, and placing in it two very powerful pumps, capable of supplying the village most abundantly with water. This plan was carried into effect. A large pipe was laid up into the lake, commencing at a point just south of the cemetery, and running thence to a well in the pump house; engine-pumps of the most approved make were purchased, and new and larger pipes laid through the streets.

1880.—The Journal's publication by S. M. Shaw & Co., was announced on the first day of January, Edward S. Brockham, for many years connected with the office, having become one of the proprietors and publishers at that date.

The contest between several eager candidates for the Postmaster-ship, was ended in January by the appointment of Mr. Harvey I. Russell to that office.

The contract for building the Court House was let to S. R. Barnes and the McCabe Brothers for $24,995, in the latter part of January.

Much alarm was manifested at the discovery on the morning of May 1st, that several points on "the Vision" were on fire, and a large number of men were employed till late at night in subduing the flames. The damage would have been serious, had there been any wind. The sight at one time was a grand and exciting one.

The Round House of C. & S. V. R. R. Company, in this village, was destroyed by fire on the 5th of June. Two engines belonging to the Company were badly damaged and the baggage car burned. Loss estimated at fully $6,000; no insurance.

A large number of families in this village and vicinity opened their houses, in July of this year, for the reception of the poor children of New York, sent into the country by the "Fresh air Fund," for a fortnight's stay in the country. About 136 of these little waifs were thus most kindly cared for, or boarded out by others, the large brick house south of the village, owned by Hooker & Spafard, being temporarily fitted up and opened for that purpose.

At an expense of about $2,000, Mrs. Jane R Carter caused several noted improvements to be made on the property of Christ Church, in July. Mrs. Carter's liberality caused the erection of the beautiful cloister, connecting church and chapel, and the artistic interior arrangement of the chapel is also due her. About $1,000 were expended on improvements of the church proper, by the parish.

In October, occurred the annual reunion of the 121st and 152d regiments, N. Y. Volunteers, in this place. There was a large attendance, and interesting proceedings.

As an evidence of the esteem in which Prof. J. G. Wight was held by his pupils, a gold watch was presented their faithful instructor, by the school, at the close of the fall term.

Laying of the Corner Stone of the Court House

On the 15th of June occurred the laying of the corner stone of the new Court House, with imposing ceremonies. Between eight and ten thousand people were in attendance. The Masonic Order was represented by the Grand Master and other high dignitaries of the State Lodge, the Utica Commandery, K. T., fourteen different Masonic Lodges, and representatives from several other lodges; the 10th Regiment Band of Albany, the Utica City Band, and two other bands were in the procession, with the Board of Supervisors, Building Committee, Village Trustees, and others. The sight was a very imposing one, as this procession filled the entire length of Main street. Major Walter H. Bunn, D. G. M., was Marshal on the occasion. The large arch erected on the Court House grounds, through which the procession passed, was beautifully covered with evergreens and flowers. In this work several ladies kindly assisted. A hard shower seriously interfered with the ceremonies planned for the laying of the corner stone. An ode was sung by a choir of gentlemen and ladies, and then Principal Architect, Capt. H. G. Wood, addressed the Grand Master in the prescribed terms of the Order, closing with the request that he proceed to lay the corner stone. The corner stone was then put in its proper position by the McCabe Brothers, builders, and the Grand Master and his associate high officials stepped forward and conducted the ceremonies in the usual form. At the close of the proceedings of laying the stone, the Masons sang the

Dedication Ode. The Grand Master then briefly addressed the assembly present, and Rev. Dr. Lord pronounced the benediction.

The address prepared for this occasion by Hon. Hezekiah Sturges, was as follows:

"Ladies and Gentlemen, Fellow-Citizens: On the 16th of February, 1791, the Legislature of the State of New York created out of the territory theretofore embraced in the county of Montgomery a political division of the State called the county of Otsego. There were then two townships in the county, one called the town of Otsego, organized in 1788, and Cherry Valley, organized in 1791. The town of Otsego was made the shire town. The village that bears the honored name of its founder was selected as the site for its Temple of Justice, where for more than 89 years it has remained, and still does remain.

Assembled on this spot, at this hour, to lay the foundation of a new Hall of Justice, thick thronging shadows come flitting over us, freighted with historical recollections, and with memories of men who have left the impress of their minds and their characters on the history of the country for more than three-fourths of a century.

The first Court House for the county of Otsego was built in 1791, located on the southeast corner of what was then known as Second and West streets of this village, now familiarly known as the location of the Davis block. Its historian describes it as a structure 30 feet square, two stories in height; the first or lower story of squared logs containing four rooms, and used as the jail; the second story frame work, and used as the court room. The entrance to the court room was on the north front, two flights of steps on the exterior of the building, meeting on a platform before a door that opened to the air.

This was superseded by a brick structure erected in 1806-7, on the site in the then extreme western limits of the village, 56 feet long and 50 feet wide. The jailer had rooms in the building, and the jail was in the lower story. That Court House was destroyed by fire on the evening of December 17th, 1840, and in 1841 another was erected on the same site. And now, after forty years, the dilapidating power of decay, and the instability of its ground rest, necessitate the construction of a new Temple.

The first court of record, called the Court of Common Pleas, and the first criminal court of record, called the Court of Sessions, was held at the first-erected Court House, the 21st of June, 1791. The Hon. William Cooper was the first Judge of these Courts. He became a resident here in 1788, was the founder of the village, and efficient in procuring the legal organization; was conspicuous in establishing the judicial, literary, and religious institutions of this part of the county, and in promoting the comfort and welfare of the pioneers to this then nearly primeval forest. He presided over those Courts until October, 1800; and from the beginning he impressed upon the Court of Common Pleas of the county of Otsego a character for dignity, ability and impartiality which it retained and maintained till its last session, in June, 1847.

Jedediah Peck was the Assistant Judge at the first term of the Court. He was a native of Connecticut, of but little legal learning, but remarkable for his sound judgment and quick perception. He was an itinerant surveyor in the county, then new and uncultivated. Judge

Hammond says, "he would survey your farm in the day time, preach a sermon in the school-house in the evening and on Sunday, and talk politics the rest of the time. If not the projector, he was the efficient and persevering advocate of the common school system, and through his exertions the foundation of the common school fund was laid." These acts entitle him to, and will ever secure to him, the gratitude of the people of this county.

Associate Justices of the Peace at that term of the court, were Ephraim Hudson, Joshua H. Britt, John Mathias Brown and Miller Johnston. The Court of Common Pleas was continued in this State from the Colonial period of our history, and from 1777, the number of Judges and Associate Justices of the Peace differed in the various counties of the State; in some counties as many as twelve each, constituted that Court. But an act was passed in March, 1818, limiting the number of Judges to five, and abolishing the office of Assistant or Associate Justices. The Court thus constituted was continued without material change till the adoption of the Constitution of 1846.

It was the duty of the county Clerk to act as the Clerk of the Court of Common Pleas. Gen. Jacob Morris was the clerk of this Court in 1791 for this county. He had distinguished himself as aid of Gen. Lee in the Revolutionary war. He came to reside in this county in 1787, as the agent of the owners of Morris patent. He was distinguished for his high culture, sound judgment, courteous manners and manly bearing. He was prominent in all the early enterprises in founding the religious and literary institutions in the south part of the county. These with other eminent pioneers made this county, from its earliest organization, distinguished in the State as the home of industry, intelligence, intellectual refinement, and high moral character. Abram Ten Broeck, John L. Morgan, James Cochran, Christopher P. Yates, Amaziah Rust, Andrew Wemple, Anthony I. Merwin and Jacob J. Fonda, were the members of the Bar for the Court of Common Pleas, in this county in the year 1791.

The office of District Attorney was created by law, on the 4th day of April, 1801. Prior to that time, this officer was called the Assistant Attorney General. Under an act of 1796 the State was divided into seven districts, and an Assistant Attorney General was appointed by the Governor and Council of Appointment, during their pleasure, in each of these districts. The seventh District was composed of the counties of Herkimer and Otsego, and Thomas R. Gold, who became a member of the Bar of the Court of Common Pleas of Otsego county in 1792, was appointed Assistant Attorney General in 1797. In 1801 the office of District Attorney being created, the State was divided into seven districts as before, and subsequently several new ones were created. That division placed Otsego in the sixth district, and Nathan Williams was made the District Attorney therefor in August, 1801. In 1818 each county was constituted a separate district, for the purposes of this office, and on the 11th of June of that year, Ambrose L. Jordan was appointed District Attorney for the county of Otsego.

During the existence of the Court of Common Pleas, Wm. Cooper was First Judge from 1791 to 1800; Joseph White from 1800 to 1823;

John C. Morris from 1823 to 1827; George Morell from 1827 to 1832; James O. Morse from 1832 to 1838; Jabez D. Hammond from 1838 to 1843; Charles C. Noble from 1843 to 1847.

The records of the Court of Common Pleas and the Court of Sessions, held at the same terms, during the fifty-six years of its existence, disclose that this Court performed a very large amount of judicial labor. That Court commanded the respect and confidence of suitors, of advocates, and of the people. It was abolished by the constitution of 1846, and what is denominated the County Court was established to take its place. And now, after the experience of thirty years, it may be seriously questioned whether the change has been any improvement of our local judiciary.

The first Circuit Court and Oyer and Terminer, in this county, was held on the 7th of July, 1792, Hon. John Lansing, one of the Justices of the Supreme Court, presiding. This Court was held here but once a year, till the reorganization of the judiciary in 1821, and thereafter two terms of this Court were held here—and in September 1823, Hon. Judge Nelson first presided in that Court in this county.

The history of the Otsego Bar commences with the organization of the county, and nearly dates with the period when the foundations of our State and National governments were laid. This is no time to individualize and eulogize. It is enough, on this occasion, to say that the members of the Bar of this county have maintained the high character of the profession for legal learning and forensic ability. It has at all times contributed to preserve civil and social order, public and private justice, to keep alive sentiments of obedience and reverence, and the supremacy of the calm, grand force of the law over fitful passion and ungoverned license. It has been seen and felt in the establishment of the civil, political, literary and religious institutions of our country, the outgrowth of which has been the peace, good order and moderate prosperity that prevail in our borders, till here, within our county, we answer the inquiry of Sir William Jones:

> "What constitutes a State?
> Not high-raised battlement or labor'd mound,
>   Thick wall, or moated gate;
> Not cities proud, with spires and turrets crown'd;
>   Not bays and broad armed ports,
> Where, laughing at the storm, rich navies ride;
>   Not starr'd and spangled courts,
> Where low-browed baseness wafts perfume to pride.
>   No: Men, high-minded men,
> With powers afar above dull brutes endued,
>   In forest brake or den,
> As beasts excel cold rocks and brambles rude:
>   Men who their duties know,
> But know their rights, and knowing, dare maintain.
> *   *   *   *   *   *   *   *   *   *
> These constitute a State."

Of such is the county of Otsego.

But the interest attaching to the construction of a Court House, does not all lie in the reminiscences of the past. It has another, if not a higher and nobler significance, that is to be seen and felt, not only by the generation that now is within the geographical limits of our own county, but by all the generations yet to come. Such a structure is the physical personification, or rather the material symbol, of liberty protected by law. It is the forum where unlicensed liberty on the one hand is restrained, and where despotic power on the other is repressed. The history of the centuries gone is replete with the description of men, of factions, of parties, to maintain an undefined liberty or unrestrained license on the one side, and despotic power on the other. Indeed, during the entire political history of the world, whole nations, in every age and in every clime, have been tinged with the blood of their people in maintaining the one, and in overthrowing the other.

During nearly the whole of the 16th century and part of the 17th, the people of France were engaged in contests for religious liberty, and its rulers were engaged in repressing it by the enforcement of edicts upon the lives and property of its citizens in such manner of cruelty and barbarity, that I fear its parallel cannot be found in the unwritten records of savage life. Yet in the 18th century the pendulum swung to the other extreme, till the events that followed hard on the death scene of Louis XVI. engulfed all liberty and all law, all social order, in one common ruin.

Liberty is a theme that has called forth the loftiest strains of the poet, the sweetest songs of the lyre, and the most eloquent periods of the orator. The statesman uses it as the watch-cry from the walls of the political edifice against danger; the demagogue, to awaken political jealousies, and finds it powerful to raise the demon discord; and yet liberty, when unrestrained, rushes on to anarchy more destructive to human society than despotic power itself. Hence law is essential to liberty, in that it defines and secures the right, and spreads its shield over the weak as well as the strong; for law is made for those who are not a law unto themselves; for the lawless and disobedient. It, for the most part, is a body of rules and enactments, portions of which may be traced to inspired wisdom, others to Rome, the lawgiver of nations, others to the refining process of reason, perfected by the learning of more modern times. It so far restrains and circumscribes liberty, that "it defends the helplessness of infancy, it restrains the passions of youth, it protects the acquisitions of manhood, it shields the sanctity of the grave, and executes the will of the departed."

Hence the only safety of the body politic lies in that condition of society in which liberty is restrained and protected by law. Yet without administration and enforcement of law, there would be in effect no law. Therefore, the whole order of society rests on its sure administration.

Here, therefore, in this rising Temple, may the law be always administered in the solidity of justice, and in the stability of fortitude, so long as the shadow of these walls shall follow the rising or setting sun. So long as that lake shall mirror on its placid bosom yon classic mountain, may liberty here be protected by law. *Esto perpetua!*"

The box for the reception of the articles was made of copper, 20 inches in length, 10 inches wide and 4 inches deep. To enumerate the records and articles placed in it, would occupy several pages of this book. The box was covered by a marble slab, fitted into the stone,

12 by 22 inches in size, and bears the following inscription, artistically executed by Henry J. Hollman of this village, an employee of the Mc-Cabe Brothers: "June 15th, A. L. 5880, M. W. Jesse B. Anthony, Grand Master of the State of New York."

The building committee was: Luther I. Burditt of Otsego, Henry G. Wood of Oneonta, Lewis McCredy of Richfield.

The Postoffice, which had been kept in the Phinney block for many years, was this year moved across the street to the Bundy block.

During this year there was much active and practical Temperance work done in this village, in which many ladies were efficient laborers.

A census of Cooperstown, made this year, "shows the number of inhabitants to be 2,198, of whom 1,180 are females, and 1,018 males—majority of females 162, of whom many are widows. Also, that there are 72 persons on the corporation who are upwards of 70 years of age, three of whom are 90 or upwards. Number of dwelling houses 268, occupied by 466 families."

Out of this population of 2,200 souls, there were only 21 deaths during the year of whom six—rather above the yearly average—were children; one of the deceased residents was 67, one 70, two 74, one 83, one 85, one 90.

CHAPTER XII.

FROM 1881 TO 1886.

During this half decade, which brings our record down to the present time, the village of Cooperstown saw little or no increase in its general business; but there was a steady though slow growth in population, as evinced in the fact that each year witnessed the erection of a few additional dwelling houses, some of which are of the better class; three new brick stores were built on Main street; the brick Orphanage and "Templeton Lodge"—a large summer boarding house—were erected; a section of the proposed sewerage system constructed; the Hotel Fenimore changed hands and was opened as a business hotel; Dr. Mc-Kim of New York built an unique summer house on the corporation, and Dr. Fowler and Mr. Waller of that city built the handsome large cottages standing a little east of the village, in the edge of Middlefield; Mr. Schuyler B. Steers purchased "the Lakelands," and spent a large amount in building a handsome stone and wood cottage, in enlarging and improving the mansion, &c., Mr. E. F. Beadle of New York laid out "Nelson Avenue," and he and Dr. C. F. Campbell made other improvements in that locality; upper Main street has witnessed marked growth and improvement.

1881.—During the last week in January, the County Musical Convention held a very successful session here, under the conductorship of H. R. Palmer.

Otsego 4 per cent. town bonds were sold here in February, at a small premium.

At the opening of the winter term, Union School had the largest number of pupils enrolled up to that time, 426, and another addition to the building became a necessity, as voted at a special meeting held in May. It cost about $4,000.

In March the sale of the Cooper House by the executors of the late H. F. Phinney, to Mr. S. E. Crittenden, was effected, for $16,000, including furniture.

Judge Bowen held the first session of court in the new Court House in March. In the erection of this building, it was shown that the contractors, who had done considerable work not specified in the contract, had received about $5,000 less than they expended; the Board of Supervisors, in consideration thereof, voted to pay them $4,955—an act of equity and justice.

In the early part of this winter the "Cooperstown Literary Society and Debating Club" was inaugurated, and held regular weekly meetings during the winter and spring, with Jas. A. Lynes as president. It is still maintained.

The question of a sewerage system for this village was much discussed this spring.

The Second National Bank of Cooperstown reduced its capital to $200,000 in May, and the First National to $150,000 in September.

S. M. Ballard, who had been for several years the proprietor of the hotel bearing his name, purchased from the Story estate the entire hotel property, in October. Soon after, John R. Millard became a partner in the business.

Miss Cooper began this fall to solicit subscriptions for aid in raising funds for the erection of a new Orphan House, the building occupied at that time being much too small.

G. M. Grant & Co., were established in their new building in time for the Holiday season.

The Lakewood Cemetery Association purchased for $4,000 the thirty-acre lot adjoining their property on the north, during the spring.

An exhibition of the fine cattle and horses kept on the two farms of Mr. Edward Clark occurred in August, and attracted a great deal of interest and attention.

A public meeting of the citizens of this village was held September 20, to take action with reference to expressing the sentiments of this community on the death of the President of the United States. The attendance was large; the feeling one of evident deep sympathy. Mr. Edward Clark was made chairman of the meeting, and briefly expressed his high appreciation of the character and abilities of the deceased President. Rev. Dr. Lord then offered prayer, and was followed by W. H. Lunn, who spoke with much feeling of the nation's great bereavement in the death of President Garfield, and after stating the object of the meeting to be the making of preliminary arrangements for public ceremonies to be observed by this community, in view of the President's death, moved that a committee of fifteen be appointed by the Chair to attend to the carrying out in detail of such services. The motion was adopted and the committee selected by the chairman. On the morning of the same day the church bells of this village were tolled, flags were raised at half mast, and the public buildings, stores, and most of the private dwellings, were draped in mourning.

Generous aid was sent to the sufferers from the Michigan fires, in September, by our citizens.

1882.—A bill passed the Assembly, in February, amending the charter of the village of Cooperstown; its chief provision being the giving to the Trustees power to raise by taxation $2,000 instead of $1,000, as heretofore.

Mr. E. F. Beadle and Dr. C. F. Campbell effected several noticeable improvements on their property in the western part of the village during this season, and these led to other improvements in the years following.

The Trustees of the village voted an appropriation to cover the expense of ascertaining the probable cost of constructing a system of sewerage, and placed the matter in the hands of Messrs. McElroy & Son, Civil Engineers of Brooklyn, who made a survey, map and specifications.

The first stereotyping was done in Cooperstown in 1830, by H. & E. Phinney, and the last by them in 1849. The first done since then was by Mr. E. S. Brockham, in the latter part of June, 33 years afterward.

The State Inter-Academic Union held its seventh annual meeting in this village in July, with a very large attendance at its most interesting sessions. A trip around the lake, in the "Natty Bumppo," was made during the time by most of those present.

Hon. Isaac N. Arnold of Chicago delivered a most interesting lecture in Bowne Hall, in July, for a local object, on "Lincoln and Congress during the Rebellion."

The Trustees of the Orphanage decided in August to erect a substantial brick and stone building, to accommodate about eighty children, about two-thirds of the amount necessary for the completion of the entire work being already subscribed at that date. In October, the corner stone was laid, Bishop Doane delivering the address.

Mr. John Worthington of this village, recently appointed U. S. Consul at Malta, sailed from New York for that island, in September.

During the month of August, a gang of burglars visited many of the towns in this county, including this village, where after an unsuccessful attempt to enter the house of Dr. Lathrop, they, the same night, effected an entrance into Mrs. Carter's residence, and although frightened off by the movements of some person in the house, managed to get away with a quantity of silver-ware, a part of which was recovered, some days later, at Richfield Springs.

A meeting of the citizens of Cooperstown was held at the Court House, October 16th, to take some appropriate action with reference to the death of Mr. Edward Clark. Judge Bowen presided, and a committee consisting of Messrs. S. M. Shaw, Andrew Davidson and Prof. J. G. Wight presented a series of fitting resolutions, which were adopted, expressive of the loss sustained by the community in Mr. Clark's decease, and tendering sympathy to his family.

In October, Mr. E. F. Beadle opened a new street, named "Nelson Avenue" in honor of the late Judge Samuel Nelson, and extending from Main to Lake street.

1883.—On the first day of the new year, J. Warren Lamb & Co., moved into their new quarters, in the fine building erected by them on Main street.

There was, during the winter, some discussion of a new railroad project, looking to the connection of Cooperstown with the New York Central at Fort Plain, and several public meetings for the consideration of this matter were held in that village; but no action was taken in the matter.

The completion of the Westlake block, one of the finest improvements made on Main street for many years, was effected in February. It is now owned by L. I. Burditt, Esq.

Cooperstown was connected by telephone with several near and remote villages during this winter, and the system has been largely extended since that time by the active manager, Mr. Paul T. Brady.

The death of Mr. James I. Hendryx, late editor of the Republican, and since a resident of Minnesota, was announced in February. He was a man of good natural abilities, and at one time held the office of County Treasurer.

In response to communications from the Cooperstown Board of Health to the State Board, Dr. Elisha Harris, secretary, and Mr. Emil

Kuichling, C. E., visited this village, June 15th, and were shown about by the local authorities. In the evening, a meeting was held, and Doct. Harris, on invitation, gave his views upon the sewerage question and other matters of like interest to Cooperstown.

There was an elaborate celebration of the Fourth of July in Cooperstown, in which the Third Separate Company of Oneonta, commanded by Capt. Wood, participated. In the afternoon a series of games (in which prizes were contended for) were played, and a fine display of fireworks was given in the evening. Rev. C. K. McHarg delivered the oration of the day, and gave an unusually interesting and able address.

Beautiful "Lakelands," just across the river from Cooperstown, was sold in August by H. J. Bowers, as agent for the estate of the late John M. Bowers, to Schuyler B. Steers, who was then the occupant of the premises, for $35,000. The purchase includes the homestead lot, and land near, amounting in all to 22 acres.

The Orphanage received a substantial benefit of about $100 in August, as the result of an amateur dramatic entertainment, given by the guests of the Cooper House.

A gala day for Cooperstown occurred in the latter part of August, on the occasion of a visit to the Cooperstown Fire Department, from the Military Company and Fire Department of Oneonta. The Military Company entered camp on the Lake immediately, and during the day there occurred the handsomest parade witnessed here for many years, two of the finest bands in the State furnishing most excellent music. The reception and escort were by the Cooperstown Fire Department.

Early in September, Doct. E. P. Fowler of New York, then spending his third summer in Cooperstown, purchased of Mr. H. K. Jarvis forty acres of land, lying east and a little south of this village, in Middlefield, on which he has since erected a most beautiful summer residence, commanding, from its sightly location, an extensive view of the Lake and upper Susquehanna valley. He sold a few acres of this land to his friend, Mr. Frank Waller, a landscape painter of New York, who has erected a fine lodge on it.

The murder trial of Mrs. Sergeant, accused of poisoning her child, was in process before Judge Follet in the latter part of September. The prisoner was acquitted on the ground of insanity at the time of the act. Mrs. Sergeant was committed to the Utica Insane Asylum, where a thorough examination by the physicians of the institution proved her mental condition was such as to justify the verdict of the jury. She remained in that institution about one year, when she returned to her friends, cured of her malady.

The County Bible Society held its annual meeting in the Methodist church in October. Rev. Dr. Swinnerton of Cherry Valley and Rev. Mr. Babcock of Richfield Springs, delivering able and interesting addresses.

People in Cooperstown at all versed in astronomy, were interested in the reappearance of an old friend, the comet of 1812, in December of this year.

A public meeting was called by the village Trustees, in the latter part of December, to consider the sewerage question. The prevalent feeling was in favor of the system, and its early adoption if a satisfactory plan could be agreed upon, was decided. Subsequently, under the bill passed by the Legislature, a section of the system was built, at a cost of about $5,000.

In December, the Presbyterian church narrowly escaped destruction by fire, caught near the furnace, and fortunately discovered before it had made progress.

1884.—The Semi-Centennial Celebration of the Baptist church of this village occurred in January, at the morning and evening services on which occasion the audience room was crowded to its utmost capacity by those interested in the exercises attending the close of this half century of the existence of this ecclesiastical body. Rev. Mr. Sawyer, a former pastor, preached in the morning.

The sale of the Central Hotel to W. N. Potter of Oneonta, was effected in February, $24,500, being the amount paid for house, furniture, stores, omnibus, team, &c.

A fitting tribute to the late Judge Samuel A. Bowen was paid by James A. Lynes, in the County Court, during the latter part of February, and on behalf of the committee previously appointed, this gentleman submitted to the court a copy of most feeling resolutions, after which brief and touching remarks were made by different members of the Bar.

The pupils of Union School, in March, placed on its walls an excellent portrait of the late Judge Bowen, for many years chairman of the Board of Education.

The Hotel Fenimore was reopened under the management of Jesse B. Brown in April, and immediately took rank as a first class hotel. Mr. Edwin M. Harris was the purchaser of the property, as the financial backer of Mr. Brown.

In April of this year, the following party of fourteen residents of Cooperstown sat down to tea together, on the 68th anniversary of the birthday of Mrs. Peter S. Sayles. We also give their respective ages at this date, February, 1886, as all are still living: Peter Becker, 80; Mrs. Becker, 72; William Brooks, 72; Mrs. Brooks, 70; S. W. Bingham, 79; Mrs. Bingham, 79; Peter P. Cooper, 70; Mrs. Cooper, 66; Lorenzo White, 68; Mrs. White, 67; Peter S. Sayles, 75; Mrs. Sayles, 70; Isaac K. Williams, 74; Mrs. Williams, 71. Total years 1013—being an average of about 72 1-3 years. Of this party, none are regarded as in feeble health; indeed, with one or two exceptions, all are now enjoying excellent health.

Building operations were unusually active this season, especially in the north and south portions of the village. Delaware street was rapidly built up with small and neat cottages, and Mr. L. I. Burditt added to his cottages on Beaver street. Dr. Robert McKim of New York commenced the erection of his large summer cottage on Lake street. Plans for Mr. Constable's fine mansion on the Lake, about a mile north of this village, promised the erection of such a notable building as this beautiful residence proves to be.

The sad announcement of the sudden death of Mr. Frederick A. Lee, startled the town on the 29th of May. Only three hours before, he had left the Journal office, having made a pleasant call on his friend, the editor of this book.

The death of Mrs. Philena Butts, the oldest resident of the village—having completed her 98th year—occurred in June. Mrs. Butts had been for 65 years a resident of this village.

A Teachers' Institute for the county of Otsego was held here in August, the State Instructors being Dr. John H. French and Prof. Chas. T. Pooler. There was a large attendance of teachers.

A. H. Gazley drove a well in his yard, at the foot of Bay street, in August, in which, after attaining a depth of 53 feet, the well flowed freely 20 inches above the surface of the ground.

In July, Mr. Davidson purchased the interest of his partner, H. I. Russell, in the Republican, and has since carried on the business alone. His son is an assistant in the office.

In July and August the summer visitors here were more numerous than for the past two or three years.

The Hop Growers' Association of Otsego county held its annual convention in the Court House during the month of August on which occasion the questions of picking hops and prices for the same were discussed by different members of the association. No practical good of any moment resulted from the efforts of this organization, and but few meetings were held.

The family at the Orphanage sustained a severe loss in the death of the beloved matron, Mrs. Eliza M. Stanton, in August. During the twelve years of her service in this orphan household, this lady had endeared herself not only to the children in her charge, but to many sincere friends, who admired her intelligence, faithfulness, and her beautiful and symmetrical character.

An entertainment and fair, given by the guests of the Cooper House for the benefit of the Orphanage, in August, netted about $413. An entertainment given by Madam Pupin, the previous week, netted S112.

Edgewater was the principal point of social attraction for two evenings during the latter part of August, when Mr. Keese, his daughters and a few friends united in giving a very pleasing amateur dramatic and musical entertainment in aid of the Orphanage, which netted about $100 for the worthy object in view.

The Skating Rink of this village was formally opened early in September, under the auspices of the Fire Department, about 700 people being present, and the entertainment netting the Department about $100. For a few weeks this attraction remained in favor, and drew to it large numbers of the young people who take pleasure in skating. Of late, it has been a very convenient place for the holding of entertainments of different kinds where ample room is required.

In laying the corner stone of his residence, in September, Doct. Fowler placed therein, copies of the village papers, together with copies of the New York daily papers, of that date, and other interesting matter.

The Orphanage narrowly escaped destruction by fire the second Sunday in September, but the flames were arrested without heavy damage to the building, by the prompt and efficient Fire Department, and a good supply of water from the hydrant near the building. The loss on building, about $700, was fully covered by insurance. The furniture was damaged to the extent of about $200.

A benefit at the Rink for the Orphanage, under the kindly auspices of the Fire Department, netting $117.53, was of great service to that institution in assisting to repair the damage of the fire, and several of the churches of the village generously donated their Sunday morning collections, amounting to about $90, to this worthy object, with which aid the furniture destroyed by the fire was replaced.

At a meeting of the directors of the Cooperstown Railroad, held in the latter part of September, the telephone was reported completed, and to be answering a very good purpose, telegraph operators being no longer required.

October 4th, a special election occurred, for the determination by the taxpayers in regard to the issue of bonds for the construction of sewerage in Cooperstown. Less interest was excited than was expected, only 124 votes being cast, 74 for and 50 against the system.

A handsome tribute to a faithful and devoted teacher, in the shape of a substantial gift of $50, was presented Miss Ball an instructor in the Union School since its opening, by her appreciative pupils, in October.

The sad though not unexpected death of the Hon. Hezekiah Sturges occurred December 4th, after an illness of about forty days. At a session of the County Court held in the Court House, Dec. 15, resolutions were submitted to the Court, and eulogistic remarks on the deceased Judge were made by different members of the Bar, in which the grandeur of his Christian character, his high standing in his profession, his genial and kindly disposition and true and noble manhood, were eloquently referred to.

Christ Church was the recipient of a valuable and gracious gift, on Christmas day; a new altar of polished oak, a brass cross, beautifully carved with the passion flower, and white hanging, heavily embroidered in gold, surrounded by rich silk bullion fringe, were seen and in use for the first time that day. While no publicly announced name accompanied these costly gifts, it was well known that they were contributed by the same generous hand that made complete the beautiful memorial chapel.

1885.—The trial and conviction of Jas. F. Clayton, of Middlefield, for the murder of his little child, in August last, occurred in January of this year, before Judge Murray, and very naturally excited a great deal of interest. This crime was a most unnatural one, and was committed while the defendant was under the influence of liquor; he had no motive for killing the child, had never shown any aversion to it; on the contrary, in his sober hours, and generally, he evinced his attachment for it. He was for the moment a partially insane man, but not wholly irresponsible for his acts. His own bad habits had brought him into that condition. Rum had been his ruin, and he suffered the just penalty of his crime. He was sentenced to State prison for life. He was very ably defended by Mr. James A. Lynes, and the prosecution by District Attorney Barber and Mr. Edick was also strong.

A highly successful Musical Convention assembled here during the last week in January. The attendance was large, Prof. Case, the conductor, gave evidence of his experience and high qualifications in his able instructions to the large class, and the presence of Mrs. Helen E.

H. Carter of Boston and several other soloists of a high order, at the concerts, gave assurance of most excellent entertainments at the close of the session.

A most admirably managed and largely attended Ball was given by the Fire Department, the first week in February. The music by the Tenth Regiment Band of Albany, was the best ever furnished on a similar occasion; about 500 persons were in attendance.

The report of the State Board of Health showed the death rate in Cooperstown in December to be considerably less than that of fourteen other places enumerated, only one place named making a better showing than Cooperstown.

The snows during the month of February were unusually heavy, the railroad being snow-bound for the first time in several years.

One of the village papers made the following statement this winter: Strangers who visit Cooperstown often speak of it as "a place containing a great many very wealthy people." That is a mistake. There are say 16 to 18 persons on this corporation who are worth from $40,000 to about $60,000, several of whom are ladies, and none of whom would be called very wealthy; few are adding to their capital. One gentleman who resides here a few months in the year, ranks among the wealthiest men in the country, being worth many millions of dollars; a lady is at the head of an estate, partly unproductive, worth say $2,500,000, and there are six gentlemen whose wealth is estimated about as follows: $450,000, $250,000, $200,000, $120,000, $100,000, $85,000.

A slight shock of earthquake was felt in this place and some of the surrounding towns, on the last day of February, buildings being shaken, windows rattled and water disturbed. It however created no alarm.

In March of this year Mr. J. Fred Reustle bought out his partner Clark, a non-resident, and commenced the mercantile business on his own account. The same year he built for himself a handsome dwelling house on the old "bull's head" lot.

The annual report of the Treasurer of the village in March, showed that the money raised for ordinary purposes was $2,924. The sum of $915 was well spent on the Fire Department; law expenses took $400; street lights, $520; police, $108; board of health, $97; these being the heaviest items. Nearly $3,600 was expended upon sidewalks and roads. The village had no debt except that incurred for sewerage— less than $5,000.

There was a demand, which could not be met, during the spring, for dwelling houses, which could be rented at $100 to $225 a year. There were no unoccupied dwellings.

The boarding house, "Templeton Lodge," was constructed by Dr. Campbell, this spring. Pleasantly located near the lake, furnished with a view to the convenience and comfort of a summer home to its guests, and with its genial and excellent hostess, Mrs. Goodwin, this house was opened the following June, and gave most excellent satisfaction to the guests that filled the house.

March was the coldest spring month experienced in 35 years.

Mr. Delos L. Birge succeeded Mr. Russell as postmaster in this village, in April, on the resignation of the latter. He receives a salary of $1,700, and $400 for clerk hire.

Mrs. Carter this spring fitted up the old family residence on Lake street, for her son-in-law, Rev. Philip A. H. Brown of New York.

In May, Mr. Walter H. Bunn of this village was appointed to the important office of United States Marshal for the Northern District of New York. He has about 30 deputies, and holds his principal office in Cooperstown.

Memorial Day was observed the last week in May, with appropriate ceremonies. It has been the custom to observe this day in Cooperstown, since its institution.

The Nelson block, near the corner of Main and Pioneer streets, narrowly escaped conflagration on the 27th of May. The fire originated in the 3d story of one of the buildings, which was damaged to the extent of about $1,000. The furniture in the editorial rooms of the Republican office also suffered considerable damage.

The Albany Academy Cadets, a fine body of young students, visited this village on the 5th of June, accompanied by the Tenth Regiment Band. They made a good appearance and a favorable impression.

Mr. John L. McNamee this summer sold to Mr. James Bunyan the fine, sightly building lot, corner of Main and Pine streets, on which Mr. Bunyan will erect a handsome dwelling.

Bishop Doane, of this Episcopal Diocese, visited Christ Church, Cooperstown, in June, and administered the rite of confirmation to a class of 36, most of whom were young people. Bishop McNierny, of this Catholic Diocese, visited St. Mary's church during the same month, and administered the rite of confirmation to a class of 185 children.

A number of city people who came to Cooperstown this summer, came by the way of the Ulster and Delaware railroad to Stamford, thence by Tally-Ho coach to Cooperstown Junction.

The summer of 1885 was a favorable one to those whose business largely depends on the presence of city people.

In their 29th annual report, made in July, the Trustees of Lakewood Cemetery say: "The present number of lot-owners is 475, and of lots sold 602. The total number of interments made since the opening of the Cemetery is 1478, of which 509 have been removals from other grounds. During the past year there have been 51 burials and 12 reinterments. The receipts of the past year were $2,531.67 and the disbursements $2,426.60. The total receipts since the organization have been $55,446.19, and the expenditures $55,370.29."

One of the finest drives out of Cooperstown has been to "Rum Hill," about 6 miles north of Cooperstown. The name of this elevation was this season changed to "Mount Otsego" on which the proprietor, Mr. Rufus Wikoff, has erected an observatory. It was visited by a large number of people during the summer. The view from this point is one of the most noted and beautiful in the State of New York.

On the last Sunday morning in July the sermons by Rev. Mr. Denniston in the Presbyterian church, and Rev. Mr. Partridge in the Baptist church, were memorial discourses on General Grant. Rev. Father Hughes of St. Mary's and Rev. Dr. Beach in Christ Church, referred in an appropriate and feeling manner to the General's death.

On the 8th day of August memorial services were held in the Rink, to pay proper tribute to the memory of General Grant. The day was all that could be desired; the weather most delightful for mid-summer. The business places generally, and many private residences, were appropriately draped. There was quite a large attendance from this and neighboring towns. At 1:30 p. m. the line was formed on Church street, in the following order: Marshal James F. Clark, drum corps, L. C. Turner Post, thirty members uniformed and carrying muskets, members of other Posts, G. A. R., and soldiers, forty in number, with muskets. President of the day, Orator and Clergy in carriages, followed by the committee of arrangements and citizens, led by Marshal Bunn, the column marching to slow music. On approaching the rink, where the services were to be held, Commander Flannigan brought his command to "reverse arms." At the rink the soldiers were brought to company front, and stacked arms before entering. The rink was filled, seating over a thousand people comfortably. Capt. Andrew Davidson, on taking the chair to preside, made a few appropriate and well-timed remarks. The invocation was by Rev. Mr. Pitcher of Hartwick Seminary; Rev. Mr. Olmstead read a selection from the Scriptures; singing by the choir; prayer by Rev. Mr. Denniston. The address of Rev. Mr. McHarg occupied just an hour, and the speaker was, as usual, equal to the occasion. Every word was distinctly heard by the large audience, and from the opening to the close of the eulogy the closest attention was paid the orator. The speaker devoted his time principally to a deeply interesting account of the public life of the deceased hero, showing perfect familiarity with his great military career, and also his position on important measures which came before Congress during his two presidential terms. He then spoke of his trip around the world, the great honors paid him by the most distinguished people everywhere, and finally of his sickness and death. The singing, which was under the direction of Mr. Wm. H. Russell, was excellent—the choir composed of about a score of gentlemen of this village.

This season, as in several preceding summers, Cooperstown was visited by a number of large excursion parties, from Albany, Binghamton and other places. On the lake were a large number of camping parties.

The popular game of lawn tennis was more generally introduced and played in Cooperstown this summer. Several large parties engaged in this favorite out-door game, were assembled on the convenient grounds of Mrs. Carter and Mr. S. B. Steers, on the lake.

Several hundred hop pickers were brought to Cooperstown by the railroad, from Albany and other cities, the closing week in August. This has been the custom during the last few years.

The house building mechanics of Cooperstown were kept well employed during the fall on the dwellings being erected by Messrs. J. F. Reustle, E. F. Beadle, J. A. M. Johnston, E. S. Bundy, L. I. Burditt, W. P. K. Fuller and others.

The Masonic Lodge Room of this village was extensively and elaborately repaired during the summer. New carpets, curtains and fixtures were added at a large expense, and the Lodge now has a handsome room. The expense of these improvements was between $700 and $800, and shared by Otsego Lodge, No. 138, and Otsego Chapter, No. 26. The former has a membership of 150 and the latter about 80.

The first week in October, on petition of the property owners of North Fair street, the Trustees of the village commenced laying sewer pipes from Main street to a junction with the main sewer.

The American Hotel, on Pioneer street, was sold by D. M. Hunter to Albert Palmer, in November, and the latter took possession the same month.

A meeting of the drafted men of Otsego county was held in this village on the 3d of December, the object being to obtain legislative enactment which will enable the towns to pay the expense to which these men were put during the late civil war.

The village papers published in December contained this mention of the sale of a handsome and desirable piece of real estate on the lake, near Cooperstown: "The 'Leatherstocking Falls' property, comprising 88 acres, which has been in the Johnson family nearly all the time for 80 years, has been sold by Edward H. Johnson, the present occupant, to Walter Langdon of Hyde Park, Dutchess county, who designs it for his nephew, Woodbury Kane of New York; consideration $10,000."

Several Cooperstown people went to Florida, to spend the present winter.

Said a village paper, at the close of this year: "Dwellings of the value of about $40,000 have been erected on this corporation during this year; and a few just off of the corporation to the value of about $22,000. Both exclusive of lots and out-buildings. We do not include Mr. Constable's fine residence on the lake, completed this spring, and which alone cost about $20,000."

The "Willow Brook" place, in the village, was sold by Mrs. F. A. Lee to her nephew, Mr. Henry C. Bowers of New York.

Some of the predictions which Mr. Cooper made, in 1838, in the closing paragraphs of his "Chronicles," are now being realized. Accommodations have been provided, in hotels and boarding houses, for those who wish to spend the summer season here; others, who desire a furnished private house, are readily accommodated, some of the most desirable dwellings in the village being placed at the service of city families, and generally at a fair rent. Although the shores of the lake are not yet "lined with country residences," these have commenced to make their appearance, several having been built within the last two years, two or three near the head of the lake. Others will follow; slowly, it may be, on account of the difficulty of obtaining desirable locations, of five to twenty-five acres or more of land, at what would be deemed a reasonable price. It is more than probable that within the present decade Cooperstown will have direct railroad communication with the Hudson river, and that will invite a far greater number of summer visitors to Otsego lake and its beautiful shores. It is not likely that Cooperstown will ever become a manufacturing place, for several evident reasons—a potent one being, its capitalists do not wish to see it such. But the village is likely in the future, as in the past, to witness a steady and solid growth.

There is one improvement we should be glad to chronicle—one which we at least hope will be chronicled by the next editor of the History of Cooperstown—and that is, the erection in this village of note in the United States, and of all others in this country best and most widely known throughout Europe, by reputation, of a Library and Art Building worthy the name of the place. In time, and probably at no very distant day, a Village Hall and Firemen's Building will doubtless be erected; let it be a credit to Cooperstown.

THE HISTORY OF COOPERSTOWN
FROM 1886 TO 1929
By Walter R. Littell

FOREWORD

In the following pages it is the purpose of the author to bring the History of Cooperstown, so adequately treated by Mr. Cooper and Mr. Shaw, down to the present.

"The Chronicles of Cooperstown" by James Fenimore Cooper, which make up the first section of this volume, form a monumental contribution to our local bibliography. Mr. Cooper has told of the beginnings of the village as no man of lesser talent or intimate association with its early development could have done.

None the less valuable is the contribution of Samuel M. Shaw, which forms the second section of the history. To a fine sense of relative values in local affairs Mr. Shaw brought all the equipment which many years in the editorial chair of a local newspaper could furnish together with the advantage of more easily reached sources of information than were available in Cooper's day. This, together with the difference in the nature of the periods covered, made Cooper's task the more difficult, but the worth of both records to all interested in the growth and development of our village is invaluable.

Both works are now, however, out of print and it is scarcely possible to secure a copy. The present volume makes both Cooper's Chronicles and Shaw's History available to the general public at a reasonable cost together with the chronological record brought up to date.

No attempt is made by the author of the third section to make the history other than a record of the succession of events which seem to have importance in the village development, although we have at times yielded to the temptation to include brief references for their curious interest alone.

On the whole, however, it is intended that the book shall be primarily valuable for reference purposes, so that therein may be found, through the foresight of the publishers in supplying an exhaustive index, an easily used storehouse of information upon the affairs of Cooperstown from the day of the arrival of the first white man to the year 1929.

And, finally, the present author wishes to emphasize the point that it has been his endeavor, as it has seemed to be that of Mr. Cooper and Mr. Shaw, to record facts, not personalities. No names appear in the portion of the history for which he is responsible on account of the individuals, *per se;* but solely because of their connection with events, that by reason of their relative importance, are worthy of inclusion. Therefore, there will be found in these pages no eulogies or estimates of character of the many heroic, distinguished, lovable, generous and otherwise worthy citizens who have made our village what it is. This, we feel, should be left to the biographers.

CHAPTER I

FROM 1886 TO 1890

1886.—Cooperstown this year rounded out its first century. Judge William Cooper first visited Otsego Lake in the autumn of 1785, and in January, 1786, he took possession of the property known as Cooper's Patent. In the summer and fall of that year emigrants from the East commenced to arrive.

The company owning the telegraph line from Cooperstown through Richfield Springs to the Mohawk Valley sold out to the Western Union Telegraph Co. The stock was owned by a few persons at Richfield Springs. Possession was given January 1st. Cooperstown was made a telegraph money order office April 1st. During the summer of this year the company added a direct wire to New York City thus improving its service to a considerable degree. The new poles erected for the telegraph wires some of which were characterized by a village paper as "short, ugly, ill-shaped sticks", occasioned a good deal of adverse criticism about the village. They were painted during the year.

The good old custom of New Year's Day "calling" had practically disappeared. Very few of the village ladies were "at home" on the 1st of January of this year. The game of progressive euchre was very popular and formed the chief means of entertainment at most of the social gatherings.

Lotteries still flourished in the county although it was an indictable offense to hold one.

The Cooperstown Railroad company reported a net profit of $2,-623.23 for the year 1885. In the last three months of that year the company paid off $3,000 of its floating debt.

Jan. 30th Francis C. Smith purchased the interest of A. M. Beadle in the boot and shoe business at the corner of Main and Pioneer streets. The firm name became F. C. Smith & Co. The latter part of the month Philip H. Potter purchased Paul T. Brady's interest in the insurance business, in order that the latter might devote more attention to his increasing telephone interests.

Over 125 people were registered at the musical convention held the last week in January at the Rink and the affair proved a decided success under the direction of a leader from Boston. Concerts were given on two evenings.

Cooperstown was well represented at a meeting held February 3d at Oneonta at which a resolution was adopted urging the members of the state assembly and senate from this district to favor the passage of a bill for the extension of the Ulster & Delaware railroad from Stamford to Oneonta by the way of Bloomville and Davenport with a connecting line to Cooperstown Junction.

With one of the judges of the district too ill to perform his duties and two others overworked the Otsego County courts became crowded with litigation to such an extent that it became necessary to make an appeal to Governor Hill for relief.

The decline of the hop growing industry in Otsego county began to be noticeable. Figures show that from September 1, 1884, to February 1, 1886, 12,200 bales of hops were shipped from the Cooperstown station. The first of the year hops brought from 5 to 10 cents per pound.

E. F. Beadle sold a newly erected house on Nelson Avenue to J. G. Fowler for $7,000. The latter sold Mr. Beadle his large lot and cottage on Pine street for $4,000.

Preliminary work on two new business blocks on the south side of Main street, one for William H. Michaels and one for Charles E. Moore, was started in March. The latter was opened July 17th and the former November 10th.

Otsego Lodge, No. 138 F. & A. M. purchased the Phinney block on Pioneer street for $5,500 about the middle of March.

In April of this year J. A. M. Johnston was appointed agent of Alfred Corning Clark to succeed James Bunyan, who for twenty years preceding the death of Edward Clark, has acted as the local agent of the Estate.

Hunter & Ayres opened a grocery store on Main street April 17th.

The ice left the lake April 14th, having been closed since January 11th or 92 days.

Late in April initial steps were taken for the organization of a co-operative fire insurance company to operate in the towns of Otsego. Middlefield and Hartwick. The first meeting was held at the Court House in Cooperstown April 24th with the following present: L. I. Burditt, William A. Thayer, R. H. Bates, Thomas H. Pitts, H. M. Pierce, Oliver Wood, S. L. Derrick, A. O. Parshall, R. B. Brownell, Dr. J. E. Leaning, R. Brown, George Brooks and L. H. Bowen. At a meeting held a week later Messrs. Thayer, Burditt, Brooks, Pitts, Pierce, Luce and Brownell were elected directors. The first officers were: William A. Thayer, president; Horace M. Pierce, vice-president; Ambrose C. Shipman, secretary and treasurer.

Discussion of the sewer question waxed earnest from the opening of the year and the matter came to a head May 3d when at a special meeting of the Board of Trustees it was voted to place the defective main sewer in proper condition at the earliest possible moment. This work was done the latter part of the month and on June 5th on petition of citizens the trustees voted the construction of a more complete sewer system for the village. As a result of this action a little over a mile of new sewer pipes were laid during the month of October at a cost of $2,633 as follows: Chestnut and Lake streets, 2,577½ feet; Susquehanna avenue, 1,781 feet; Pioneer street, 1,350 feet.

"The Central Shoe Store" was opened by W. J. Moak during the week of May 8th in the new building erected by him on Main street.

The Cooper House, thoroughly repaired and renovated, was opened for the season June 22nd.

The trial of John M. Schuyler of Morris on the charge of murdering his three-year-old child, was completed June 9th and the jury, after deliberating from 2 until 11:30 p. m., returned a verdict of guilty in the first degree. Schuyler was under the influence of liquor and committed the deed while in a rage because his wife had left the house. Seizing the little one by the ankles he took it out of doors and three times swung its head against a block of wood. Justice Celora E. Martin presided at the trial and sentenced Schuyler to be hung Tuesday, July 27th. District Attorney C. L. Barber and E. M. Harris tried the case for the People and A. P. Barber and S. S. Edick represented the defendant.

The contract for the new parsonage of the Presbyterian church was let about June 15th to Charles Root and Murty Keough. About the same time ground was broken for the new Susan M. Hughes block on Main street adjoining the Court House grounds.

The old "Town Pump", for many years an object of note on the corporation and of great use to three generations of residents was removed in June and covered with a large stone forming a part of the new side walk being laid on that part of Main street. During the fire of 1862 the old pump did noble service when all other sources of water failed.

It was estimated that 10,000 people attended the Firemen's Tournament held in Cooperstown June 30th. This tournament was not confined to Otsego county firemen but departments were invited from all this part of the state. Cherry Valley, Morris, New Berlin, Richfield Springs, Cobleskill, Delhi, Franklin, Oneonta, Schenevus, Troy and Walton were represented. Dinner was served at the Rink for the visiting firemen 500 being seated at a time at well laden tables. The ladies of the village had the meal in charge and the great crowd was fed in a complete and satisfactory manner in about two hours. Lee B. Cruttenden was the chief of the Cooperstown department.

Through week-end sleeping car service from New York to Cooperstown was given a trial during the summer but was soon discontinued as the patronage was poor.

July 9th the Central Hotel fire took place. The proprietors, Potter & Whipple, suffered a total loss of the building and much personal property although the supplies in the cellar were but little damaged. Mr. Potter purchased the interest of his partner and rebuilt the hotel which was reopened later in the year.

A leading industry in the village at this period was that conducted by Peter, Laurence, Bryan and Michael McCabe, under the firm of McCabe Brothers, contractors, builders, and dealers in headstones. They employed about sixty men with an annual payroll of $15,000. In July E. A. Potter purchased their marble and granite business and they moved to a location nearer New York which was more advantageous to the large building contracts which they were carrying out in that vicinity.

Neptune Engine Co. No. 3 was formed to operate the new "Fernleigh" fire engine. The company tested the new engine July 13th.

July 23d the citizens of the village were startled by the ringing of the bell on the county jail and it was announced that five prisoners had escaped. With a saw made of a case knife they had sawed through a hinge on the inner door of the lower corridor and then with a strong piece of wood had sprung the door sufficiently for a man to get through, then pried open the outer door in the same manner, smashed down the door into the kitchen and escaped. Three of them, named Connerty, McClure and VanEvera were captured in the town of Middlefield near the home of Charles Bowen, who recognized them when they applied for food. The other two, Beers and Wilfred, escaped.

More than 400 teachers attended the teachers' institute held here the week of August 15th.

Following freely expressed dissatisfaction with the gas supply the village trustees in August granted a franchise to R. H. Johnson of Brooklyn to manufacture gas from coal oil and water and supply it to the residents of the village for a period of twenty years. Residents of the village subscribed $8,000 towards the capital stock of $25,000 and Mr. Johnson with a fixed period in which to begin operations returned to Brooklyn to sell the rest of the stock.

The Ballard House barn was burned to the ground September 13th and was rebuilt at once.

During the fall a debt of $3,000 that had been embarrassing the Orphan House for some time was paid in full as the result of a popular subscription campaign conducted by the Freeman's Journal, a fund of $600 raised for the construction of a play room, and a start made upon an endowment for the institution.

The failure of the firm of Robert Russell & Co. which had done business here since 1862 was announced the last of the year. There were no local creditors.

The village continued to enjoy a steady and sound growth. In April it was reported that every dwelling on the corporation except two were either occupied or engaged.

During the year buildings were erected on the corporation at an aggregate cost of about $54,000. These included five stores and one dwelling on Main street, five on Nelson avenue, four small dwellings on Delaware street and five on other streets. About $10,000 was expended in rebuilding the Central Hotel after it was burned. Among the new residences erected were those of John G. Fowler, W. J. Chrisler, Allen Gallup, E. F. Beadle on Nelson avenue, Sands Shumway on Elm street, and the new parsonage of the First Presbyterian Church at the corner of Elm and Church.

Dr. E. P. Fowler's "chateau", occupying high grounds comprising thirty acres on the eastern shore of the Susquehanna river a half mile southeast of Cooperstown was completed.

The year proved very satisfactory from the standpoint of the village as a summer resort. The cottage colony increased in numbers; the Cooper House did a good business, and the three hotels on Main street, the Hotel Fenimore, Carr's and the Ballard House reported that they were filled to capacity on more than one occasion. Hotels at Five and Three-Mile Points flourished.

In April the proprietors of the Central and Fenimore Hotels put men and teams on Main street and cleared it of stones and the surrounding "drives" were kept in good condition. Considerable stone flagging was laid in the form of sidewalks and the first steps were taken by the village authorities in the establishment of a policy of steady construction that should at a not too distant date provide permanent walks for the entire village.

A unique census conducted by one of the village newspapers showed that 104 residents of the corporation were over 70 years of age and that there were 72 persons who had lived in the village for fifty years or more. The paper expressed the opinion that there was not another place of its size in the state that could make an equal showing—surely an evidence that health and living conditions were good in those days.

The mean temperature for the year was 43½ degrees. The lowest temperature was recorded February 4th, 15 degrees below zero.

1887.—Paul B. Boden leased the Five-Mile Point House from John D. Tunnicliff for a term of years. Possession was given February 1st. Mr. and Mrs. Tunnicliff had kept the house for thirty-six years. It was a popular resort under their management.

A union meeting was held in the Presbyterian church in January to consider furnishing backing for the newly organized Y. M. C. A.

In this year there was marked sentiment at Oneonta to erect a new county with that village as its center, and to include several towns of Otsego and Delaware. It was proposed to call the new county "Unadilla." Nothing ever came of the project but talk.

It was reported in February that the debt of the Otsego County Agricultural society amounted to $2,600 and that $1,400 was needed for improvements.

A new steeple was placed on the First Presbyterian church edifice, new roofs on both the church and chapel and both buildings were painted this Spring at a cost of $7,176. Repairs to the interior were also made at an expense of $475. The sum of $2,635 was also raised towards the parsonage fund leaving this debt only $1,530.

Dr. Mary Imogene Bassett, recently graduated from Medical College, announced that she would practice in Cooperstown. She was the daughter of Dr. W. T. Bassett, at that time the senior physician of the village.

New quarters for the Y. M. C. A. were fitted up in the Michaels block and the Woman's auxiliary organized.

The "Skating Rink", which was opened in 1883 and served not only for skating but as a valuable assembly hall, fell under the weight of a large body of snow during a storm on April 1st. At the last of its life the building was owned by Shaw & Quaif and used for the storage of hops. Fortunately no one was in it at the time. The net loss was about $1,600 after the lumber and equipment were sold.

During the winter from November 25, 1886, to April 7, 1887, inclusive, there was good sleighing in and about Cooperstown— a period of 134 days. This exceeded by one week any record of any year in the preceding thirty-five.

April 20. The assignment of George Clarke and G. Hyde Clark, his son, was filed in the county clerk's office. Judgments on record against the former amounted to about $300,000. The obligations of the son were mainly in the form of endorsements of his father's paper.

During April a portrait of Miss Susan Fenimore Cooper by Curtz, the gift of Mrs. Alfred Corning Clark, was placed in the Orphan House.

May 15. At a special Village election the project to erect a new Village Hall and Firemen's building was carried by a vote of 109 to 67. At a special meeting of the Village Board on the following evening it was voted to buy the rink lot adjoining the one already owned by the Village for $1,500. A committee composed of Messrs. Bunyan, Lynes and Keese was appointed to confer with the Firemen's committee as to the requirements of the department and to inspect buildings in other places.

In May James Bunyan leased all the Cooper Grounds east of Fair street and cleaned them thoroughly. The practice of making them a loafing place, dumping ground, etc., was discontinued.

Lake navigation opened May 29th with the steamers, Natty Bumppo, under Captain Watkins, and The Gem, under Captain Cooper, serving the public.

The name of the Otsego, Middlefield & Hartwick Insurance company was changed in May to the Otsego County Farmers' Cooperative Fire Insurance company.

June 1. The large barn of E. F. Beadle between Pine street and Nelson avenue and contents were totally destroyed by fire.

The appointment of Richard Freeman as commissioner of the U. S. Deposit Fund for Otsego county was confirmed by the Senate in June.

The Susquehanna river bridge on Main street was repaired by the towns of Otsego and Middlefield in July at an expense of several hundred dollars. At this time the timber stringers which had been used were replaced by iron.

Henry C. Bowers tore away the old tenant house on the grounds of Willowbrook during the summer which greatly improved the appearance of the place.

At its last meeting in June the Village trustees entered into a contract with H. L. Browning of Albany, representing the Edison Electric Light corporation, to furnish electric lights for the village streets. He agreed to furnish the 35 posts in use on the corporation with light for the sum of $500 annually and give additional lights at $18 a post. The company contracted to have service in operation by September 15.

July 1. Sewer bonds in the sum of $3,250, the longest of which had only two years to run, were sold at auction at a premium of $77.94. James Bunyan was the purchaser.

The Hotel Fenimore had 120 guests August 1 and the Cooper House was also well patronized. ·

Aug. 16. The sum of $400 was added to the rectory fund of Christ church as the result of a garden party at Edgewater.

The fence in front of the Baptist church was removed in August, an example which was followed by a number of property owners of all faiths.

The village board erected three new fire hydrants, one each on Pine, Nelson and Main streets. The Board also engaged the services of a night watchman.

In August David A. Avery was elected cashier of the Second National Bank of Utica and moved to that city.

Aug. 29. A children's fair originated by Spottswood D. Bowers and W. Lord Reed, netted the sum of $80 for the Orphan House. Others who participated were Ransom S. Hooker, Russell Starkweather, Robert R. Reed, R. Grant White, G. Benjamin White, Laura Fish, Kate Starkweather, Mary Denniston, Edith Welch, Mary Bowers and Serita Wright.

Sept. 20. Frank A. Robbins' circus and menagerie exhibited in Cooperstown.

Sept. 19. The Otsego County Fair, which opened on this date was a success from a financial standpoint. The receipts were $3,800 leaving a surplus to apply to a reduction of debt and other purposes.

In September the $19,000 issue of Village Hall bonds were sold to George H. Han of New York City at 101½.

Oct. 2. The corner stone of the new Village Hall was laid. The speaker of the occasion was Samuel M. Shaw, editor of the Freeman's Journal. The block was cut by E. A. Potter and contained a list of the village officers, full record of the fire department, history of Cooperstown, Supervisors' Proceedings, records of the Otsego County Fair, etc.

This Fall the new road through the "gulf" leading west from Cooperstown to Fly Creek was opened. In this project the village was assisted by the people of Fly Creek.

Nov. 17. Glimmerglen, the summer home of William Constable on Otsego Lake, was burned to the ground with a loss of $50,000. A gas explosion was the cause

Violation of the fishing law led to the passage of an act shutting out all nets from Otsego Lake for a period of five years.

In December Alfred Corning Clark bought the large house and lot on the southeast corner of Main and River streets, for $4,150 and the Cooper Grounds on which had stood Otsego Hall with a small lot on Church street for $7,350.

Monday evening December 19th marked the opening of a new era in the history of Cooperstown when its streets were partly lighted by electricity under the Edison three-copper-wire system. Between 7 and 8 o'clock the streets on this pleasant dark winter's evening were unusually crowded with people. A few minutes after 8 a strong white light on the faces of hundreds of watchers was received with shouts of greeting. The gas jets were burning with a strong yellow light and the contrast was marked. Large numbers of people visited the "factory" to see the machinery in operation.

1888—January 13th it was announced by the village press that "a fine new bridge" had been built over the Susquehanna river by the towns of Middlefield and Otsego near the pump-house.

In January the J. P. Sill estate sold 300 acres of land that had been a part of the George Clarke property at the head of the Lake to Lewis Barton Strong for $18,470, the best sale of real estate in Otsego county in some time.

Feb. 1.   Henry F. Button, convicted of murder in the second degree for killing his wife, Letitia Button at Plainfield, Sept. 24, 1887, was sentenced to Auburn State prison for life by Judge Gerrit A. Forbes. The trial took place in Circuit Court at the Court House in Cooperstown and lasted from January 17th to January 27, the jury deliberating four hours.   District Attorney Charles T. Brewer with Judge Albert C. Tennant of counsel represented the People and Townsend & Kellogg of Oneonta with S. L. Huntington of Leonardsville of counsel, for defendant.

January 28.   Total eclipse of the moon was viewed in the evening by many residents.

In February Clarence William Davidson became associated with his father, the Hon. Andrew Davidson, as editor of The Otsego Republican.

A debt of $1,500 on the Presbyterian manse was paid early in the year.

The issue of one of the local newspapers dated February 17th said: "There was a terrible amount of drunkenness about town after the polls closed last Tuesday night.   We pity the poor women and children who have to meet such husbands and fathers on their return home."

Feb. 14.   Town Meeting Day.   James F. Clark elected Railroad commissioner after a most exciting campaign in which the town was deluged with circulars for various candidates.   Personal feelings ran high and political considerations were lost sight of in the oncoming "railroad warfare."

March 12th and 13th.   Snow commenced falling this (Sunday) evening and continued uninterruptedly for forty-four hours.   Two feet of snow fell, the greatest amount in any storm since the noted storm of May, 1857.

March 18.   Clinton House sold at Sheriff's sale to Farrant Pratt for $5,400.

In March the Central Hotel was leased to ex-Sheriff Olcott McCredy and Paul B. Boden by William M. Potter for a term of years.

In May a fund of over $2,000 was raised by The Freeman's Journal for the "Orphanage."

It was noted that by this year the tendency to remove the front fence was becoming very apparent about the village.

June 6th in Circuit Court before Judge Walter Lloyd Smith, John M. Schuyler pleaded guilty to the charge of murder in the second degree, nearly three years after he killed his child in the town of Morris. Upon his first trial he was found guilty of murder in the first degree but the case was appealed and the higher courts sent the case back for a new trial.   He was sentenced to Auburn state prison for life.

In June the old Otsego County Bank stone building on Main street was purchased by Alfred Corning Clark of E. F. Beadle. Mr. Clark was the then owner of the Cooper Grounds which the building adjoined.

F. W. Spraker of Canajoharie became first bookkeeper of the Second National bank during the summer.

June 22. Lenox, five-year-old son of the Rev. and Mrs. Newell Woolsey Wells of Brooklyn, was drowned in the Susquehanna river near their summer home, Riverbrink.

Building of "camp houses" on Otsego Lake had a real start this summer. The Eldred brothers erected a cottage on the west shore and Mr. Hall of Starkville leased from the Hoke estate a piece of property with 100 feet frontage and erected Lakeview. William Clark of Fort Plain leased for thirty years a piece of property with 300 feet frontage from the same owners and erected Arcadia.

August 8. Edgar H. Lake was elected secretary and treasurer of the Cooperstown Railroad company to succeed George M. Jarvis, resigned.

In September Leslie Pell-Clarke sold his college associate and friend, Henry L. Wardwell, the J. F. Scott farm near the head of the Lake for the sum of $22,000 being $75 an acre.

Oct. 26. Mr. and Mrs. H. C. Bowers entertained Governor David B. Hill and a party at dinner at Willowbrook.

Dec. 1. The apparatus and equipment of the Cooperstown Fire department was moved to the new quarters in the newly erected Firemen's building.

In December a fine new barn was completed on the Fernleigh Farm of Alfred Corning Clark. It was an extension of the large and commodious barn that stood there for years. The whole length was 154 feet by 40 feet wide with a large basement under the whole. Charles L. Root, was the boss carpenter and Charles J. Tuttle, the mason.

Paul B. Boden sold his interest in the Central Hotel late in the year to his partner, Olcott McCredy. Fowler & Son sold their real estate and coal, flour and feed business near the depot to Lathrop, Austin & Co., John Paule having become a general partner in the concern.

The Cooperstown band was organized during the year and was giving well received concerts by Christmas.

During the year only five or six new dwellings were erected on the corporation; two new stores in the place of a couple of old-shops; the Village Hall was completed but not formally opened.

1889.—Jan. 18. The new Village Hall on Chestnut street near Main; or Firemen's Hall, as it, perhaps, more properly should be called, as it was originally projected for the purpose of meeting the wants of the Cooperstown Fire department, was opened and over 700 people attended the concert and dedication ball, the music being furnished by the Albany Lyceum Concert company and Gartland's Tenth Regiment orchestra. The building was of brick with rooms for the fire apparatus on the ground floor which also had a room for the Village Trustees' headquarters where the meetings of that body have regularly been held and the records kept. The second floor contained the assembly or auditorium with a good sized stage and with the gallery was capable of seating 500 people. In those days it was regarded as admirably meeting the requirements.

Jan. 29. A new Village Charter retaining the desirable features of the charter in existence and embodying a few amendments to fit the conditions of the day was approved at a meeting of the Board of Village Trustees and was recommended to the Legislature for adoption. The bill was passed and signed by the Governor June 15th.

In March the "brick hotel" or "Skeleton hotel" as it was called, passed into the hands of Mr. Alfred Corning Clark. The hotel was partly built twenty years before at the corner of Main and Fair streets at a cost of about $57,000, including the value of the lot, and then collapsed for want of funds with which to carry on the project. The stockholders received back about $9,000 on its purchase at auction a few years later by George Clarke. Later the east wing of the building was taken down and the brick sold. The only use to which it was put was for hop storage. At a judgment sale in 1887 it was purchased by the Hon. George VanHorn for about $2,800. Mr. Alfred Corning Clark, a short time previous to acquiring this property, had bought the Cooper lot where once stood Otsego Hall, the home of the Cooper family, the old Otsego County Bank building, and two or three other lots near it. The building was removed, the site graded, and the other property similarly improved.

Late in March Richard E. Bolton retired from the grocery business and Frank Mulkins formed a partnership with Charles H. Mason and took over the business.

In April the plans for a new church edifice, drawn by Architect M. H. Hubbard of Utica, were accepted by the Board of Trustees of the First Baptist church. Subscriptions in the sum of $7,500 had been made by the members and friends of the church before the project was started. The corner stone was laid June 15th.

April 29. The citizens of the Village were invited to meet at the Village Hall in the evening to confer on the celebration the next day of the centennial anniversary of the inauguration of the first President of the United States. The movement came too late for any elaborate observance, but the bells were rung at 8 a. m. and flags displayed throughout the streets during the day. The Cooperstown Band gave a concert on Main street in the afternoon and special services were held in the Episcopal, Catholic and Presbyterian churches.

This summer the village contributed the sum of $1,000 for the relief of sufferers in the Johnstown flood. Few villages did more liberally for this worthy object.

June 28. Work on the new Alfred Corning Clark gymnasium at the corner of Main and Fair streets was well under way. Charles J. Tuttle was in charge of the mason work and Charles L. Root of the carpenter work.

The mortgage given by the Cooperstown Railroad company in 1869 for $100,000, on which $140,000 interest had been paid in the twenty years, was retired by July 1st of this year.

July 5. The building at the corner of Main and Fair street, orig inally erected for the old Otsego County Bank was formally turned over by Mr. Alfred Corning Clark to the Cooperstown Y. M. C. A. and opened with a reception under the auspices of the Ladies' auxiliary. No expense was spared by Mr. Clark in the extensive work done to make it all that could be desired for the purpose.

General William T. Sherman with his daughter was at the Cooper House over the week-end from the 9th to the 13th of August. Saturday night the resident veterans of the Civil War, headed by the Military Band, marched to the hotel and serenaded the General who came out on the piazza and gave expression to his pleasure in seeing them. At the conclusion of his remarks, which were in a very happy vein, he came down and shook hands with each of the old soldiers.

The hotels at Three-Mile Point, Five-Mile Point, and Vibbard's at the head of the Lake all reported good business during this season. It is interesting to note that rates at the summer hotels here this summer were about three dollars per day.

Dr. C. F. Campbell sold to Mrs. Walter Rutherford of New York City, the brick house at the corner of Lake and Pine streets for a consideration of $9,650. The property included the large lot bounded by three streets and a cottage on Nelson avenue.

A large and handsome stone mansion, "Cary-Mead," was completed during the summer by Mrs. Harriet T. Slayton.

In August and September the ties and rails were laid on the Cooperstown road between Cooperstown Junction and West Davenport.

F. L. Gilbert became postmaster, October 1st. J. Fred Murphy and Miss Mary Bingham were named assistants.

Work on the new orphanage building was approaching completion in September, and in this month Charles H. Tuttle erected the wall between the Village Hall and the Court House grounds. It was four feet thick, ten feet high and 72 feet long.

"Real estate in the rural districts, all over the state, has for several years past depreciated in value, and there are no prospects of any immediate change for the better. Otsego county is no exception to this general condition of things; indeed, it has suffered more than some others as to farm lands, on account of the large amount of such property on the market. There is a great deal of village property for sale in the county—much more than is put openly upon the market." The above is a quotation from one of the village newspapers which will throw some light upon the business conditions here during this period.

We learn that the salary of the postmaster at this time was $1,700, with allowance for clerk hire of $300; rent, fuel and lights, $285; total, $2,285. He paid for clerk hire, $900; rent, $225; fuel and lights, $85; political assessments about $75; total $1,285, leaving the postmaster about $1,000, if lucky.

The bell was hung in the tower of the Firemen's Hall and the town clock installed the latter part of September.

Sept. 11. The people were stirred by an unpleasant sensation when it was announced that Robert MacKie of Fort Wayne, Ind., would not be here to keep his engagement to wed an estimable and attractive young lady of the village. The engagement had lasted about a year. MacKie was known to be respectably connected and not a lisp had ever been heard against his reputation. That he expected to be married on the day set was believed by his relatives and friends who were present from a distance. On the eve of his wedding day he left for Albany where he met a married woman and eloped with her to Canada. A letter was received on the next day stating that he could not meet his engagement. At first it was thought that he was deranged but later the true state of affairs was revealed to the surprise of everybody.

Sept. 24. The Cooperstown railroad was opened to West Davenport. The preceding five or six years were filled with rumored railroad projects of more or less interest to Cooperstown. Besides the extension of the road above named, the proposed line to Fort Plain was being strongly advocated, and there was talk of the extension of the Cooperstown line to Catskill and of lines between Oneonta, Gilbertsville and New Berlin. A survey was made from Oneonta to Oneida.

Sept. 24. The drowning of the aeronaut, E. M. Walrath of Ilion in Otsego Lake was a sad winding up of that day's proceedings of the Otsego County Fair then in progress. The parachute dropped into the Lake between Two and Three-Mile Points, about thirty rods from the shore. Persons watching the descent with field glasses from points of observation said that both aeronaut and parachute—which had several pounds of iron in its construction—struck the water simultaneously. The young man was only 22 years old and the performance here was the third he had ever given. After a long search expert divers from New York discovered the body September 28th between 300 and 400 feet from the shore in about 45 feet of water.

Oct. 11. The Phinney Hose company was incorporated. The directors were Lynn J. Arnold, William L. McEwan, James H. Seeber, Ed. L. Sliter, Charles I. McCabe, Charles W. Bunn and Clarence W. Davidson.

Nov. 1. The large additions, alterations and repairs to the original building of the Orphan House of the Holy Saviour, including a new heating plant and electric lights, were completed at a cost of $7,500.

Nov. 1. Erastus F. Beadle, senior member of the firm of Beadle & Adams, publishers of New York City, sold his interest in the business to his partner, expecting to spend the greater part of his time henceforth at his summer home, Glimmerview, located at Cooperstown.

Mr. Beadle exerted a distinctive influence in the development of that part of the village, between Main and Lake, west of Pine street. He purchased of J. L. McNamee a valuable tract of land lying in the corporation, opened Nelson avenue and put up two dwellings thereon. Sites on this street, Upper Main and Pine street were sold and a number of new and handsome dwellings erected. Originating in his purchase this section of the village had a fine development.

Alfred Corning Clark contributed $18,000 for the endowment of Thanksgiving Hospital. The institution had been closed since 1876 when the financial panic crippled some of its most liberal supporters. Miss Susan Fenimore Cooper had always cherished the hope that a small hospital bearing the old name might be opened to meet the needs of the community but she had been advised against taking any step in that direction until an endowment of at least $25,000 was secured. During the Fall of this year she placed the matter before Mr. and Mrs. Clark with the success above stated. With the $6,000 already on hand and an additional gift by Mrs. Clark of $1,000 the required endowment was completed. Erastus F. Beadle, the next week, offered a site for the new institution in the rear of Nelson avenue.

Mrs. Rutherford caused the sidewalk on the north side of the lane in the rear of her home at the corner of Pine and Lake streets to be removed and the line fence set back several feet claiming ownership to the center of the lane. Twice the village trustees had the fence removed and replaced the walk and three times the agent of Mrs. Rutherford caused it to be taken up. In November the trustees decided to commence a suit at law in defense of what they regarded as the rights of the corporation.

The annual report of the Cooperstown Railroad company for the fiscal year ending September 30th showed net profits of $8,697.

Nov. 2. The Phoenix Knitting Mills property, including the machinery, owned by the First and Second National Banks of this village, was purchased by Theodore Frelinghuysen of New York City, whose father was a member of President Arthur's cabinet.

Nov. 10. At the annual meeting of the Otsego County Agricultural society it was reported that the debt of the society after all available cash was applied in liquidation would be about $1,200.

At the close of the year the sum of about $1,160 had been subscribed toward the debt of the Orphan House.

Nov. 18. A public meeting was held at the Village Hall to adopt measures to arrest the taking of fish illegally from Otsego Lake. As a result of a vote that the existing law prohibiting the use of nets be enforced, a committee of fifteen of which George VanHorn was chairman, was appointed. For two years preceding this action parties in Otsego, Cherry Valley and Springfield had been engaged in illegal fishing. Nets were being openly drawn over the spawning beds and thousands of little bass taken and sold in nearby markets. The same condition also existed with relation to trout, and line fishing practically disappeared from the lake.

Early in December Samuel L. Warrin, who had been a resident of Cooperstown for about two years, having come here from New York City, purchased the residence of E. S. Bundy on Main street at a consideration of $7,000.

1890.—The four children of the late Jane R. A. Carter united in the generous gift of $10,000 for the proposed Thanksgiving Hospital. The gift was made by Mrs. P. A. H. Brown, Mrs. G. Hyde Clarke, Miss Anna Grace Carter and L. Averell Carter to form a memorial to their deceased mother. The announcement was made early in January.

At meetings of the directors of the Cooperstown and Susquehanna

Valley and Cooperstown & Charlotte Valley Railroad Companies early in the year voted to close the double accounts running between the two companies. The work of grading beyond West Davenport, new locomotive, etc., had been covered by the issue of $100,000 bonds and $15,000 paid in by the stockholders of the C. & C. V. R. R. Most of the bonds had been sold.

January 25. Committee interested in forming Farmers' Cooperative Creamery met at Village Hall and announced that $2,550 had been subscribed with assurance that the remaining $450 would be forthcoming. Committee on plans was appointed composed of M. H. Wedderspoon, W. Kendrick Warren, A. H. Clark, Bartlett Rogers, A. S. Potts, Thos. Laidler, L. J. Parshall, Chas. Hubbard and Fenimore Whipple.

In February a village paper said that in 25 out of 36 years the mean temperature of this place had varied but one degree; grouping the years in periods of five there was a variation of only one degree or less from a mean of 44 degrees. During that period of 36 years, the lowest temperature occurred 17 times in December and January and 19 times in February and March.

The new First Baptist church edifice was dedicated on Elm street, February 6th. The building was commenced the preceding Spring, the corner stone having been laid June 15th. It was a beautiful building of Romanesque style of architecture, 60x100 feet. M. H. Hubbard of Utica was the architect. The auditorium comfortably seated 430 persons. Contractors: George A. Hines, general construction; John C. Smith, mason, both of Cooperstown; George Hathorne, Oneida, slating; Paul Kallies, Utica, frescoing and hardwood finish; C. P. Davis & Sons, Utica, cathedral glass; Furniture Manufacturing Co., Northville, Mich., pews; Pierce, Butler & Pierce, Syracuse, steam heating; H. M. Hooker & Co., Cooperstown, plumbing, tinning, etc. The total cost was $14,500. Debt, about $4,000.

In February hops were selling at 20 cents a pound for best quality.

"The Railroad War" was renewed at the annual town meeting held on February 11th and was fought with vigor on both sides. Herbert Wedderspoon was supported for Commissioner by those who sustained the existing management and Everett A. Potter by those opposed. The former had a majority of 3 in a vote of 1,100. Feeling ran high during the election and two or three arrests were made.

At a meeting held on the 12th the Cooperative Creamery project was successfully launched. A site was selected on the banks of the river near the water works. The first board of directors was made up as follows: G. Hyde Clarke, Robt. L. Davidson, A. S. Potts, L. G. Parshall, A. W. Thayer, M. C. Bundy, Jas. Bunyan, M. H. Wedderspoon and F. C. Whipple. Mr. Clarke was elected president; Mr. Bundy, vice-president; C. W. Davidson, secretary, and W. H. Peake, treasurer.

In the suit brought before Judge Merwin in Supreme Court by G. Pomeroy Keese, Jas. Bunyan and others, "praying for an order"— establishing the election of the petitioners to the office of directors of the C. & S. V. R. R. Co. and setting aside the election of the defendants (the acting board of directors) or directing a new election to be held, the Court granted an order directing a new election to be held March 21st. An appeal was taken.

Otsego bass fishing was reported as exceptionally good in February. One man took 54 in one day.

Great fear for the ice crop existed March 1st. On Feb. 17 and again on March 3d hopes were entertained that the cold weather was at hand but in vain.

The winter was the most remarkable in 36 years. Not one day of good sleighing existed up to March 5th. The first eight or nine days of the month brought the first cold weather and the work of harvesting the ice crop for the year began, but a thaw followed and cut short what promised to be a very active harvest. A hundred tons of ice were shipped to Oneonta.

Charles H. Lathrop established a steam laundry on Lake street in March.

Capt. Andrew Davidson, editor of the Otsego Republican, was appointed by the President, March 14th, first deputy commissioner of pensions at a salary of $3,600.

The law partnership of Carlton B. Pierce and Lynn J. Arnold was formed in March.

March 28. There were 10 or 12 unoccupied dwellings on the corporation with several furnished houses to let during the summer.

At the election of directors of the C. & S. V. R. R. Co. held 21st pursuant to an order of the Court the following were chosen: Horace Lathrop, Albert Lane, Thomas W. Thayer, Wm. H. Michaels, Sands Shumway, John Wood, Francis Hecox, Lancelot Taylor, Orren Benton, Peter P. Cooper, Allen Gallup, Peter Parshall, Reuben H. Bates. The board afterwards met and organized by choosing Dr. Lathrop, president; Albert Lane, vice-president and E. H. Lake, secretary and treasurer. The net result was the re-election of the old board with two exceptions, one in the place of the late W. E. Cory and one in the place of Mr. Reynolds.

Another suit was commenced late in March by substantially the same parties who brought the action for a new election for directors. The complaint was signed by James Bunyan, one of the plaintiffs in the action, and C. B. Pierce as attorney. It recited the organization of the two railroad companies, matters related to the elections of directors and commissioners, alleging fraud, an illegal corporation, etc., and asked that the lease of the C. & S. V. by the C. & C. V. Co. be set aside and a receiver appointed. The local newspapers took an active part in the discussion arising over the suit, the Freeman's Journal and Otsego Republican on one side and the Otsego Farmer on the other.

The death of Capt. Peter P. Cooper took place on Monday, March 31, at the age of 75 years. Capt. Cooper was widely known as the owner of one of the Otsego Lake steamers and a fleet of small boats, also as one of the old time fishermen of the place.

After a faithful service of over 21 years as a member of the Board of Education, during which time he acted as its president, Dr. Horace

Lathrop resigned, April 1st, the office to which he had been elected eight different times without opposition.

April 14. Dr. Horace Lathrop received $10,000 for the Thanksgiving Hospital building from an anonymous donor.

April 14. Three prisoners escaped from the county jail by sawing through an iron hasp fastening the inner door with a small saw made from a pocket knife.

May 6. The new locomotive made by the Baldwin Works in Philadelphia arrived and was placed on the Cooperstown road.

RAILROAD LITIGATION

In January, confidently expecting to elect the town railroad commissioner to be chosen the following month, the gentlemen who were previously voted for and failed to be elected directors of the C. & S. V. R. R. Co. commenced a suit against the acting board to depose them from office on the charge that they had not been legally and properly elected. The judge did not establish the election of the fourteen petitioners as requested but did order a new election. The election was held and the acting board was re-elected—their party having unexpectedly to their opponents elected the commissioner in February. The legality of the Board therefore was established and a new lease of the road was made by the directors with the avowed object of curing any possible defect therein.

This lease was made by the C. & S. V. R. R. Co. which operated the road from Cooperstown to Cooperstown Junction, a distance of sixteen miles, to the C. & C. V. R. R., which proposed to build a line from the Junction to meet the new road from Catskill to Stamford and which afterward became the Ulster & Delaware. At that time there was no thought that the Ulster & Delaware would make Oneonta its terminal point. In September, 1889, the C. & C. V. R. R. was completed to West Davenport but not far enough to make the proposed connection with the Stamford line.

Another suit was brought in March to take the C. & S. V. R. R. out of the hands of the directors and place it in the hands of a receiver. The complaint referring to the lease of 1889 charged that the control of the road had been illegally and improperly obtained by a fraudulent and corrupt scheme designed by the directors to secure for themselves valuable property and divide the profits among themselves in salaries; that the defendants misapplied, diverted and converted to their own use moneys belonging to the lessor company of which no account had been rendered; and also that the assistance of certain local newspapers—referring to the Freeman's Journal and Otsego Republican—had been secured by the defendants to assist them in the so-called scheme. As a matter of fact the local newspapers took a marked interest in the matter. The Otsego Farmer backed the interest of the plaintiffs with all its might while the two older and more conservative newspapers mentioned above favored the defendants.

Describing the conclusion of the railroad war we quote the following from "The Story of Cooperstown" by the Rev. Ralph Birdsall: (See Page 381 1st edition.):

"Toward the middle of May, 1891, the stage was set for the case against the railway management. The interest of a controversy which had kept the community in a ferment for the better part of six years was now centered at the county court-house in Cooperstown, and all eyes were turned toward the symbol of justice, the scales and the sword, which the court-house tower uplifts above the village.

"The first few days of court week were taken up with unimportant cases. Both sides in the impending suit against the railway management realized that the books of the two companies, the C. & S. V. R. R. Co. and the C. & C. V. R. R. Co., showing the accountings between them, and the financial affairs of both for six years previously, would be of great importance at the trial. On the morning after the opening of court the plaintiffs' attorney asked for an order to be allowed to see the books of the company before the case was called. Judge Charles E. Parker, of Owego, who presided, said that the plaintiffs should be allowed to see the books. Judge E. M. Harris, for the railway management, stated that Edgar H. Lake, secretary and treasurer of the railroad companies, was confined to his room in the Fenimore Hotel by illness, and that the books would be produced at the trial. However, at the suggestion of Judge Parker, Harris wrote a note to Lake, directing him to permit the attorneys of plaintiffs to have access to the books. To the bearer of this note Lake gave a verbal message, saying that he would be ready to show the books in the evening, or on the next morning, which was Wednesday, the thirteenth of May. At the close of Wednesday afternoon, which was taken up with another case, Carlton B. Pierce, attorney for the plaintiffs, stated to the judge that he had been unable to get a sight of the company's books, and asked for an order to have them deposited with the county clerk, and for an attachment against Edgar Lake as a non-appearing witness. The Judge said that he would grant the attachment, returnable next day. Lake could not be found, and the attachment was not served.

"In the evening Judge Harris sought for Lake in vain. He was not in his room, and no one had seen him about the hotel. Harris waited for him until midnight, but he did not appear. At seven o'clock the next morning Judge Harris went to Lake's room, and saw that the bed had not been occupied during the night. Lake did not appear at his usual place at the breakfast table, and after leaving orders that a thorough search should be made for the missing secretary and treasurer, Judge Harris went to the court-house.

"Another search of Lake's room in the hotel revealed the following letter, in Lake's handwriting, addressed to Judge Harris:

"Office of
"Cooperstown and Charlotte Valley R. R.

."Cooperstown, N. Y., May 13, 1891.

"Judge—You will have to put the case over the term, as it is impossible for me to be in attendance.

"You will find great disorder in my affairs, but there is no money missing.

"When I took the position I thought I could fill it, but I was incompetent.

"(The letter was written on the official stationery of the company, office. The next paragraph was written in a lighter shade of ink.)

"I have always intended to employ an expert to write the books up, but have neglected it.

"(The rest was added in lead pencil.)

"This is the only way that I can see whereby I can quit the world even. You will now have time to have the books written up, and when they are in proper shape you are sure to win. If I should stay and go on the stand you would be embarrassed, to say the least.

"This is another case where your kindness and faith have caused you trouble.

"My father and mother—may God pity them.

"Lake was found on the top floor of the hotel in an unused room, in which there was a bed with only a mattress upon it. Upon this bed Lake lay prostrate, fully dressed, and in a dying condition when discovered, having cut his throat with a razor. Physicians were hastily summoned, but nothing could be done for him; within a few minutes Edgar Lake was dead.

"Lake's tragic end was a terrible blow to Judge Harris, whose iron nerve had never failed him until now. For six years he had lived calm and unruffled amid scenes of strife, but this fatal issue of the drama broke him completely down.

"In Lake's pocket the sum of sixty dollars was found, but nothing was discovered in his rooms to throw any further light upon the tragedy. At his office a strange state of affairs was revealed. The place was in the utmost confusion. The table was stacked with letters; express packages and messages were lying in chairs and around the room in every direction; packages of money and uncashed cheques were scattered about in wild profusion; many letters and messages remained unopened, some of which bore dates of two and three months back. At the post-office Lake's box was found to be overflowing with a week's accumulation of mail.

"Lake's dead hand stopped the machinery of the law at the court-house. It was as he said in his farewell letter. He had compelled the court 'to put the case over the term.'

"An expert accountant was set at work upon Lake's confused affairs. It was a slow task to bring order out of such chaos, but when it had been done the situation was found to be exactly as Lake had described it. There had been great disorder in his affairs, but there was not one cent of money missing.

"The rest of the story is soon told. The celebrated case came to trial at the next term of court. Judge Parker filed his decision against the contention of the plaintiffs that the lease was fraudulent and void. The lease was sustained, and the railroad war was over."

Nearly 60,000 feet of plank were put down on the village walks during the Spring by the trustees; and several substantial crosswalks were built. The roadway on several avenues was improved.

The Tunnicliff Inn was leased for the season by J. H. McDonald of Albany and Saratoga.

Walter H. Bunn was selected clerk of the commission to revise the judiciary article of the State constitution. Judge A. C. Tennant was a member of the commission which met at Albany during the summer.

In this year it was estimated by a village newspaper that it required about $11,000 a year, on the average, to meet the ordinary expenses of the several churches of the village, and that they were contributing about $1,500 annually to their several missionary, educational and philanthropic societies.

The trustees in June offered a reward of fifty dollars for evidence leading to the conviction of the persons who painted red the memorial stone set up on Fair street.

The Cooperstown Aqueduct association installed a new boiler and steam pump in July.

Early in the month the Postoffice was moved to the Masonic block on Pioneer street, affording increased accommodation for the public.

In July it was reported that there were eight or nine parties camping on the shores of Otsego Lake, some of them from a distance.

Dr. John C. Wight resigned as principal of the Cooperstown Union and High school to become principal at the opening of the school year of the High school at Worcester, Mass. Dr. Wight had been head of the local school since its organization as a Union Free School in October, 1871, and his departure was a matter of great regret to all in the community. As a leading and successful educator, Dr. Wight achieved a prominent position in the State, and endeared himself to scores of young people who came to do honor to their alma mater.

Ransom Hooker, Stuart Patterson, Fred Scott and Samuel Bunn started July 2nd on a canoe trip from Cooperstown to Wilkes-Barre, Pa., which they completed successfully.

The textile business was good in 1890 and operations boomed at the Phoenix Mills.

The school census of this year showed 532 children in the district between the ages of 5 and 21 years.

The Cooperstown Athletics lent fame to the village for baseball prowess.

Survivors of the 121st and 152nd N. Y. Volunteer regiments of the Civil War met in Cooperstown for their annual reunion August 21st. Dinner was served by the village for the visitors at the Village Hall and the occasion was made a notable one.

In August the village trustees ordered the opening of Fair street through the old Fair grounds to Beaver. The land was donated by James Bunyan and associates.

Plans were completed in August for the new First National bank building designed by Frank Waller and work commenced at once.

George VanHorn was nominated for Congress on the Democratic ticket September 27th, and elected by 200 plurality.

The four children of the late Mrs. Jane R. A. Carter contributed

$8,000 to the enlargement and improvement of Christ church as a memorial to their mother.

At the close of the year 41 dwelling houses and 7 or 8 stores were for sale. Not a single building was erected on the corporation during the year and only one commenced.

CHAPTER II

FROM 1891 TO 1895

1891.—The new Alfred Corning Clark gymnasium was opened to the inspection of the public on February 10th with Prof. W. H. Martin in charge.

Tens of thousands of new hop poles were being brought to Cooperstown this year indicating that many new yards were being set out.

The "Mabel Coburn" was the name of a new 12 x 60 foot pleasure steamer constructed here by Capt. George Coburn for use in connection with his boat livery on Otsego Lake.

The Ballard House property was purchased in March by the popular landlord, George J. Vandewerker. He obtained real estate that was once valued at $45,000, and the furniture in the hotel, for $12,000.

The village purchased for $1,000 the vacant lot adjoining Firemen's Hall on the South following a special election.

The following significant item appeared in a village newspaper dated April 2nd. "An easy money market here the first of April. A class of fortunate hop growers are paying up obligations."

April 20. Fire destroyed the storehouse of Austin, Bolton & Bronner near the railroad tracks on Railroad avenue. Between 400 and 500 bales of cotton belonging to the proprietor of the Knitting mills at Phoenix, 50 tons of hay belonging to D. J. McGown and E. A. Potter, 8 tons of straw belonging to Thomas Taylor and a small quantity of coal and salt belonging to Austin, Bolton & Bronner were destroyed. The cotton was fully insured and there was $1,000 insurance on the building.

April 28. The Court of Appeals denied a motion to reopen the case of D. M. Hunter et al, adm'rs., etc., against the Cooperstown Railroad Co., for causing the death of Henry S. Hunter in 1884. This case became a noted one in the Courts of the State. It was four times tried before a jury, and each time a verdict was rendered for the plaintiffs: first in 1885 before the Hon. H. Boardman Smith; the verdict being set aside at the General Term and a new trial granted; second, in 1886 before Judge Martin, General Term denied a new trial but the Court of Appeals granted one; third in 1889 before Judge C. E. Parker when the General Term ordered a new trial; fourth, in 1890 before Judge Walter L. Smith, new trial denied by Special and General Terms; taken to Court of Appeals, which set aside the judgment and ordered a new trial. When the matter came up at the May term in 1891 the plaintiff did not appear and the case was dismissed with costs.

Hops were bringing 32 and 35 cents per pound on the local market.

There were on the corporation twenty places licensed for selling liquor (not counting the Cooper House)—6 hotels, 7 saloons, 4 drug stores, 3 stores. They paid $640 in license fees.

A direct telephone line was constructed to Utica in the summer of this year.

The corner stone of the Carter Memorial Chancel of Christ church was laid July 2nd, at 4 o'clock.

The First National bank opened in its new building on Monday morning June 29th. It was a solid brick and terra cotta structure of renaissance design, three stories in height, fronting 44 feet eight inches on Main street and eighty-seven feet from front to rear. The building was divided into two parts, one for the bank at the west and the other for a store which was leased to the Bundy Brothers. John C. Smith did the mason work and Fayette Houck the woodwork.

July 6. Special Election held pursuant to notice upon the question of whether or not the village should own its own water works. For the proposition 91, against 199.

The number of fire hydrants on the corporation was increased from 34 to 40 by the Aqueduct association at their own expense, the total charge for hydrant rental remaining at $1,000.

Charles P. Thompson, for many years head of the Intermediate department of the Union school resigned that position in July. At his departure the school lost a teacher of experience, acknowledged ability and faithfulness.

The management reported that not since 1883 had the Cooper House had so good a season as this year.

Work was commenced on the summer residence of Mrs. George Clarke at the head of the Lake facing Hyde Bay.

In August, William Constable and Edward S. Clark proposed to erect at their joint expense a new, larger and more convenient grandstand for the Athletic association, which was a popular organization at this time, supporting a strong baseball team, conducting tennis tournaments, etc. The offer was accepted and the stand built without delay.

The Cooper House was destroyed by fire Saturday morning, August 8th. The flames were seen at about 3:45 a. m., and a few minutes later the alarm was sounded. The fire starter in the bake room and kitchen which was located in the basement. S. E. Crittenden, the proprietor, who had put much money into the improvement of the property suffered a grievous loss which was estimated at over $50,000 with insurance of $22,500 on building and contents. It was estimated that the property could not have been replaced at that time for less than $75,000. There were about 200 guests in the house at the time all of whom escaped without injury. Several in the north wing, however, lost all or nearly all of their clothing together with some valuable jewelry and two or three watches. Among those in the house at the time were the following: The Rev. Dr. Morgan A. Dix, rector of Trinity church, New York; Rear Admiral D. L. Braine, U. S. N.; Frederick J. dePeyster, New York; Charles W. Ridgeway, New York; R. R. Perkins, New York; A. E. Wright, New York; Charles P. Buchanan, New York, with their families and guests. This ended the existence of the building built in 1854 as the Cooperstown Seminary. Its original cost was about $55,000 including furniture. It was not a financial success, and after having two or three different principals was closed in the Spring of 1858, and remained so until the Fall of 1859, when by the assistance of Cooperstown citizens it was purchased by R. C. Flack at a nominal price and reopened in November. He conducted it until 1865 when William M. Clinton bought the property, spent a large sum of money on it and placed the Rev. Dr. Kerr at its head, but relinquished control in two years and then it finally closed. Mr. Clinton sank many thousand dollars in the venture. The property then passed into the hands of the Second National bank which held a mortgage on it, and they sold to H. F. Phinney in January, 1869. Mr. Phinney made extensive improvements to fit it for the purposes of a summer hotel. When completed it was named "The Cooper House" and was first leased to C. A. Watkins and afterwards to Coleman & Maxwell. Mr. Phinney sank about $65,000 in the venture in one way or another. In 1878 the entire property was sold to S. E. Crittenden for about $17,000.

A public meeting for the purpose of considering plans for rebuilding the Cooper House was held at the Court House, August 19th, when a committee of 22 citizens was appointed to take up the matter. Subcommittees were appointed to solicit subscriptions with the desire of securing pledges amounting to at least $15,000. It was thought that a suitable structure larger than the old one might have been built at $50,000 with $15,000 more for furniture. The project finally failed on account of the inability of those interested to obtain the necessary loan and the decision finally arrived at by the contractors, that a suitable building could not be erected at the figure at first proposed.

In the fall of this year it was estimated that there were upwards of 8,000 people at work in the hop yards of the county.

New 70-foot poles for the telephone and telegraph wires were put up in Main street in September making a considerable improvement over the heterogenious collection of "sticks" that had been in use.

The Index Mills at Phoenix were running night and day in the fall of this year employing 120 people in all The payroll amounted to $1,000 a week.

The taxpayers voted on the 17th, 80 to 6, to purchase a steam fire engine. The committee appointed for that purpose decided to purchase a No. 3 La France Steamer built at Elmira. The steamer weighed 5,800 pounds and cost delivered $3,150. It was determined by the trustees to retain the Fernleigh engine in the department.

The Winning Hose Co. leased two large rooms in the First National bank building of the Bundy Bros. and fitted up handsome club rooms there for their enjoyment.

The report of the Athletic Association Oct. 6th showed a deficit of $836.42. S. L. Warrin was the treasurer and the report was examined and found correct by a special committee composed of A. J. Butler and W. C. Flanders. Leslie Pell-Clarke, the president, submitted a report outlining plans for the next year and for reducing the indebtedness.

The Rev. Brewer G. Boardman on Oct. 22 resigned the pastorate of the First Baptist church to accept a call to the Baptist church at

Geneva. Mr. Boardman's pastorate extended over a period of five and one-half years and was successful along all lines but its greatest achievement was the erection of the new church edifice very largely through his own indefatigable efforts.

The consecration of the Carter Memorial Chancel of Christ church took place on the morning of the festival of St. Simon and St. Jude, October 28th. The Rt. Rev. Wm. Coswell Doane, Bishop of the Albany Diocese officiated. The sermon was preached by the Rt. Rev. Leighton Coleman, Bishop of Delaware. Besides the rector, the Rev. Mr. Olmsted, and the Bishops, there were seventeen clergymen present from other parishes.

The Bundy Bros. moved into their new store in the First National Bank Building Nov. 26th.

The Rev. C. E. Nichols of Skaneateles was called to the pulpit of the First Baptist Church the 1st of December to assume his new duties January 1st.

In the last month of the year a new sewer was laid on Lake street from Chestnut to Pine.

In December Mulkins & Mason bought of Mrs. Chas. E. Moore the building in wh'ch they were doing business. Consideration $8,000.

On the morning of December 4th one of the women in charge at the Orphanage discovered Paris Green in the milk that was to be used at breakfast and it was discovered that two of the older girls, aged about 13 years, had planned a diabolical scheme mainly directed against one of those in charge.

On December 18th fire broke out in the upper part of the steam laundry of H. W. Thayer on Lake street and the greater part of the building was consumed. It belonged to Wm. H. Collins and was valued at $1,200; insured for half that amount.

In 1889 and 1890 no buildings were erected on the corporation. In 1891 Mr. Beadle put up two, and D. M. Hunter and Mr. Crittenden one each—four in all. The First National Bank building was commenced in 1890 and completed in 1891.

Weather conditions in 1891 were remarkable in some respects. An autumn unusually fine and prolonged with a month of September 7 degrees above the mean for that month; and a December with the highest temperature in 38 years. The Lake on the first of the month was lower than at any corresponding date but one in 25 years.

1892.—About $125 was realized by the presentation of the home-talent play "Longfellow's Dream" by about 100 persons at the Village Hall on the two opening evenings of the New Year and under the auspices of the Universalist society.

A new and substantial dock was erected by the village trustees at the foot of Fair street in February. It was ten feet longer than the former dock and was a permanent improvement.

E. F. Beadle sold the Dr. Wight house on Church street to the Universalist society for a parsonage early in February. Consideration $3,500.

There was a large attendance at the fox chase on February 6th in which there were fifteen entries includ'ng some of the finest hounds in the county. Unfortunately the fox, which had been a long time in captivity, could not stand the long journey and had to be carried most of the last half of the intended course which broke up the trail. As far as the trail was connected the dogs followed it perfectly, and the chase was quite exciting.

The report of the treasurer of the Otsego County Agricultural society showed a balance of $1,680 on hand and liabilities of $1,616.

2,000 yearling Michigan Lake trout hatched at Northville, Mich., were placed in Otsego Lake March 2nd.

Enumerators for the census of the town of Otsego filed their returns in March for the census of 1890 showing a population of 4,342 a decrease of 348 since 1880. The population of the village of Cooperstown was 2,657.

In the interest of the creditors Walter H. Bunn was appointed temporary receiver of the Cooperstown Illuminating Co., March 9th, with instructions to operate the plant. April 3d Judge Herrick granted an order dissolving the company and Mr. Bunn was appointed permanent receiver.

April 2nd the Second National Bank building was vacated the business being moved to the building one door east while extensive additions and improvements were being made. Charles J. Tuttle and Charles L. Root were the contractors. The work was completed and the bank returned to occupy the new quarters the last of August. The improvements made it one of the handsomest buildings in this section. The improvements consisted of an entire new front of red sandstone with a large window affording excellent light for the banking room, 20 x 42 feet, formed by combining two former front rooms; and a brick addition in the rear for the president's and directors' room with the cashier's office between that and the banking room. A large fire and burglar proof safe was added to the old one affording adequate facilities in this respect.

300,000 whitefish fry and 200,000 trout fry from Government hatcheries were placed in the Lake in April.

April 26. Work was commenced on a new residence for W. H. Michaels on Nelson avenue.

During the year the Cooperstown Aqueduct association put down 3,600 feet of new water mains.

Capt. Geo. E. Coburn's new steamer, "The Mabel Coburn" was launched April 28th.

May 16. Forty men commenced work on the extension of the Cooperstown railroad with the idea of completing the extension to Davenport Center by the middle of July.

An experimental strip of concrete road was laid on Pioneer street from Main to the foot of the hill in June.

William C. Bailey retired from the retail business in June after an active career of 48 years. Benj. F. Kipp who commenced business in 1834 and P. G. Tanner, who started in 1843, alone were Mr. Bailey's seniors when he retired.

A nine made up of the young men of the village and the New York "Giants," made up entirely of young women played a game of base ball on the Fair Grounds, June 21st. The teams were quite evenly matched and played fairly well the score being 16 to 15 in favor of the fair sex.

The Hope factory at Index was sold in July to Mrs. John P. Doane, whose husband was the agent and superintendent of the Phoenix Mills.

On Sunday, July 10th, at the morning service at the First Baptist Church Henry G. Trevor of New York City offered a contribution of $2,000 toward lifting the church debt of $3,800 provided the balance was raised in a week's time. The effort met with success among the more liberal givers besides Mr. Trevor being Col. Charles S. Stewart, Edward S. Clark and C. W. Smith.

The Cornell University Musical clubs gave a concert at the Bowne Opera House on the evening of July 16.

B. F. Murdock, Jr's., new house was erected in the fall of this year on Chestnut street.

The payment into the treasury of the Orphan House of the Holy Saviour in the spring of the $3,000 bequest in the will of Mrs. Lucy Chase put that institution out of debt for the first time in years and also permitted the carrying out of many necessary repairs to the interior of the building. These included new floors, the wainscoting of the dormitories on the third floor, replastering many of the ceilings, installation of fire escapes, etc.

George M. Jarvis was elected cashier of the Second National bank to take effect November 1st succeeding Henry L. Hinman, resigned.

H. I. Russell sold his interest in The Otsego Farmer to Charles H. Parshall and Henry Scott. Arthur H. Crist retained his interest in the business.

The Cooperstown Electric company was incorporated late in September with a capital stock of $12,500, with Oliver R. Butler of Cooperstown, Robert E. Drake, Paul T. Brady of Syracuse, Charles B. Staats and Frederick B. Wadhams of Albany as directors. The Cooperstown Gas Co. was incorporated at the same time with the same capital and directors.

A most unnatural and repulsive crime was committed at Hyde Hall at the head of the Lake on Sept. 18 when the private vault of the Clarke family was entered and the lead casket containing the remains of a child placed there in 1856 was opened by being cut into with a knife. Four hoppickers from Albany were arrested the next day and brought to Cooperstown and committed. Two were discharged on Tuesday and the other two held by Justice Cook.

The death by drowning in Otsego Lake of Elihu Phinney, a highly esteemed and prominent citizen, took place on Sept. 20th. Mr. Phinney spent much of his time fishing generally going to the upper part in the morning and returning in the evening his row boat being towed by the Natty. He had done this on the day the tragedy took place. When the steamer touched the dock, he stepped from her deck down to his boat, made a misstep and fell into the water. It is thought that he hit his head on the side of the boat or suffered a sudden shock as he made practically no effort to save himself. He was about twelve minutes in the water. Mr. Phinney had passed his 70th birthday. He represented one of the first families that settled in and greatly aided in the upbuilding of this village.

Following the annual Fair this year it was announced that the County Agricultural society could pay its debts at maturity from funds now on hand and show a surplus of about $1,500. In 1891 about $1,000 was expended on permanent improvements. The total receipts for 1892 were nearly $4,000 the greatest in the history of the society.

In September S. J. W. Reynolds sold the Corner Book store business to H. I. Russell.

New sewers were laid in October on Beaver street west from Susquehanna and also the entire length of Eagle street.

After being operated for eight years as a year-round hotel, The Hotel Fenimore was closed for the winter, October 1st.

The sale of the Cooperstown Electric Co. and the Cooperstown Gas Co. took place October 5. In December the companies were reorganized with a capital of $25,000. The officers were: President, C. B. Staats of Albany; vice-president, Lee B. Cruttenden; secretary, treasurer and general superintendent, O. R. Butler; directors, C. B. Staats, James Bunyan, L. B. Cruttenden, O. R. Butler and P. T. Brady. The report of the receiver showed that the company paid expenses.

Columbus Day having been set aside as a holiday this year Cooperstown celebrated on an extensive scale and a large number of people gathered from the surrounding country. The program consisted of a parade with exercises at the Village Hall when addresses were made by the Rev. Father Daniel O'Connell and the Rev. Chas. K. McHarg. In the evening there was a fine display of fireworks on the Court House grounds with a concert by the Cooperstown Military band.

It was evidently a prosperous time for farmers. A village paper said in November, "the surplus profits on the hop crop of Otsego county will this year amount to about $600,000. The good prices obtained for butter, cheese, etc., will add say $400,000 to that sum—which will make the net earnings from the farms about $1,000,000, being an average of $200 each to 5,000 farmer families."

Twenty arc lights replaced the incandescent electric lights in the streets of Cooperstown in December.

The Maddox Wire Belt Co. was projected to manufacture wire belting at the Hope Mill at Index and $15,000 stock was purchased locally to finance the concern. The company had a capital stock of $75,000. The local directors were Albert Lane, John P. Doane and Jas. F. Clark.

Only three or four houses were erected on the corporation during the year.

1893.—January 8. A train of cars for the first time passed over the extension of the Cooperstown road which had been built to Davenport Center. The line was never operated having been built with the idea of connecting with the U. & D. which at that time had been extended to Catskill. The U. & D. went to Oneonta instead.

Upon invitation of Albert C. Tennant, Lee B. Cruttenden, E. R. Carr, C. L. Burlingham, S. S. Bowne, Carlton B. Pierce, Walter H. Bunn, Lynn J. Arnold, J. A. Ward, Edwin S. Bundy, C. E. Roberts, M. C. Bundy, Frank L. Smith, Philip H. Potter, C. R. Burch and J.

F. Reustle, James A. Lynes, a prominent Cooperstown Attorney delivered a lecture on the Keeley treatment for intemperance at the Village Hall, January 13th, which was largely attended by citizens of the village.

George A. Hinds commenced the erection of a large new house on Pine street early in the year.

In January the Rev. Dr. Morgan A. Dix, rector of Trinity church, New York City, presented Christ Church with a bell as a memorial to his father, General John A. Dix. Dr. Dix was a summer visitor in Cooperstown in those years.

The machinery for the Maddox Wire Belting Co. arrived and was placed in position early in March.

W. H. Michaels took possession of his house just completed on Nelson avenue. Chas. L. Root did the carpenter work and Charles J. Tuttle was the mason.

The Hotel Fenimore was sold in March to J. E. Whipple of Carbondale, Pa., by Judge E. M. Harris.

Tunnicliff Cottage at Five-Mile Point was leased for the season to Frank Pierce.

The new summer residence of Henry L. Wardwell at the head of the Lake was built during the summer.

The Three-Mile Point House was not opened during the summer.

The new arc light system of illuminating the village streets went into effect April 1st and was regarded as a great improvement.

The Hotel Fenimore was opened to the public on April 11th.

While excavating the cellar for the addition to the Ballard House in April the workmen dug up a petrified piece of wood about 15 inches long and 7 inches in diameter, which weighed 19 pounds. It was evidently the end of a chestnut fence post.

Work for the enlargement of the Ballard House was commenced April 9th and was completed early in July. An addition, 60 x 25 feet, matching the rest of the building added a number of rooms and a new steam heating plant for the whole building was installed.

The Clinton factory situated about five miles south of Cooperstown and which had been lying idle for several years, was leased of Short & Luther by Rufus Steere for the manufacture of cotton yarn.

Capt. P. P. Cooper built and placed in operation on Otsego Lake, a new steamer, "Cyclone."

The new bell at Christ church was rung for the first time, June 1st.

Dr. Henry D. Sill opened an office for the practice of medicine in this village in June. Dr. Sill became one of the leading surgeons of Central New York and as a citizen of Cooperstown was noted for his charity and good works.

E. A. and Frederick Schneider, Jr., in July purchased the bakery business of their father, Frederick Schneider, and continued it.

Mrs. George Clarke opened the Dower House overlooking Hyde Bay on Otsego Lake August 1st with an "at home."

Estli avenue received its name by authority of the village trustees in July.

The Cooperstown Athletics again flourished and there was great interest in baseball. Several games were played a week and seem to have been well patronized.

A phonographic concert was given at the Village Hall, October 12th, by Lyman H. Howe under the auspices of the Y. M. C. A. that both surprised and pleased the audience.

October 10. The 46th meeting of the Archdeaconry of the Susquehanna and the first annual festival of the choirs of the Archdeaconry opened at Christ church.

The Seventeenth annual convention of the Otsego County S. S. association opened on October 17. The sessions were held at the Presbyterian and Baptist churches.

At a meeting of the Cooperstown Athletic Association held late in October, it appeared from the report of the treasurer that after crediting a very generous gift to the association from Wm. Constable, there remained a debt of almost $800, a portion of which was created by permanent improvement to the grounds. The entire amount of the deficit was subscribed by the end of the year.

In November water mains were extended by the Cooperstown Aqueduct association from Elm to Beaver street down Susquehanna avenue and also on Lake street from Chestnut to Nelson avenue.

The Cooperstown Military Band was reorganized in November with G. B. Snyder as bandmaster.

At a meeting of the Board of Managers of Thanksgiving Hospital held late in October plans for the building prepared by Architect W. H. W. Young of New York were submitted and adopted

Robert R. Converse purchased the Manhattan Villa property on Pine street of E. F. Beadle in November. Possession April 1st following.

The Index Mills at Phoenix Mills were shut down in part in November on account of the refusal of the men employed to consent to a ten per cent reduction in wages demanded by poor business conditions. The women of whom there were 100 employed earning $8 to $9 per week readily agreed to the proposal but 30 men earning $1 to $3 per day would not do so. The shutdown was only temporary as the plant reopened Nov. 27.

In November the Maddox Wire Belt Co. was closed out by the sheriff to satisfy a judgment of $400 held by a Massachusetts cotton concern.

Cooperstown did not stand entirely still during the year 1893. The Ballard House was enlarged, as were the storehouses of Austin, Bolton & Bronner and Edick, Grant & Park. H. I. Russell put up a new building on Main street, George Hines one on Pine street, G. A. Thayer one on Elm street and Mr. Brady one near the Pioneer Mills. E. A. Potter and E. Wattenberg put up storehouses near the railroad depot; a large depot for the reception of milk was put up on lower Chestnut street; the Cooperstown Lumber company's factory on Grove street; and a small building near the depot was changed to a grist mill.

With the close of 1893 G. Pomeroy Keese completed a continuous weather record for forty years in Cooperstown. There were but two or three of older date in the United States. He writes: "In all these years the climate of Otsego has not changed. However extreme the temperature may be, either hot or cold, at any particular season, the yearly average never varies. Closely proved by the year just ended, the mean temperature of 1893 is but one half of a degree less than the average of the thirty-nine years previous. In the matter of rainfall it requires a period of five years to make an average."

1894.—During the latter part of January a field of ice developed on Otsego Lake which for skating purposes surpassed anything enjoyed in years. While the Lake always freezes it is seldom that the skating is good on account of the snow, etc. The pleasure of this phenomenon, however, was lost sight of when on the morning of January 20th it was announced that James H. Pitcher, aged sixteen years, son of Aaron Pitcher of the village and two brothers, Arthur and Floyd Griffin, aged 15 and 17 respectively, sons of Burle'gh Griffin who lived in the Double-day house opposite the Fenimore Farm, had been drowned the night before while skating. The Pitcher boy went through the ice while skating across the Lake from the Tower in company with a companion, Harry Farquharson, a lad of about his own age. The Farquharson boy saw his playmate go into the water and went to get a pole to pull him out but before he returned the unfortunate lad had disappeared. The body was recovered the next day in about sixty feet of water by Capt. V. P. Cooper.

While preparations were being made to recover the Pitcher body Gordon Schermerhorn, skating up the west side, was horrified to see through the clear ice the bodies of the two Griffin boys and near them their hand sled. He summoned assistance at once and Lorain Benton, Charles Gray, Fred Rogers, and Capt. Cooper assisted him in recovering the bodies. The boys had gone to Cooperstown on an errand and when they did not return in the evening the father thought they had gone to spend the night with their grandfather at Toddsville, as they had spoken of going there. They left the village, as a matter of fact, about 4:30 o'clock, one wearing skates and pushing his brother on the sled. When about 200 feet off the Fenimore Farm shore they struck a large air hole, about six feet in diameter, and the sled and both boys went into the icy waters.

At a meeting of the managers of the Thanksgiving Hospital held February 4th the bids for the work of erecting the new building were awarded to the lowest bidders as follows: carpenter work and painting, Fayette Houck, $15,443; mason work, Charles J. Tuttle, $2,500. At a later date the contract for the plumbing, gas fitting, etc., was awarded to M. M. Millis at $1,025.

"The last of the George Clarke lands in the state of New York will be sold at public auction about April 1st, a decree of foreclosure having been obtained by the Equitable Life Insurance Co. of New York." These lands consisted of 1,300 acres of valuable farming property in the town of Pine Pla'ns, Dutchess county. Title to them was obtained by the first George Clarke from Queen Ann of England on April 10, 1706.

The work of making the excavations for the new hospital building was commenced in April.

Judge A. C. Tennant resigned the office of Surrogate of Otsego county in April after discharging the duties of that office for ten years during which time in no instance was a decision made by him set aside by an Appellate Court. Judge Tennant entered the well known law firm of Matthew Hale & A. T. Buckley at Albany. Chatfield Leonard of this village was appointed as Judge Tennant's successor.

Lee B. Cruttenden purchased an interest in the dry goods business conducted by the Bundy Brothers and early in May the firm title became Bundy Bros. & Cruttenden.

The cornerstone of the Thanksgiving Hospital building was laid May 16th.

The Winning Hose Co. disbanded as an arm of the Cooperstown Fire department May 2nd. It was organized June 21, 1874. The members at the time of disbanding were: Samuel S. Bowne, Charles T. Brewer, Edwin S. Bundy, Hugh J. Brady, Wm. D. Boden, Lee B. Cruttenden, S. E. Conklin, Dewitt Delong, W. P. K. Fuller, Geo. L. Gould, Clement T. Huyck, Chatfield Leonard, R. P. Lane, W. H. Michaels, Philip H. Potter, Charles Page, Adolph Schoen, Henry Schneider, Fred P. Tanner, Chas. J. Tuttle, Chas. P. Thompson, L. E. Walrath and Samuel Warrin. The name of the club established by the Winning Hose in 1892 with elegant rooms in the First National bank building was changed to "The Mohican Club."

Strong Comstock tendered his resignation in May as principal of the Cooperstown High school to take effect June 22nd after four years in that position which he filled in such a manner as to maintain its high rank among the schools of the state. W. D. Johnson, head of the Morris Union school was secured as his successor.

Burglars, supposed to be professionals, blew open the safe of Austin, Bolton & Bronner May 11 and helped themselves to about $110. They then rode away in a wagon which had been standing in an adjoining shed. Officers tracked them to Emmons and then lost the trail.

The game law was so amended as to read: "Fish may be taken from the waters of Otsego Lake between the first day of May and the first day of September of each year, with seines having meshes not less than 1¾ inches provided however that such fishing shall only be done in the daytime between sunrise and sunset." The provision of the law as to the size of the mesh was evidently a mistake as there at once began to appear on the streets of Cooperstown quantities of Otsego bass averaging three and four to the pound.

A sewer was laid on Fair street from Elk to Main in June.

The celebration of the Fourth of July drew a great crowd. One of the features of the occasion was a parade of the Cooperstown Bicycle club having 40 wheels in line. The oration was delivered by the Hon. John M. Bowers. There were athletic contests, a parade of the Fire department and other organizations and a base ball game.

Ringling Bros. Circus showed in Cooperstown July 30th.

Ten steamers, big and little, public and private, were plying the waters of Otsego Lake in 1894.

The appointment of Samuel S. Bowne as postmaster at Cooperstown was confirmed by the U. S. Senate, July 23d.

July 21. Four persons were drowned in Otsego Lake about a third
of a mile from shore and about 1 mile north from five-Mile Point. Joseph R. Edwards, wife and child by a previous husband and a picture
agent named George Lewis of East Worcester, who had been living on
the Lake shore, capsized in a boat in which they were rowing. Efforts
were made to rescue them but they went down for the last time before
help could reach them.

On August 30 Henry C. Hinds, a well known resident and former
business man of the village, aged about 50 years, was accidentally shot
near the Dugway on the east side of Otsego Lake and died on the
steamer, Mabel Coburn, soon after she reached the dock at the foot
of Fair street. The shot was fired by the twelve-year-old son of C. J.
Rumsey of Ithaca who aimed at a bird.

The game of golf was first played in this locality during the summer of 1894 the links being located at the head of the Lake.

The close of the base ball season showed the Athletic association
with a deficit of about $1,150.

During the year a new field and garden hoe, the blade of which
was bent in the form of a scoop, and which was patented by Menzo A.
Smith of Cooperstown, was put on the market and its sale grew with
leaps and bounds. The manufacturing was done at the large implement factory at Clayville and Mr. Smith received many attractive offers
to make the tool.

Rockmere Cottage, a gothic wooden structure erected by Cutler
Field in 1848, sold by him to Dr. Beresford in 1851, purchased of his
estate by Mrs. Morehouse, purchased of her estate by Mrs. Alfred
Clark, who willed the same to her cousin, Mrs. Davenport, of Rochester
who became its owner on the death of Mrs. Clark in 1889, was destroyed by fire at an early hour October 26th. The cottage presented
a picturesque appearance as seen from the Lake as it stood at the corner of River and Lake in full view from the water front.

During 1894 the new Thanksgiving Hospital building was erected
on Grove street. C. B. Hartson erected a large bottling factory in
the rear of his house on Pioneer street. Dwelling houses were erected
by F. W Spraker on Nelson avenue, Lynn J. Arnold on Elk street,
John C. Smith on Beaver street, Clark Kinney on Susquehanna avenue,
O. I. and L. E. Walrath on Chestnut street, Albert Stocking on upper
Main street. Two new buildings for the use of the Cooperstown railroad were erected and Henry Williams put up a building on Grove
street for carpet cleaning. Austin and DeLong built an addition to
their brick block including the two stores fronting on Main street.
Repairs, additions and improvements were made to a large number of
other buildings. All of which it was estimated cost in the neighborhood of $45,000.

1895.—A great storm which commenced on the evening of February 7th continued until the 9th with 18 inches of snow and a very
high wind that blocked all the roads and tied up rail traffic for a short
time.

A series of religious meetings which excelled in interest and results any such held in Cooperstown in half a century closed after
three weeks duration, March 1st. The services were under the management of the Rev. E. E. Davidson. It was expected that at least 150
persons united with the churches in which they were held.

March 8th. A gymnastic meet between the team of athletes of the
Cooperstown gymnasium and one representing Union College at the
local gym. resulted in a victory by 12 points for Cooperstown. J. W.
Taylor, captain, S. D. Bowers, W. F. Martin, S. E. Cronkhite and
E. Tucker represented Cooperstown. Over 200 spectators were present.

March 9. Total eclipse of the moon. Practically obscured by
clouds.

The Village Trustees this year established the custom of collect-
ing the corporation tax in April instead of August.

A local newspaper dated April 11 contained the following item:
"The bicycle has 'come to stay.' There are now 30 or more factories
in the United States that are turning out thousands of them a month.
Women as well as men are learning to ride the bicycle; it is the popular thing of the day."

April 4th. The Village Board of Trustees endeavored to elect
a president without success. After balloting fifty times they went into
executive session.

A bill amending the charter of Cooperstown so as to allow the
people to elect the village president, commencing in 1896, became a
law.

April 15th. George C. Kellogg, aged 63 years, a Pierstown farmer,
committed suicide by hanging himself in his stable.

In April it was announced that the indebtedness of the Cooperstown Athletic association had been cleared, two subscriptions of $250
each having been received and $500 subscribed in smaller amounts.
A schedule of baseball games was announced which included ten with
Richfield Springs.

April 29th. The Leatherstocking Falls farm was sold at auction
to Charles I. Thayer for $4,255. The farm contained 78 acres.

May 6th. After spending two months in an effort to organize,
M. R. Stocker was elected president of the Village Board of Trustees.
At a meeting held on May 3d, M. Kraham was elected president but
resigned following the resignations of E. A. Potter and L. I. Burditt,
which took place after an extended season of balloting had resulted
in Kraham's election.

June 3d. The Hotel Fenimore which was first opened to the public in June, 1874, was sold by Mrs. E. M. Harris to Menzo W. Baker
of Middleburgh.

July 17th and 18th. The second annual tournament of the Otsego County Fireman's association was held in Cooperstown and brought
a large crowd to the village.

July 23d. Another great crowd was drawn to the village to attend the Ringling Brothers' Circus and Show.

July 31st. A benefit entertainment given by the Cooperstown

Athletic association for the Orphanage netted about $400 and completed a fund of $1,000 which freed that institution of debt.

August 14th and 15th. Celebration of 100th anniversary of Otsego Lodge, No. 138 F. & A. M. Most Worshipful John Stewart, Grand Master of the Grand Lodge of the State of New York, was present with several other officers of the Grand Lodge and many visiting brethren from lodges in this part of the state.

During the last week in August a memorial window was placed in the Presbyterian church the gift of Mrs. Phinney in memory of her husband, the late Elihu Phinney.

September 12th. Theresa, the daughter of Moses Maschke, was killed in an accident in which she collided on a bicycle with a team driven by Joseph Mitchell. She fell heavily and was hit on the head by a hoof of one of the horses.

During the 1895 base ball season, the Cooperstown Athletics won 19 and lost 10 games. The report of the treasurer showed "quite a large deficiency."

In September it was proposed to turn Hartwick Seminary into a full fledged college.

September 29th. J. F. Brower of Brooklyn presented Christ church with a beautiful brass Processional Cross in memory of his mother, Jeanette Catherine Brower.

Sept. 16. L. A. Kaple, after twelve years of service, retired as conductor on the C. & C. V. R. R. Merton Barnes, then station agent succeeded Mr. Kaple and Edward Martin, assistant agent, succeeded Mr. Barnes.

Several extensions of the water system were made in the fall by the Cooperstown Aqueduct association. The main pipe in Pioneer, below Main, was replaced by a larger one, the pipe extended from Nelson avenue up Main to the foot of the hill, and also in Lake street a considerable distance.

October 15th. Through the generosity of a local citizen a marker suitably inscribed was placed in the sidewalk on Main street designating the site of "the old town pump."

October 22. H. K. Jarvis and S. T. Bliss sold their drug business in the Ironclad block to Charles E. Winegar, a native of Middlefield.

Additional repairs and new machinery at the Index Mills cost $10,000.

December 2. On this date the Mohican club voted to take over from George Brooks the Raymond building on Main street adjoining the Hotel Fenimore on the east. Mr. Brooks had recently purchased the property for $5,000. The club gave him a mortgage for that amount payable without interest at the end of ten years.

In December the Hotel Fenimore was sold by Mrs. E. M. Harris to Clayton Weeks of Hobart.

Dec. 22. William D. Van Slyke, aged 32 years, committed suicide by hanging in the garret of his house on Elm street.

CHAPTER III

FROM 1896 TO 1900

1896   Jan. 1.—A beautiful and appropriate window to the memory of Susan Fenimore Cooper, purchased by admiring personal friends for Christ .church, of which she was a life-long member, was dedicated with appropriate services.

May 11th.   The Mohican club formally "opened" its new home on Main street.   About $2,000 was spent previously in putting the building in shape for club purposes.

May 11th.   At a meeting of the Board of Village Trustees a petition was presented, signed by seventy taxpayers, asking that a Board of Water Commissioners be appointed with the power given them by statute to submit the question to the vote of the people as to whether the village should purchase the present system of water works or construct a new one.   A motion was made that the village president appoint such a commission.   Two members voted aye, one no, and four declined to vote.   The motion was declared carried and the president appointed G. P. Keese, George M. Jarvis, Wm. H. Michaels, L. E. Walrath.   Philip H. Potter and Dewitt Delong.   A short time later this body unanimously resigned and the Village Board of Trustees organized as a Board of Water Commissioners and a special election was called for June 23d.   The question presented was whether or not "the taxes authorized by section 21 of Chapter 181 of the laws of 1875 relating to the 'Village Water Works' shall be levied and collected."   This, it appeared, meant not that the village purchase the water system then operated privately or acquire it by condemnation, but that the village should be bonded and a new system constructed; in short, that the village enter into competition with the private corporation.   The vote resulted, yes, 147; no, 142.   The village never acted on the matter, which seems to have had its start in excitement growing out of a set of increased rates for water and rules to prevent the waste of water. In August the Board and the water company got together and settled their differences by agreement on rates and the company agreeing to keep the pressure at the Firemen's building at not less than sixty pounds.

May 29.   The Hotel Fenimore, after being closed twenty months, was reopened under the management of Clayton Weeks, as owner.

For forty-eight hours ending June 10th Cooperstown experienced the greatest rainfall in sixteen years.   A total of 3½ inches was recorded in that period.

Over 800 hoppickers were employed in the yards of J. F. Clark near this village during the harvesting season.

August 27th.   The members of Otsego Chapter, D. A. R., with the Sons of the American Revolution, Lafayette Chapter, C. A. R. as guests, celebrated the damming of the Susquehanna river at the outlet of Otsego Lake with suitable exercises held on the steamer, "Natty

Bumppo." Suitable addresses on General Clinton's expedition, the work of the D. A. R. and local points of interest were given by the Rev. E. A. Perry, G. Pomeroy Keese and Miss Forsyth of Kingston, the State Regent.

The Phinney Memorial window in the Presbyterian church was taken out in September by the makers, Tiffany & Co., of New York, who were disappointed in it as was Mr. Phinney, and a new one put in called "The Victory of Faith."

Oct. 1. Thanksgiving Hospital was opened with a formal reception attended by about 250 people.

Enlargements and improvements of the Second National bank building were completed in December.

1897.—Jan. 1. Lynn J. Arnold and Harris L. Cooke, who had been engaged in the real estate and insurance business since the preceding August when they succeeded William H. Potter, formed a partnership for the practice of law.

Jan. 18. The Shakespearean Reading club, organized in 1877 through the efforts of J. G. Wight, O. A. Coleman, G. S. Coleman and the Rev. D. N. Woolsey Wells, observed its twentieth anniversary.

Feb. 8. Fire, thought to have caught from the heating plant, caused damage estimated at over $4,000 to the First Baptist church edifice.

In February Wm. M. Potter exchanged the Central Hotel property for property in Syracuse with W. T. Rooney.

The work on the old stone Otsego County Bank building, which was enlarged and fitted up for the offices of the Edward and Alfred C. Clark estates, was completed in March.

Late in March the Governor signed a bill which had been passed by the Legislature empowering the Village Trustees to vacate and discontinue that portion of Fair street lying between Main and Church streets so long as it is maintained as a park for the use of the public. The act provides that "whenever it cease to be used as such park * * * such street shall immediately revert to its former use."

April 6. The Village Board of Trustees unanimously adopted resolutions authorizing the discontinuance of the section of Fair street above referred to and the control thereof passed to Mrs. Elizabeth Scriven Clark for the purpose of including it in a public park into which she proposed to convert the "Cooper Grounds."

April 13. Excavations were commenced for the Library and Museum building at the corner of Main and Fair streets.

April 18. (Easter Sunday). A beautiful new pulpit erected to the memory of "Father" Nash, first Rector of Christ Church and for several years previous thereto Rector of several churches in Otsego county, was used for the first time. The pulpit was of quartered oak, octagonal in shape and raised four steps above the floor. Standing on a panelled pedestal surrounded by short columns at the angles. On this occasion the Rev. Dr. Shreve, the Rector, preached an historical sermon dealing with the ministry of the Rev. Daniel Nash.

The name of Templeton Lodge was changed to Otsego Hall in May.

The house was rented to Mrs. K. M. Price of Albany by John A. Rutherford, who resumed possession after an incompleted sale a short time preceding.

May 23. A large flock of plover migrating to the northward settled down in Cooperstown for the night at about 9 o'clock and remained until morning when they departed as suddenly as they came. All the trees were filled with the birds and their songs awakened the curious interest of the village.

June 1. The name of the Ballard House was changed to the "Park" Hotel. The hotel was originally known as the "Globe" but when it was purchased by S. M. Ballard he gave it his own name. George J. Vanderwerker had been proprietor for eight years when the construction of "Cooper Park," nearly opposite was commenced and inspired the name.

May 27. A slight earthquake shock was felt. Buildings were shaken so that the windows rattled but no damage was done.

June 30. About 300 veterans of the Civil War, mostly members of the 121st and 152nd regiments, with their families attended a reunion held in the village.

This summer the Clinton Mills Power company completed its plant located at Clintonville and began furnishing Cooperstown with electric power. The officers of the company were: George Brooks, president; E. V. Adams, vice-president; Geo. M. Jarvis, secretary and treasurer; Russel Warren, general manager; T. J. Myers, superintendent.

After being closed for the purposes of worship since the fire of February this year the edifice of the First Baptist church was reopened August 20th. During the interim the congregation worshipped in the Village Hall. Marked improvements were made in the Main auditorium the greatest of which consisted of a new organ, installed by Frank Beman of Binghamton at a cost of $2,500. It was opened on the above date with a concert by Prof. F. W. Riesberg, organist of the Rutgers Presbyterian church of New York, and Miss Katherin Hilke, soprano soloist, of St. Patrick's Cathedral, New York.

A large excursion from Cohoes on August 19th brought 1,400 people to this village and another on 21st from Wilkes-Barre, Pa., brought 1,500 more.

In August all night street light service was instituted by the village trustees through an arrangement with the Clinton Mills Power Co.

This year a number of people either failed or refused to pay the annual 75-cent poll tax and the corporation counsel was instructed to sue all delinquents.

Sept. 22. Governor Black arrived by special train at 1:15 p. m., was met at the station by a committee of citizens and officers of the Otsego County Agricultural society. Under the escort of the committee and Phinney Hose company, headed by Derring's Military band, the Governor was taken to Fernleigh where he dined as the guest of Mr. Edward Severin Clark. There were also present a few guests from this village and Oneonta. The Governor spoke at the Fair grounds in the afternoon and returned to Albany at 5 o'clock.

In September the sale of the tract of land near the head of the Lake by Leslie Pell-Clarke to S. S. Spaulding of Buffalo was consummated.

The parcel contained twenty-four acres for which Mr. Spaulding paid $6,000. The contract for a Mansion of 175 feet frontage was let in the same fall to Fayette Houck of this village. The grounds were laid out by L. G. Parshall.

Oct. 5. At the annual meeting of the Cooperstown Athletic association held at the close of the baseball season the treasurer reported a deficit of $1,000. It was decided to raise the money by subscription and next year to put a home team in the field to replace the professional club supported for several years past.

Overlook Cottage on Beadle avenue, later Pine street, was purchased of Mrs. E. L. Raymond by George B. Woodman in October.

Oct. 15. The machinery of the Clinton Mills Power Electric company's plant at Clintonville was first operated on this date. It was located six miles from Cooperstown at the site of the old Clinton Cotton Mills. The equipment consisted of two turbine water wheels capable of upwards of 200 h. p., arc and incandescent dynamos, switchboards and indicators, and was considered very complete and up-to-date. It was one of two companies of the state capable of sending 5,600 volts over its wires. The company brought about the beginning of the general use of electricity for lighting dwellings in this village. There were 2,500 incandescent lights in use by the first of the year.

Oct. 21. The Reustle house at the corner of Main street and Beadle avenue was bought by H. C. Church for $4,700 from the First National bank.

In November through the favor of Mr. Edward S. Clark a nine-hole golf course was laid out on the Cory farm on the Fly Creek road, and provision made for a club house.

1898.—Jan. 20. The village census completed by Albert T. Van Horne on this date showed 2,358 inhabitants, a decrease of six since the census six years before. There were 11 Italians, 2 Chinese, 20 colored.

Feb. 19. The Central Hotel property was bid in at auction by B. F. Murdock as surviving executor of the estate of the late Calvin Graves for the heirs interested at $11,500 which was about $1,500 less than the mortgage and accrued interest.

Feb. 23. Wm. Festus Morgan purchased the stone building on Fair street of Mrs. E. L. Raymond, daughter of its builder, E. F. Beadle.

In March Mrs. Russel Warren sold the brick house at the corner of River and Elk streets to Dr. J. H. Moon for $4,500.

March 18. E. A. Potter completed the moving of the large granite boulder to mark the site of Otsego Hall at the Cooper Grounds from the hill on the western line of the village. The boulder weighs over thirty tons and is about eight feet high. Four weeks were consumed with the moving.

In May a local newspaper had the following significant paragraph regarding fishing: "It used to be a very rare occurrence for an Otsego bass to be caught with a hook and line. This season, it is said, many of good size are being taken in that manner. Is it because the Lake has been so freely stocked with 'white fish' which now pass for bass?"

May 28. A replica of J. I. Ward's masterpiece, the statue entitled

"The Indian Hunter," was placed in position on the boulder recently moved to the Cooper Grounds at the site of Otsego Hall. Representing an Indian of life size, one hand holding the bow from which he has just discharged an arrow, the other resting upon and restraining his dog, his earnest gaze fixed upon the distant animal which he has been hunting, it typifies the literary achievement of the greatest writer of purely American romance, James Fenimore Cooper.

In June friends paid the $900 deficit of the Cooperstown Athletic association and with a fund of $1,000, $800 of which was presented by a generous lady, it was decided to engage a base ball team for the season.

The Hon. Edward D. White, Associate Justice of the United States Supreme Court, and then the youngest member of the Court, occupied the Browning house on Lake street this summer.

June 17. The birth of the first child since its reopening occurred at Thanksgiving Hospital.

June 17. Cooperstown Band organized. The officers were Fred M. Tilley, president; George Hall, vice-president; Michael Kraham, secretary; Ephriam Stevens, treasurer.

July 4 The new Cooperstown Golf course was opened as an annex to the Otsego Golf Club. The total distance for the nine holes was 2,000 yards, "bogie" being 36.

July 6. The "Cooper Grounds" were fully opened to the public as a park.

Aug. 2. A Red Cross auxiliary was opened. Mrs. Henry L. Wardwell was president and Mrs. Leslie Pell-Clarke, secretary.

Aug. 17. The new stone building erected by the Clark family at the corner of Main and Fair streets to be used as a Y. M. C. A , library and museum, was formally opened with a ball given by Mrs. Alfred Corning Clark for her son, Mr. Robert Sterling Clark, who had lately reached his twenty-first birthday. Parlati's orchestra of Albany furnished the music and the supper was served by Sherry of New York.

Sept. 13. A deficit of about $800 was shown at the close of the base ball season.

In September Albert S. Potts was appointed postmaster in Cooperstown to succeed Samuel S. Bowne.

This fall the steamer Natty Bumppo, which carried thousands of people safely over the water of Otsego Lake, was dismantled after making her last trip. The boat was built in 1872 and made her initial trip June 3, 1873.

Oct. 27. Hope Mills, the factory building near Cooperstown, was sold to the owner of the Index Mills at Phoenix, Theodore Frelinghuysen by Mrs. G. Hyde Clarke.

In December M. Ernest Lippitt purchased and took possession of the jewelry business of Charles R. Burch.

1899—In January Charles F. Zabriskie of New York purchased the property known as Glimmerview on Lake street. Consideration $17,500.

Jan. 15. Monroe F. Augur purchased the business and lease of the book store conducted at the corner of Main and Pioneer streets by S. F. Lang.

In March Hollet Abrams leased the Cooperstown Gas Works for a term of five years. The building and plant damaged to the extent of $4,000 in February was repaired and the gas service of the village continued. The streets of Cooperstown were first lighted by gas in 1861.

March 12. The Cooperstown Y. M. C. A. held its first meeting in the new building erected by Mrs. Alfred Corning Clark at the corner of Main and Fair streets. The Village Library and Museum were also housed in th's building.

April 1. Charles A. Scott became a partner in the drug business known as Church's Pharmacy and the firm title became Church & Scott. Mrs. H. C. Church reta'ned a portion of the interest of her deceased husband in the business.

In April work was commenced on the large new stone barn of Mr. Edward S. Clark on the Fenimore Farm.

In April the American Hotel on Pioneer street was sold by Mrs. James H. Kelly to George Strachan. Consideration, $4,900.

May 15. Frank Lettis and La Vern F. Saxton opened a dry goods business in the store owned by James Bunyan on Main street, in the block East of Pioneer on the South Side. About the same time William Osborn and Thomas Shay opened a meat market in the basement at the corner of Main and Chestnut streets.

May 6. Horatio L. Olcott of Brooklyn, a native of Cherry Valley, died from taking a large dose of laudanum at his room at the Central Hotel.

In May the following item appeared in The Freeman's Journal: "Those of our readers who feel favorably impressed with the proposition to purchase for the village the Three-Mile Point property and who are able and willing to aid in carrying it out, are invited to send $5 to $20 to the editor to consummate the bargain."

For many years the Point was held by the village under a lease given by William Cooper to the Village Improvement Society of Cooperstown. The lease was for a period of years expiring in 1900 and it was regarded as of the highest importance that the ownership lodge in the village itself. G. Pomeroy Keese, acting for the society, at about this time secured an option from Mr. Cooper at what was regarded as a very favorable figure.

In response to the appeal the property was purchased the latter part of the month. The funds were contributed by the following: Mrs. Alfred Corning Clark, Mr. Edward S. Clark, L. Averell Carter, The C. & C. V. Railroad Co., Bundy Bros. & Cruttenden, The Clerks of the First National Bank, G. P. Keese, S. M. Shaw, George M. Jarvis, D. H. Gregory, General J. H. Patterson, Robert Quaif, Mr. and Mrs. R. Warren, Andrew Davidson, Richard Freeman, H. M. Hooker & Co., B. F. Murdock & Sons, William H. Michaels, George Van Horn, Mulkins & Mason, Miss F. I. Bunyan, George Brooks, Church & Scott, John P. Doane, R. Heber White, Spingler & Gould. Twenty dollars was taken from the funds of the Village Improvement society to complete the fund.

One of the village papers in May said: "The comparatively few robins seen in this locality this year is a noticeable fact, and a matter of regret. The bobolink and the blue bird have about disappeared; it is three years since we have seen either near here."

July 1. The Park Hotel, for nine years conducted by George J. Vanderwerker, passed into the ownership of the Park Hotel Company and opened under the management of George H. Wilber.

July 4. Thousands of people attended a great Independence Day celebration. The address of the day was given by the Hon. Walter H. Bunn.

July 6-7. The third annual tournament of the Central New York Golf League was held at the Otsego Golf club at the head of the Lake. Otsego won the Championship cup. Syracuse, Rochester and Utica also competed.

The first week of July Mrs. Alfred Corning Clark came to the relief of the defunct Cooperstown Athletic association assuming the liabilities and taking a bill of sale of its building, grandstand and personal property.

During this summer Mrs. Alfred Corning Clark caused a gray granite slab to be placed on the Indian mound on "Fernleigh Over" bearing the inscription: "White man, greeting: We near whose bones you stand were Iroquois. The wide land which now is yours, was ours. Friendly hands have given back to us enough for a tomb."

Aug. 2. William Nevells, aged thirty years, of Toddsville was drowned in Otsego Lake near Point Florence when the boat in which he and Henry Carey and Lynn Goodenough were rowing overturned. Nevells was attempting to swim ashore. The others clung to the side of the boat and were rescued.

Aug. 28. Lineal descendants of Judge William Cooper, John Russell and Mrs. Metcalf, pioneers of Cooperstown, held a picnic at Point Judith on the eastern shore of Otsego Lake in celebration of the 100th anniversary of the first recorded picnic held on the Lake.

Sept. 21. Col. Theodore Roosevelt, governor of the State of New York, spoke at the Otsego County Fair.

Dec. 4. Simon Uhlmann of New York, who had recently purchased the Albert Van Horn farm west of Three-Mile Point, donated to the village the right of way across a strip of his property which was needed as an entrance to the village property at the Point.

During the year Contractor Fayette Houck built eight new residences in the village.

1900:—Early in January the new house erected by M. H. Bronner on Pine street was completed ready for occupancy. E. D. Boden purchased the residence of J. A. M. Johnston on Main street opposite the Court House grounds.

In February after some time in litigation the sum of $5,000 was paid to the Cooperstown orphanage from the estate of William H. Gage of Yates county.

The appearance of the landscape at the outlet of the Lake was greatly improved by the removal of the ruins of the old brewery building.

March 7. Four farms, property of James F. Clark and all located near the village, were sold at mortgage foreclosure. The home farm was sold a few weeks later.

March 17. Col. Andrew Davidson was appointed commandant of the New York State Soldiers' and Sailors' Home at Bath.

March 22. The report of a special committee embracing the plans and specifications for a new and fireproof county clerk's building on the Court House grounds were adopted at a special meeting of the Board of Supervisors. The plans were drawn by Architect Linn Kinne of Utica.

In April the large model of Otsego Hall built at the shop of Fayette Houck by Eugene Eckler from a smaller one constructed by G. Pomeroy Keese, was completed and placed in the Museum.

April 26. The Otsego County Farm Products Company to deal in milk and its products was organized with the following directors: Datus E. Siver, Harris L. Cooke, John B. Conkling, Melvin C. Bundy, E. S. Bundy, George H. White, S. L. Warrin, Frank Mulkins, Albert S. Potts, John P. Doane, Lynn J. Arnold, Charles S. Barney and Walter C. Flanders. Datus E. Siver was president; Lynn J. Arnold, vice-president; Harris L. Cooke, secretary and treasurer and John B. Conkling, superintendent. The Pioneer Mills property was taken over and machinery installed for making condensed milk, pasteurized milk, butter, etc.

In May Harry P. Nash became proprietor of Carr's Hotel.

Early in the year the balance of the indebtedness of the Lakewood Cemetery association was paid in full.

In May Michael Hanlon purchased the Pioneer Hotel of Mrs. M. L. Clark.

May 22. Contract for the new county clerk's building let at $26,-000 to Butts, Ingalls & Co., of Oneonta. As this amount was $1,000 in excess of the limit set by the Board of Supervisors the citizens of Cooperstown agreed to make up the difference.

June 13 and 14. The Centennial celebration of the organization of the First Presbyterian church took place.

A new X-ray machine purchased through public subscription was first used at Thanksgiving Hospital in June; and a new operating table was ordered.

July 28. The corner stone of the new county clerk's building was laid at the Court House grounds. The ceremonies were in charge of Most Worshipful Charles W. Meade, Grand Master of Masons of the State of New York and were participated in by twenty-five officers of the Grand Lodge. The address of the day was made by the Hon. George W. Ray, Judge of the Federal Court. A beautiful souvenir trowel was presented to M. W. Meade by Otsego Lodge, No. 138, F. & A. M., of Cooperstown with fitting remarks by Worshipful Master Frank Hale.

This summer was characterized by an exceptionally large number of severe electric storms.

The Hotel Fenimore property including the Fenimore barns off Chestnut street was sold by Mrs. E. M. Harris to Bundy Bros. & Cruttenden. The property was taken over by a stock company called the Fenimore Hotel Co. in October, 1900. The directors were E. S. Bundy, M. C. Bundy, L. B. Cruttenden and L. J. Arnold. The Fenimore was built in 1873 by Edward Clark, and opened as a summer hotel in June 1874. Ten years later, after being for some time closed, it was purchased of the Edward Clark Estate by Edwin M. Harris, and was for a few years kept by his brother-in-law, J. B. Brown, and then leased to different parties. It was again closed in the fall of 1899.

The first week in September the contract was closed for the erection of a fine new residence and stable for Arthur Ryerson at the head of the Lake.

Oct. 18. The Cooperstown gas works, operated for some time by H. Abrams, was sold at mortgage foreclosure to the First National Bank.

In the latter part of October the Elk street stables of the Clark Estate were completed.

The contract for the erection of a new residence for Simon Uhlmann at Three-Mile Point was let in November.

CHAPTER IV

FROM 1901 TO 1905

1901.—In January two new pumps were installed at the pumping station by the Cooperstown Aqueduct association.

March 1. The Empire Cheese company commenced operations having leased the old Pioneer Mills plant for a period of five years and doubled its capacity by additions to the building, installed new machinery, etc. A fund of $1,000 was presented to the company by Cooperstown citizens as a token of good will.

March 2. Charles E. Winegar, who had been doing business as a druggist in the Ironclad building since October, 1895, sold out to Hubbard L. Brazee and Edward D. Boden, who formed a partnership and did business under the title of Brazee & Boden.

April 9. About 150 persons assembled at the Village Hall to discuss the question of allowing the electric line then being built from Oneonta to Richfield Springs, and later extended to Mohawk, to enter Cooperstown via Chestnut street and run down Main.

In April Robert R. Converse purchased the Park Hotel of Mrs. M. E. Taylor Smith of Binghamton and James Bunyan. Mr. Converse had operated the hotel under a lease for two years and made many improvements to the property.

April 19. The Village Trustees unanimously voted a franchise to the Oneonta, Cooperstown & Richfield Springs Electric railroad to enter Cooperstown via Chestnut street to Main. It was provided that no freight car or cars carrying freight should run on the village streets except from the southern boundary of the village line to the Chestnut street crossing of the C. & S. V. railroad.

May 1. Work was commenced on the erection of the residence of J. A. M. Johnston at the corner of Lake and Pine streets.

May 7. Phinney Hose Co., No. 1, of the Cooperstown Fire department disbanded. It was organized in August, 1871. Of the twenty-four charter members only one, P. H. Hotaling, continued his membership throughout the entire thirty years of its life.

May 8. The Hotel Fenimore under the management of H. E. Bissell of Brandon, Vt., was opened with a reception.

In May the firm of H. M. Hooker & Co., in active business in the hardware trade in Cooperstown for 31 years was succeeded by D. Jefferson McGown, who was a clerk in the store for eight years previous to 1870 and then became one of the partners.

June 4. General Walter C. Stokes' automobile made several trips through the village streets in the afternoon. One newspaper commented as follows: "Considering the fact that it was a new attraction for the horses to meet they as a rule behaved very well. The exhibtion offered an amount of amusement for a lot of people.

The large piazzas on the Park Hotel were completed in June.

June 19. The jury which heard the testimony in the case of the

People against Mrs. Samuel Hillsinger of West Oneonta in Supreme Court in Cooperstown brought in a verdict of guilty of murder in the second degree. Mrs. Hillsinger was tried for killing the preceding September a girl named Anna White who lived in her home and of whom she is said to have been jealous. She was sentenced to Auburn State prison for life. District Attorney Merritt Bridges of Morris with Judge Lynn J. Arnold of Cooperstown of counsel represented the People and Gibbs & Wilbur of Oneonta the defendant.

July 1. The new residence of Simon Uhlmann at Three-Mile Point was completed.

July 15. John Conners, aged 21 years, a groom, and Michael Hurley, aged 24 years, a footman, employed by John M. Bowers at his summer place, Lakelands, were drowned at the outlet of the Lake in the Susquehanna river in about six feet of water. It is thought that they had entered the water for a cooling plunge and had been seized with cramps. Both were residents of New York City.

Aug. 1. Mrs. Alfred Corning Clark celebrated the coming of age of her third son, Mr. Frederick Ambrose Clark, by giving a barn dance in her new Elk street stables, a very appropriate action on her part as the young man was very fond of horses and became one of the leading steeple-chase riders and polo players of two continents. The dancing was in the large carriage house, a room 115 feet long by 30 feet wide, occupying the entire north front of the building. It was simply and artistically decorated with whips, coach horns and other articles of horsemanship with a few vases of cut flowers and some potted plants. Towards midnight there was an unique surprise. A large panel, forming the center of the carriage house ceiling, was opened, and the carriage lift slowly descended, filled with a group of young people seated around two tables set for supper. At this signal, the guests walked along a passageway between the saddle and harness rooms—used as cloak rooms—to the stable where supper was served. During the repast David H. Gregory proposed the health of young Mr. Clark, who responded in a few words of thanks. About 200 guests were present. The music was by Gioscia's orchestra of Albany and the supper by Lucas of Troy.

The large new residence of Mr. Arthur Ryerson at Ringwood at the head of the Lake was completed in the fall of the year by Contractor Fayette Houck.

Judge Albert C. Tennant, lecturer at the Albany Law school on Real and Personal Property, Criminal Law, and Sales was appointed by the trustees of that institution of learning to deliver seventy lectures during the next school year on the Law of Contracts. Judge Tennant, besides his duties at the Law School, maintained offices for the practice of law at Albany and Cooperstown, devoting at this particular time Mondays and Saturdays, at least, to his Cooperstown office.

Aug. 20. A "cloud burst" did great damage at several points on both the east and west sides of the Lake, carrying away bridges, washing out highways, etc.

The new residence of Judge Albert C. Tennant on Main street was completed this fall.

Sept. 2. Otsego Chapter, D. A. R., with appropriate ceremonies unveiled the marker it had caused to be erected on the site of the dam erected by General James Clinton at the outlet of Otsego Lake. On the preceding Saturday a reception was given at the home of the Regent, Mrs. Theodore Ernst, in honor of the Regent of New York City Chapter. The unveiling was done by two girls and a boy all dressed in Indian costume, viz: Jennie O. Mason, Fannie M. Converse and F. Hamilton McGown, descendants of soldiers who helped build the Clinton dam. At the Village Hall in the evening the historical address was delivered by Mr. G. Pomeroy Keese and he was followed by Mrs. Donald McLean, Regent of the New York City Chapter, who spoke in a happy vein. The marker is a huge boulder, placed on the east side of the outlet on which is mounted an old mortar which saw service in the Civil War. On the face of the boulder is a tablet with this inscription: "Here was built a dam, the summer of 1779, by the soldiers under Gen'l Clinton, to enable them to join the forces under Gen'l Sullivan at Tioga. (D. A. R. signia). Marked by Otsego Chapter, Daughters of the American Revolution."

Sept. 28. The first electric train on the Oneonta, Cooperstown & Richfield Springs railway ran into Cooperstown.

This fall Mr. F. Ambrose Clark commenced the development of the Iroquois Farm south of the village.

Sept. 30. The new County Clerk's building on the Court House grounds was practically completed and the Surrogate held his first term of Court there.

Oct. 1. The ownership of the Freeman's Journal passed from S. M. Shaw & Co. to Edward S. Brockham and George H. Carley the firm name being Brockham & Carley. Announcing the change in a signed editorial Mr. Shaw wrote, "For the first time in fifty-three years I am not the entire or part owner of a newspaper establishment." Mr. Shaw remained for a time at the head of the Editorial department.

1902.—Early in the year Robert R. Converse, after conducting a meat market in this village for eighteen years, sold same to George N. Smith, who had been in the same line of business, enabling Mr. Converse to devote his entire attention to the Park Hotel of which he was the proprietor.

Charles A. Francis commenced the erection of a large carriage shop on Railroad avenue in January.

Jan. 27. The Central Hotel passed into the hands, under a lease, of Alfred Marshall, of Cherry Valley.

Feb. 5. The block on the south side of Main street, east of the Pioneer street corner, was sold by Mrs. G. Tyley to Mrs. W. S. Basinger. It is one of the oldest and most substantial structures on the corporation, probably erected—no one knows by whom—about the year 1800, as was the block adjoining on the west, previously occupied by the old Court House and county jail, in 1811. Dr. Thomas Fuller, who came here in 1791, and John M. Bowers, who came here in 1803, both for a time occupied the dwelling parts of this block.

Feb. 25. The trustees of the Methodist Episcopal church in anticipation of erecting a new house of worship, acquired from John Pank, the Crafts property, at the corner of Chestnut street and Glen avenue, consisting of a large dwelling and spacious and well located lot. The society exchanged its parsonage on Eagle street and paid $2,100 as consideration.

William L. McEwan, who had been in business at Carlsbad, N. M., purchased the hardware and plumbing business long conducted by J. Warren Lamb, taking possession late in January.

In April M. H. Wedderspoon and J. D. Whipple purchased the Five-Mile Point property. The Hotel was greatly improved, a large new barn and stable built, the Point filled in, graded and seeded.

The organization of the Cooperstown Telephone company to compete with the Central New York (Bell) company gave Cooperstown two telephone services. For several years business and professional men advertised that they might be called on "both phones."

Otsego Lake Park at the foot of Pioneer street was opened to the public in May. The pavilion was built this year.

Sept. 1. Simon Uhlmann of New York City, who had recently opened Uncas Lodge, his new summer home at Three-Mile Point, entertained 250 of his friends at a clam bake on the beach served by the Hine Catering company of Binghamton. The service was under the direction of Proprietor H. E. Bissell of the Hotel Fenimore. The menu consisted of fish, clams, chicken, lobster, potatoes and corn, all of which we are told "was artistically cooked," and we are also told that "the cordials were of the best brands on the market, and limited only by the good judgment of the partaker." Mr. Uhlmann responded to a toast drunk in his honor and Albert Lane and A. W. Thayer spoke.

In September a new line was laid out on the west side of Otsego Lake for the proposed Cooperstown-Fort Plain steam railroad.

Sept. 21. Merton Hokes shot a blue heron on Brookwood Point which measured nearly six feet from tip to tip.

With this season the Otsego Lake Tally-ho Co. which ran the tally-ho and boats between Cooperstown and Richfield Springs went out of business on account of the construction of the electric railroad.

Oct. 4. Mrs. Alfred Corning Clark and the Rt. Rev. Henry Codman Potter, Bishop of New York, were married at Christ church, the Rev. Dr. William M. Grosvenor, rector of the Church of the Incarnation, New York City, officiating. It was a family wedding with a few intimate personal friends and a few members of old Cooperstown families.

1903.—Jan. 1. George H. Carley became the sole owner of The Freeman's Journal.

The playing of the game "whist" which was quite the rage the year preceding, seems to have become less popular this winter, perhaps on account of the introduction of the new form "auction" bridge, another form of the game with the mastery of which society was struggling. At this time it was already popular at the Mohican Club.

The retirement of Richard Freeman after an active business career of twenty-six years was announced in February.

Jan. 28.—Announcement of the prospect of closing the Index Knitting Mills, employing over 400 hands, was made at a meeting of the Cooperstown Board of Trade. Theodore Frelinghuysen, the owner, was forced to this decision through large losses occasioned by the defalcation of a trusted employee in New York City. An ineffectual effort was made to incorporate a new company and continue the business with local capital. The mills closed the last week in February. Later in the year the Fenimore Knitting Mills was organized by New York parties with John P. Doane, who had acted as superintendent and general manager for years under the former ownership, as president. The new company took over the properties known as the Phoenix and Hope mills.

In April the contract for erecting the new edifice of the Methodist Episcopal church on the Crafts property at the corner of Glen avenue and Chestnut street was let to Fayette Houck of this village. Ground was broken for the building May 5th. The corner stone was laid June 19th, the Rev. Dr. Henry Tuckley, pastor of the first church at Oneonta, preaching the occasional sermon.

May 17. Arthur Munn, a plumber by trade, was drowned in Otsego Lake, about a quarter of a mile south of Three-Mile Point at about 9 o'clock in the morning. He was forty-four years of age and unmarried.

The village trustees this summer adopted the policy of constructing the sidewalks of concrete instead of planks.

With the issue of July 30th Samuel M. Shaw, its editor for fifty-two years, retired from the Freeman's Journal which was sold a short time preceding to George H. Carley. It was the first time in 67 years and two months that he "owed no duty to any printing office."

Aug. 17. Walter L. Main's circus exhibited in Cooperstown.

Aug. 22. Howard Kinney of New Berlin, 18 years of age, was drowned off Hutter's Point.

The completion of the new home of Mr. J. A. M. Johnston at the corner of Lake and Pine streets was marked by the celebration in the yet unoccupied mansion of the coming of age of Mr. Stephen Carlton Clark, youngest son of the late Alfred Corning Clark. There were 200 guests present and at the stroke of midnight the young man's health was proposed by the Rt. Rev. Henry C. Potter, Episcopal Bishop of New York, step-father of the guest of honor.

Sept. 16. At a meeting of the Vestry of Christ church announcement was made of a gift by Miss Florence V. Sill of a Parish House to cost $5,000 for the society in memory of her mother, Mrs. Jedediah P. Sill. The new building was located on Fair street.

Nov. 1. The International Cheese company organized by W. W. Hovey of Bainbridge took over the Rosemary creamery which succeeded the Empire Milk company.

1904—Jan. 2. After serving with distinction as principal of the High school for nine and one-half years, Prof. Willard D. Johnson, Ph. M., resigned to accept an appointment as Inspector of High schools with the New York State Department of Education. Jay P. Kinney was elected to fill the vacancy.

H. C. Tubbs was appointed to a position in the Cooperstown D. & H. station. He had served as operator and clerk at the Cooperstown Junction for fourteen years.

The official weather record showed the month of February of this year the coldest but four in fifty-four years. The mean temperature for the month was 14½ degrees F. as compared with an average of 21 degrees F. The mean temperature for the sixty days of January and February was lower than any period in 55 years save only 1875.

Cement sidewalks up to this time were laid by the village whereever property owners desired, the owner paying a portion of the cost and the village the balance.

March 25. The Village Board decided to lay about 25,000 square feet of cement sidewalks this year without any direct expense to the abutting property owners.

March 25. The newly erected house of worship of the Methodist Episcopal church at the corner of Chestnut street and Glen avenue was dedicated by the district superintendent, the Rev. Dr. T. F. Hall of Oneonta. The dedicatory sermon was preached by Bishop E. G. Andrews, D. D., LL. D., of New York City whose first pastorate had been in Cooperstown fifty years before. The pastor was the Rev. J. H. Littell. Under his leadership the location was purchased and the church erected at an expenditure of about $21,000.

April 15. Forty-one individuals and firms organized themselves into the Business Men's Protective association under the agreement that if a man owed an account to a member and showed no disposition to adjust the matter, the other members of the association were forbidden to extend that persons credit under penalty of twenty-five dollars fine. The association was short lived.

April 27. Thirty-five thousand lake trout fry from the Cape Vincent Hatchery were received and placed in Otsego Lake.

June 6. At a meeting of the Union and High school district it was decided to submit a proposal to erect a new school building to the eligible voters. No election however was held for some time.

June 12. The saloon keepers of the village entered into an agreement to observe the law.

June 16. The following item appeared in a local newspaper: "The increase in the number of automobiles that are run in this vicinity is decreasing the number of people who have been accustomed to driving horses, especially along the Lake roads. The danger of accidents is calculated to render people timid. Two gentlemen of this village owning fine horses are offering them for sale because of the 'red devils on wheels' now so frequently encountered."

July 1. An ambulance presented to the Thanksgiving Hospital by "a liberal friend" made its first trip to convey a patient to that institution. It was Cooperstown's first ambulance.

July 5. The Cooperstown National Bank opened its doors for business. The first president was Andrew R. Smith, Dr. D. E. Siver was vice-president and John R. Kirby, cashier. The bank was located a few doors west of the northwest corner of Main and Pioneer streets.

July 7. Valuable jewels belonging to Mrs. F. Ambrose Clark were stolen from the safe at the offices of the Clark Estates. Pinkerton detectives arrested William Coleman, a crook well known to the New York police, July 27th, in that city in connection with the crime and he was brought to the Otsego county jail. He was held for the Grand Jury but no indictment was returned and he was released after having been held in the county jail until November. When Coleman returned to New York City he was shadowed by detectives day by day until he was discovered taking long walks in the upper part of Harlem. Trailing him on one of these trips he was found digging beneath the viaduct on 155th street, east of 8th avenue. There the jewels were found in a glass jar. He was arrested and brought back to Cooperstown where he was indicted by the Grand Jury in March, 1905, pleaded guilty and sentenced.

Carr's Hotel was sold to Justin Lange who took possession May 1, 1905, and conducted it for years as a first class house.

July 10. The Cooperstown Country club was organized. The first officers were: David H. Gregory, president; Walter C. Stokes, vice-president; William Festus Morgan, secretary; J. A. M. Johnston, treasurer. The club occupied the house and grounds formerly known as the Otsego Golf club "Annex."

July 24. George Pitcher of New Berlin and Leon Carr of Edmeston were drowned in Otsego Lake near Five-Mile Point when a row boat in which they, with three companions were rowing, capsized. The others were rescued by occupants of motor boats near by.

Sept. 7. The Rt. Rev. Randall T. Davidson, Archbishop of Canterbury and Primate of All England, arrived in Cooperstown, accompanied by Mrs. Davidson, and spent a few days at Fernleigh Mansion as the guests of the Rt. Rev. and Mrs. Henry C. Potter.

Oct. 9. Adolphus Busch, the well known St. Louis brewer, purchased the Uncas Lodge property, at Three-Mile Point owned by Simon Uhlmann and the adjoining property of A. W. Thayer. Possession was given November 1st. It was stated in the newspapers at the time that the purchase price was $75,000. About 200 acres of land was transferred.

Dec. 1. The printing plant of the Farmer Publishing company suffered a $20,000 loss by fire. The blaze started in the basement and eating away the floor joist let the machinery fall through. The building and plant were saved from total loss by the heroic work of the Fire department.

Fred A. Martin, aged thirty-one years, was killed Dec. 1 in a railroad accident at Worcester. He had just taken up his duties as a fireman on the D. & H. railroad. Two other firemen, besides Mr. Martin, were killed.

Dec. 15. George Brooks purchased the controlling interest in the Cooperstown Gas plant. The original gas light company was formed in March, 1861, with a capital of $12,500. For many years O. R. Butler was the owner and manager of the works. Later it changed hands many times.

1905—Jan. 2. Howard N. Michaels became the business partner of his father, William H. Michaels, in the meat market which the latter had conducted for twenty-five years in this village.

Jan. 3. Surveyors from the State Engineer's and Surveyor's office

arrived here to make the survey for a new macadam road to be constructed with state aid from Cooperstown to Three-Mile Point along the
west shore of Otsego Lake. The first state road was built in this state
under what was known as the Higbie-Armstrong Act and the pieces of
highway were selected through favorable action of the Board of Supervisors upon a formal application made by any town through its member. Clement M. Allison was the representative of the town of Otsego
who made the application. At the time two or three short pieces of state-
aid highway only had been applied for in this county.

Feb. 6. Otsego Lake Transit Company incorporated. Contract
let for large new steamer, The Mohican. The original incorporators
were L. N. Wood, F. B. Shipman, M. E. Lippitt, Charles H. Mason
and Edward Martin. In April they purchased the business and stock
of Capt. Geo. E. Coburn who had been in the boat business for thirty
years.

March 14. A proposition to expend not to exceed $25,000 to pave
Main street with vitrified brick from the Clark Estate offices to
the Fenimore corner, submitted to the taxpayers at the regular corporation election, was defeated by a vote of 31 ayes and 102 noes.

In April the Fenimore Knitting company of Phoenix Mills, three
miles away, was employing 250 people and turning out 300 dozen gar-
ments daily including men's and women's underwear and men's fleece
lined overshirts.

April 10. The Village Board of Trustees purchased a ten-ton
steam roller for use in street improvement, repairs and construction.

May 1. Byron H. Burditt of New York City and Henry Hoffman
purchased the Park Hotel property of C. P. Buskirk, taking immediate
possession. The name of the Hotel was changed at this time to the
Hoffman House.

May 30. While the entire Fire department was attending a Memorial Day celebration at Fly Creek and the most of the citizens who were
not there were at the athletic grounds on the opposite side of the village
the grist mill on Railroad avenue owned by Edward Martin, and operated
by Ellra Ballard, took fire and burned to the ground. Loss about $4,000.
The firemen hastened to return and the citizens left the games and by
their united efforts saved several adjacent buildings.

July 1. The steamer Mohican, the new craft of the Otsego Lake
Transit company, licensed to carry 400 people, was launched. As the
boat slid into the water she was christened "Mohican" by Miss Osborne,
daughter of the builder. An unsuccessful effort to launch the boat was
made the preceding Thursday.

July 17. The building and contents of the lumber mill of J. F.
Brady & Co., were totally destroyed by fire of unknown origin. Mr.
Brady at once erected a new mill.

Aug. 2. James Fenimore Clayton, after serving twenty years in
prison for murder of his little child, was set at liberty and returned to
Cooperstown, his life term having been commuted by the governor.

Aug. 8. The Board of Education announced that Mrs. Henry C.
Potter would donate to the Union Free School district, No. 1, the necessary portion of the Cooper House grounds as a site for a new school

building if the voters of the district would vote the sum of $80,000 for the purpose of building and equipment and that Mr. Edward Severin Clark would also donate the sum of $10,000 for the same purpose.

Aug. 15. Twenty-seven Cooperstown boys organized themselves into a regular part of the Cooperstown Fire department, to be known as the Iroquois Hose company. The first officers were: Owen G. Clark, foreman; Arthur T. Fay, assistant foreman; Rowan D. Spraker, secretary, William H. Michaels, Jr., treasurer.

Aug. 16-19. The fifth annual Regatta of the Otsego Lake Boat club took place with races for all classes of boats, a Regatta ball and an illuminated parade as evening events.

This summer the receiver of the O. C. & R. S. trolley line, H. B. Coman of Oneida, who operated the road for a time, ran a special parlor car from Utica to Cooperstown and return daily.

Grading was begun on the hillside north of Cooperstown for the roadbed for the proposed Cooperstown & Northern Railway in which several citizens of Cooperstown and Springfield Center were interested. Nothing but a portion of the roadbed was ever completed.

Extensive improvements including a complete change in the finish of the woodwork of the interior, the removal of the two side galleries, the placing of a Gothic top over the sanctuary and the building of a new piazza connecting the church with the priest's house, were effected in St. Mary's Roman Catholic church during the summer.

Sept. 2. As a result of a heavy fall of rain the water in Otsego Lake raised 18 inches in one night. Willow Brook became a raging torrent, overflowed its banks at the Chestnut street bridge and, running down that street and Main caused great damage by flooding the cellars of business places and residences. Great damage was done throughout the county by floods and washouts.

Sept. 5. The fall term of the Cooperstown High school opened with Prof. M. J. Multer, who came here from Perry, N. Y., as principal.

Sept. 12. The proposition to build a new school house was carried at a special election by a vote of 176 to 167. A local paper, commenting on the election, said that "it was one of the warmest contests of its kind that has ever taken place in Cooperstown."

Sept. 15-16. A largely attended County Missionary Institute with speakers from the mission fields and exhibits of literature and helps was held at the Y.M.C.A. building under the auspices of the Protestant churches of Cooperstown.

The houses in Cooperstown were numbered this fall in preparation for the establishment of free mail delivery.

According to the state enumeration of the census the total population of Otsego county was 48,209, a decrease of 730 in five years. The only towns of the county to show increases were Oneonta, 1,018, and Hartwick and Laurens, 17 each. The population of the village of Cooperstown was 2,446, an increase of 78.

Dec. 1. Work on a new storage reservoir holding 166,000 gallons of water as an auxiliary fire protection was completed. The reservoir was constructed by the Cooperstown Aqueduct association and was located on the high ground above Grove street.

Repairs upon the Otsego county jail costing $17,000 were completed the last of the year.

Dec. 19. Justice A. H. Sewell in Supreme Court in Cooperstown gave judgment in favor of the plaintiff, the Knickerbocker Trust company of New York, against the Oneonta, Cooperstown and Richfield Springs Railway, the electric line connecting those places, in the full amount of its claim. The action was one of the important steps in extended litigation in which the road was involved for years.

Dec. 29. Fred Cole, a farmer residing at Pierstown, three miles north of Cooperstown, committed suicide by drinking strychnine. Financial troubles and drink were the causes described.

CHAPTER V

FROM 1906 TO 1910

Jan. 20. The new operating theatre at Thanksgiving Hospital was formally opened. The first operation was performed by Dr. B. W. Dewar of Cooperstown and immediately afterward Dr. Arthur W. Elting of Albany operated upon a patient. A new wing to the building was completed this month, bringing the total capacity up to twenty-five beds which made it possible to carry out the long cherished desire of the staff of physicians to have the Hospital registered with the Regents Department at Albany.

Jan. 23. The ice left Otsego Lake. The weather of the week preceding this date eclipsed all precedent. The thermometer stood at 60 degrees F. for three consecutive days. By February 8th, however, the Lake was closed again and the ice was nine inches thick. The Lake was cleared for the second time this winter, April 14th.

Feb. 1. Free delivery of mail in Cooperstown began. Up to this time one journeyed to the postoffice for one's mail.

March 13. The Oneonta, Cooperstown and Richfield Springs Railway was sold at auction under foreclosure at the entrance to the Court House in Cooperstown to the Knickerbocker Trust company of New York. The price was $960,000 and the purchaser assumed the payment of $250,000 of receiver's certificates and incidental expenses bringing the price up to $1,300,000. The sale was conducted by Judge Nathaniel P. Willis, referee.

March 15. The contract for erecting the new High school building on Chestnut street was let to Charles C. Ingalls of Binghamton at $67,000. The contract for heating, plumbing and ventilating was let to Breen Brothers of Utica.

April 11. The annual session of the Wyoming Annual Conference of the Methodist Episcopal church was held here opening on this date. Bishop Daniel A. Goodsall, D. D., LL.D., of Boston presided.

April 18. John Mullen under indictment for burglary of the bank at Gilbertsville, the preceding May, was acquitted by a jury in County Court.

May 8. The certificate of incorporation of the Mohawk Valley Railroad Company, succeeding the Oneonta, Cooperstown & Richfield Springs Railway company, was filed with the County Clerk. The new company had a maximum capitalization of $1,800,000 consisting of 18,-000 shares of $100 par value.

May 15. $76,000 school bonds issued by District No. 1 of the town of Otsego, drawing 4 per cent interest, were purchased by the First National Bank which was the only bidder.

June 7. Arthur Ellwell was sentenced in Supreme Court to a term of nine years in Auburn state prison after he pleaded guilty to an indictment charging attempted arson. He confessed to setting fire to the M. R. Stocker house on Eagle street and the S. S. Bowne house on Pioneer street.

June 9. William Beattie and William P. Doubleday purchased the grocery business of G. M. Grant & Co., organized in 1853 by George M. Grant, who had associated with him Benjamin Kipp. Following their death the store had been conducted by R. Heber White.

July 1. The Rev. Cyrus W. Negus of Homer became the pastor of the First Baptist church.

July 16. Corner stone of new Parish House of Christ church donated to the parish by Miss Florence V. Sill as a memorial to her mother, Levantia Wood Sill took place with fitting services in which the Rt. Rev. Henry C. Potter, Bishop of New York and the Rev. W. Y. Lord, D.D., of Albany, a former rector participated. The stone was laid by the rector, the Rev. Ralph Birdsall. The building was dedicated December 20th.

The Old Fort Dayton Band of Herkimer gave weekly concerts during the summer through the courtesy of Mr. Edward Severin Clark.

Aug. 3. The first arrest for operating an automobile beyond the speed limit occurred on this date. The defendant, who gave his name as Vincent and his home as New York City, paid a fine of ten dollars.

Aug. 8-9. The sixth annual regatta of the Otsego Lake Boat club was successfully carried out. Outstanding features were the music by the Baumline Military band, an illuminated parade and the regatta ball.

Aug. 15. Many large hauls of Otsego bass (white fish) were made this summer. One seine drawn in on this date contained more than 120 of the fish.

Aug. 25. Some men who were drawing a seine on the north side of Five-Mile Point drew in the remains of George Pitcher of New Berlin, who with Leon Carr of Edmeston was drowned in Otsego Lake on Sunday, July 24, 1904.

Oct. 18. Engineers for the proposed Cooperstown & Northern railroad completed the survey from this village to Springfield Center.

Oct. 27. A "cyclonic gust," as a local newspaper termed it, tore up by the roots a locust tree that had stood on the grounds at Edgewater, the home of G. Pomeroy Keese, for nearly 100 years.

Nov. 6. Election day brought to a climax a campaign which stirred the village. Nathaniel P. Willis, Republican, was opposed for reelection to the office of Surrogate of the County by James J. Byard, Jr. Both were residents of Cooperstown, and both strong politically. So successfully did Mr. Byard and the Democrats wage their campaign that despite the fact that Governor Charles E. Hughes, Republican, carried the county by a plurality of about 1,800, the result was in doubt until weeks afterward. The official canvass made Judge Willis' plurality 12, which was upheld by Justice George F. Lyons who reviewed the spoiled ballots in Supreme Court on a mandamus order issued to Mr. Byard, although the Court counted eight of the spoiled ballots, seven of which went to Mr. Byard and one to Mr. Willis. The board of county canvassers was evenly divided, however, and by a vote of 12 to 12 refused to certify the returns until compelled to do so by an order issued by the Court on the application of Mr. Willis.

Dec. 12. The Central Hotel, which stood on Main street, on the site later occupied by the Leatherstocking building, recently purchased by the Second National bank, was badly damaged by fire and water used in its extinction. The hotel was in poor repair and was occupied by Frank Graves, who operated the bar only.

1907—Jan. 1. Charles H. Parshall retired from the publishing firm of Crist, Scott & Parshall.

Jan. 2. The Hotel Fenimore was sold by the Hotel Fenimore Co. to Michael Hanlon, who took possession April 1st. The Hotel Fenimore company was formed by Judge Lynn J. Arnold, E. S. Bundy, M. C. Bundy and Lee B. Cruttenden in 1900 when such a step was necessary and it was through their enterprise that the hotel was kept open to the public Mr. Hanlon had been proprietor of the Pioneer Hotel for twelve years before he purchased the Fenimore.

Jan. 8. George H. White purchased the Central Hotel property, a short time before damaged by fire. The hotel was erected by Webster C. Keyes in 1864 following the fire which wiped out the hotel on the same site.

Jan. 9. C. H. Spencer leased Otsego Hall on Nelson avenue and announced that he would open it as a summer hotel this summer.

Jan. 17. John R. Kirby resigned as cashier of the Cooperstown National Bank to become assistant cashier of the National Bank of Norwich. He was succeeded by Robert M. Bush, a Cooperstown lawyer. Edward D. Lindsay was appointed teller at this time.

Feb. 2. The saw and grist mill of H. E. Lewis & Co. of Bowerstown were swept away by fire. The fire was discovered at about 11:30 p. m. and before it was under control nothing was left of the five buildings or their contents but the foundations and a few scraps of iron. The loss was estimated at $20,000 with insurance of $2,000.

Feb. 7 Manager L. A. Brainard and Lou W. Sherwood at the Village Hall presented the rural drama, "Happy Hollow," introducing a company of local stars including besides Messrs. Brainard and Sherwood, George Hall, Miss Lucy H. Chrisler, F. Harold Chrisler, Miss Mary R. Crain, Charles M. Kraham, Raymond C. Derrick, Charles Baird and Miss Margaret G. Bunn.

Feb. 25. The State Railroad commission granted a certificate of convenience and necessity to the proposed Cooperstown & Northern Railroad company, whose line was already well commenced between this village and Springfield Center.

March 10. W. I. Gardner sold the harness and trunk business which he had conducted for seven years to Arthur B. Clark.

March 25. Samuel M. Shaw, veteran editor of the Freeman's Journal and a leader in the social and political life of the county, died at the age of eighty-four years.

The preliminary survey for the construction of a state road from Oneonta to Springfield through Cooperstown along the west side of Otsego Lake took place this summer.

April 5. At a public meeting held at the Village Hall resolutions offered by the Rev. Ralph Birdsall, rector of Christ Church, were adopted providing for the celebration on a large scale of the centennial of the village. The date was set for August 4th to 10th and other plans made which were elaborated later.

April 26. John Kelley and William Reed, employees of Mrs. Leslie Pell-Clarke at Swanswick, at the head of Otsego Lake, were drowned a short distance from the shore of the estate, when a rowboat in which they were riding overturned.

April 29. Olin Wright committed suicide by hanging himself in a shed on the Averell farm a mile and a half west of the village.

May 1. The mills of H. E. Lewis & Co., destroyed by fire earlier in the year, were rebuilt and were again in operation on this date.

The old Central Hotel building purchased earlier in the year by George H. White for the First National Bank and sold by him to James J. Byard, Jr., was torn down during April and the lumber removed.

May 12. Forbidding the use of nets in Otsego Lake other than gill nets a new fishing law went into effect. Gill nets were allowed with a mesh of not less than 1¾ inch bar and not more than sixty feet in length from July 1st to August 31st, providing a license were obtained from the State Forest, Fish and Game commission.

The International Milk Products company did a large business in ice cream which it manufactured in twenty-eight different flavors, with seventeen kinds of ices, six of sherbets and brick ice cream in any combination of the above.

June 19. The stage between Cooperstown and Springfield Center was discontinued. From this date the Springfield mail from Cooperstown was carried on rural free delivery route No. 5 and the electric line to Richfield Springs.

June 15. Cooperstown's first public garage, located on the north side of Main street west of Chestnut, was opened for business by Arthur H. Crist.

June 21. The Cooperstown Fish & Game club was reorganized with Waldo C. Johnston, president; F. Ambrose Clark, vice-president and Harry H. Willsey, secretary and treasurer. It was voted to incorporate under the above title.

July 17-28. The first regiment of Lancers of the Catholic Abstainers' Union of Scranton, Pa., embracing four companies and numbering 386 men under the command of Col. Walter McNichols conducted its annual encampment on the Fair Grounds. Here the regiment pitched 200 tents. It was well equipped and brought its own choir, band, base ball teams and minstrel troupes and its manoeuvres, concerts, games, dress parade, etc., attracted large interest and admiration among the people of this community. The Military Mass, celebrated on the Sunday of the stay here, was a most impressive event.

THE COOPERSTOWN CENTENNIAL.

The week of August 4th to 11th occurred the celebration on a comprehensive and dignified scale of the Centennial of the Village of Cooperstown. There was some early objection to the selection of this year for holding a "centennial" celebration because it marked merely the 100th anniversary of the first incorporation of the village, an act which was never put into effect and, worst of all, named the village which was called "Cooperstown" always before and afterwards by the name Otsego. These objections melted away, however, before the logic and enthusiasm of the Rev. Ralph Birdsall, rector of Christ church and himself an authority on local history, who pointed out that the object primarily was not to celebrate any particular event which transpired 100 years before but the whole history of the village using the term "centennial" in a very broad and loose sense. "As an absolutely accurate centennial of Cooperstown," he pointed out, "no date can be fixed that is not reasonably open to dispute. The next really favorable date," he continued, "is 1986, when a bi-centennial may appropriately be held. But there are reasons why most of us lack enthusiasm for a commemoration so remote. For similar reasons some of us doubt whether we could be sure of taking any keen interest in a Centennial of 1912."

This problem so convincingly disposed of, the celebration was planned and brought to a complete and successful realization. Organized on the plan outlined at the outset by the Rev. Mr. Birdsall the many committees made up entirely of citizens of the village, worked tirelessly and harmoniously, under his direction and that of the executive committee of which Harris L. Cooke was chairman and it was largely due to their breadth of vision and competent leadership that the event proved perhaps the most outstanding from a literary and historical standpoint, ever held here. It is interesting to note, in addition to the fact that the management was entirely local, that all expense was met by the fund of $6,000 raised in advance by the finance committee. Thousands of people, many from distant parts of the country, including great numbers of former residents called back by the celebration to the scenes of other days were present, while the village itself gave up everything else for the time being to participate in or attend the many interesting features of an elaborate program. It was estimated that on Thursday, the occasion of the literary exercises in the afternoon when Prof. Brander Matthews of Columbia University gave his paper on "James Fenimore Cooper," and of the historical parade with a grand display of fireworks in the evening, there were 15,000 people in Cooperstown, the largest crowd which has visited the village in the opinion of students of history, before or since.

In such a celebration a chief place was naturally given to Cooperstown's most famous son, James Fenimore Cooper, but it was more than a Cooper memorial celebration; it was a commemoration of all that belongs to the history of the place.

Outstanding speakers of the week in addition to Prof. Matthews were the Rt. Rev. Henry C. Potter, Bishop of the New York Diocese of the Protestant Episcopal church and Francis Whiting Halsey, author of "The Old New York Frontier." Original poems written for the occasion were read by their authors, Clinton B. Scollard of Clinton, and the Rev. Walton W. Battershall, D.D., of Albany. In addition a poem composed for the event by Julia Ward Howe was read by Bishop Potter in the absence of the author.

Music was furnished during the week by the 10th Regiment Band of Albany. The 2nd and 3d Battalions of the 10th Regiment were present and established Camp Nelson on the Fair Grounds and with the 3d Separate Company of Oneonta provided interesting military drills and parades giving pomp and circumstance to the proceedings. The Centennial supplements to the village newspapers contained, in addition to complete reports of the addresses, poems and other exercises, many unique contributions from the pens of noted writers and former residents with reference to Cooper and Cooperstown. The loan collection of many articles of historic local interest was one of the notable features of the celebration. The complete proceedings were published in book form making a valuable addition to the Cooperstown bibliography.

Nov. 1. James J. Byard, Jr., and Orange L. Van Horne entered into a partnership for the practice of law in this village.

Dec. 15. The Rev. Edward A. Perry, pastor of the Universalist church here and at Fly Creek for thirteen years, died at Thanksgiving Hospital.

Dec. 23. A thunder storm occurred on this date.

1908.—Jan. 7. When the Union and High school was resumed following the holiday vacation the new building on Chestnut street was used for the first time. The old building on Susquehanna avenue was sold at auction subsequently to W. J. Ashton for $4,600.

Jan. 8. A death blow to the project to build a railroad from Cooperstown to Springfield Center, and later to the Mohawk Valley, was dealt by the Appellate Division of the Supreme Court which, upon appeal from the action of the Railroad commission in granting the road a certificate of convenience and necessity, handed down a decision in favor of the petitioners whose lands it crossed. Much of the right of way had been secured and thousands of dollars spent in grading, getting out ties, etc. The principal backers of the proposed road were Andrew R. Smith of Springfield Center and Amos M. Farnham of Cooperstown. The road would have been called the Cooperstown & Northern.

A bill introduced in the Legislature early in the year providing a city charter for Oneonta village created a large amount of adverse criticism about the county by reason of a provision which allowed the new city six members in the county Board of Supervisors. Heeding the storm of protest which arose on all sides the act was amended before passage to change the number to three and in this form it became a law.

Feb. 25. E. A. Potter sold the marble and granite business which he had conducted for several years to Henry J. Patrick of Cherry Valley.

March 2. The dry goods firm of Bundy & Cruttenden began business succeeding Bundy Bros. & Cruttenden, the surviving partners having purchased the interest held by the estate of Melvin C. Bundy. The Bundy Brothers started business here in 1876. The partnership with Lee B. Cruttenden was formed in 1894.

March 16. The Cooperstown brass band was reorganized. The officers were: President, H. N. Michaels; secretary, H. L. Hartum; treasurer, Edward D. Lindsay; director, F. Victor Schenk.

In March "Spaulding's Official Base Ball Guide for 1908" contained the announcement that the commission of experts appointed three years before had officially decided that Cooperstown was the birth place of baseball, having determined after a careful investigation, that the present game was designed and named by Abner Doubleday, later Major General Doubleday, of Civil War fame, in this village during the Harrison Presidential campaign in 1839. The commission was comprised of U. S. Senator Morgan G. Bulkeley, A. G. Mills, Nicholas E. Young, Alfred J. Reach, George Wright and James E. Sullivan—names of renown in the baseball world of the day. The finding was largely based upon the testimony of Abner Graves of Denver, Colo., who stated that he was a fellow student with Doubleday at Green's Select School in Cooperstown; that he saw him lay out the first diamond-shaped playing field and heard him call it "base ball." Graves, moreover, swore that he participated with other boys of the school in playing the game under Doubleday's direction. The verdict was generally accepted in baseball circles throughout the country. It is believed by some that it was at Duff's Military School that Abner Doubleday first played baseball. This school stood on "Apple Hill," the present site of Fernleigh.

One Cooperstown fisherman took 1,100 Otsego bass through the ice during the winter of 1907-08.

April 1. The United States Express Company opened an office in Cooperstown. W. C. Merrill was the agent.

April 30. Announcement made of the purchase by the Otsego Lake Transit company of the real estate at the foot of Pioneer street, known as Otsego Lake Park, owned by George Brooks. The company also purchased the fleet of row boats and motor boats and accessories and continued the business in connection with its enterprise conducted at the foot of Fair street.

April 28. A home talent cast including A. deJ. Allez, Eugene D. Stocker, R. Grant White, Miss Bessie Boden, Miss Fanny Hanlon, Mrs. Eugene D. Stocker, Miss Florence Bundy and Miss G. Louise Scowden presented the play, "Out of Town," before a large audience at the Village Hall, under the direction of Miss Frances Schermer for the benefit of the Orphan House of the Holy Saviour.

May 1. The Rev. Ralph Birdsall leased the building on Main street known as "The Stone Jug," and converted it into a club for men which he operated for a time as a substitute for the saloon which had been located there for years. The expense of organization and renovations and equipment was met by subscription, but it was operated on a business basis visitors being required to pay for what they got. Billiard tables, card tables, reading matter, etc., were provided and there were cigars, tobacco, soft drinks and sandwiches on sale.

May 1. The Hotel Fenimore, purchased a short time before by Michael Hanlon, again passed into the hands of the Hotel Fenimore Company. Frank A. Pierson of New York City was engaged as manager.

June 28. A partial eclipse of the sun was visible here under favorable weather conditions.

July 5. John R. Kirby purchased the Coal and Feed business of W. J. Ashton.

July 7. The regiment of Lancers from the Lackawanna Valley in Pennsylvania arrived for a ten-days' encampment at the Fair Grounds. This was the Lancers' second visit. They brought 300 men, full equipment, bands, base ball teams, minstrels, etc.

July 16-17. The annual convention and tournament of the Otsego County Firemen's association was held in this village.

July 21. The Rt. Rev. Henry C. Potter, Bishop of New York, died at Fernleigh, his summer home in Cooperstown. Bishop Potter came to Fernleigh with Mrs. Potter in June to complete his recovery from an illness of stomach and liver trouble which he had suffered in April. On June 23d he was prostrated and although he rallied about July 1st leading to more hope on the part of the physicians and members of the family, there was a relapse July 20th and he passed away at 8:25 o'clock the following night of arterio-sclerosis accompanied by embolism of the blood vessels. The notable career of Bishop Potter is recorded at length in other volumes and in the annals of the Protestant Episcopal church. He was born at Schenectady May 25, 1835. He was educated in theology in Virginia and became rector of Grace Church, New York City, in 1868. He was consecrated Bishop in 1887. He married Mrs. Alfred Corning Clark in Cooperstown in October, 1902.

July 26. The Five-Mile Point House, a large wooden structure located at that charming spot on Otsego Lake was totally destroyed by fire. The loss was estimated at about $12,000, with $4,000 insurance. The blaze was first discovered at about 9:30 p. m. and the flames quickly spread. Although the Cooperstown Fire department "hastened" to the scene in a special boat the building was beyond salvation when they arrived. The house was owned by M. H. Wedderspoon and J. Dana Whipple.

Aug. 1. The Freeman's Journal of this village reached its 100th birthday. Col. J. H. Prentiss was its editor for forty years and he was succeeded by Samuel M. Shaw who filled the editorial chair for half a century. Edward S. Brockham, who spent forty years in the office, became a partner of Mr. Shaw in 1880. In 1901 George H. Carley became the associate partner of Mr. Brockham and they continued the business until January 1, 1903, when Mr. Carley became the sole editor and publisher.

Aug. 2. Alexander S. Phinney caught a trout from the waters of Otsego Lake which weighed nineteen pounds.

Sept. 23. Lieutenant Governor Lewis S. Chandler spoke at the Otsego County Fair.

In October the old grist mill was removed from the Leatherstocking Falls Farm which had been purchased by Dr. William E. Guy, then of Princeton, N. J. The old mill, which was probably 100 years old, was torn down to provide stone to be used in a new summer residence which Dr. Guy erected on the property.

Oct. 7.   A certificate of incorporation was filed with the Secretary of State of "The Arthur H. Crist Company" of Cooperstown which took over the publishing business owned and conducted heretofore by Arthur H. Crist.   The capital stock was $200,000 and the incorporators were Arthur H. Crist, Charles F. White, Edward S. Clark, Stephen C. Clark and Lynn J. Arnold, all of Cooperstown.   The Otsego Farmer, owned by this corporation, a local newspaper, which had heretofore been independent in politics, at this time became a Republican newspaper.

Oct. 7.   A certificate of incorporation of the "Five-Mile Point Hotel Association" with its principal office located at Cooperstown, was filed with the Secretary of State.   The capital was $15,000 and the directors were Harris L. Cooke, Frank Mulkins, Justin Lange, J. Dana Whipple, and M. E. Lippitt, all of Cooperstown.   This corporation was formed to purchase the Five-Mile Point property and erect a new summer hotel on the site of the structure which was destroyed by fire earlier in the year.

Oct. 9.   The Oneonta, Cooperstown and Richfield Springs railroad was sold at auction once more by Referee in Bankruptcy Nathaniel P. Willis.   The purchaser was Joseph Starrett of New York City and the price $200,000.   Henry W. Bean, the last preceding purchaser, reorganized the road and changed the name to the Oneonta and Mohawk Valley railway, but upon being required by the Court to make a further payment, defaulted and the road was again advertised for sale.   Joseph K. Choate, as receiver, took over the operation of the line for the benefit of the creditors in June.

Nov. 13.   Contract for constructing the Cooperstown-Three-Mile Point macadam state road let by State Engineer to Malloy and Davis of Schenectady at $31,420.98.

Dec. 15.   The new business block erected by J. B. Slote on Main street to house his art store and photograph store was opened for business.   The building was of brick and made a decidedly attractive addition to the business section.

Early in November the new Shaw-Brooks Memorial Nurses' Home at Thanksgiving Hospital was completed and five rooms in the main building occupied by nurses were made available for patients. One of these the Presbyterian church furnished; one, the Baptist church; one, Mrs. Paddock in memory of her father, Dr. Horace Lathrop; and one, Samuel L. Warrin, in memory of his son.

1909—Jan 1.   Frank Hale was elected assistant cashier and Frank B. Shipman teller of the First National Bank.

An epidemic of typhoid fever which continued from late in 1908 into the early part of 1909 reached its height the first of the year with some thirty cases, several of which proved fatal.   Sanitary inspectors from the State and New York City Boards of Health made careful investigations of the water and milk supplies finally locating the trouble in an individual milk supply. Among the victims of the disease were Dr. Henry D. Sill, a leading physician and citizen of the village, and the Rev. Cyrus W. Negus, pastor of the First Baptist church.

Feb. 1. C. K. Lippitt purchased a half interest in the jewelry business conducted heretofore by his brother, M. E. Lippitt, and the business became known as Lippitt Brothers. Another business change was the formation of the hardware firm known as the "McEwan Hardware Co.", to succeed the business conducted by W. L. McEwan for several years. His brother, Paul H. McEwan, became associated in the new enterprise.

Feb. 9. For the first time since 1901 the liquor question was submitted to the voters at the town meeting. Saloon, store, pharmacists' and hotel licenses were voted by large majorities.

Feb. 9. The 100th anniversary of the organization of Otsego Chapter, No. 26, R. A. M., was fittingly celebrated.

Feb. 9. The Hon. John Worthington, who was for 12 years United States counsul to Malta, died at Worthington Hall, where he was born, at the age of sixty-eight. Mr. Worthington was a poet and author of more than local reputation.

March 6. Jacob Getman of Roseboom, indicted for murder in the first degree, was convicted of manslaughter in the first degree, for killing Fred Neal in that town. The trial was held in Supreme Court in Cooperstown before Justice H. B. Coman, who sentenced Getman to a term of not less than twelve or more than nineteen years and three months at Auburn State prison.

March 16. Hubbard L. Brazee became the sole owner of the drug business heretofore conducted by Brazee and Boden, having purchased the interest of his partner, Edward D. Boden.

March 25. A sizable and attractive addition to the First National Bank building, completed the latter part of the month, doubled the working space of this bank. Its revolving doors were the first to be installed in Cooperstown.

March 28. The Board of Trade appropriated the sum of thirty dollars for advertising Cooperstown as a summer resort—the first money ever used by the community as a whole for that purpose. It was all spent.

April 1. Extensive improvements in the Hotel Fenimore, completed at about this time, included the installation of an elevator, a new electric lighting system, and the complete redecoration of the upper floors.

April 13. The suicide of Arthur W. T. Back, at Binghamton caused the abrupt termination of the term of Supreme Court which had been adjourned to this date for his trial on one of a number of indictments charging grand larceny and forgery through which he was alleged to have embezzeled Broome county funds in the sum of $13,500. The trial was set down for Otsego county on a change of venue and was attracting a vast amount of attention. He had already been tried on one count, found guilty and sentenced to one year in prison. An appeal was taken and was pending when the end came.

Under the direction of Waldo C. Johnston, then superintendent of the Iroquois Farm of F. Ambrose Clark, a large experiment in forestry was started this spring with the planting of some 60,000 white pine trees. From this beginning forestry became a settled policy of the Iroquois Farm which has been carried out on a scientific basis and extensive scale to the present time.

In May the purchase of Otsego Hall by Mr. and Mrs. L. H. Spencer was announced. They had managed the popular summer boarding house for two seasons.

May 3. Work commenced on the new macadam state road from Cooperstown to Three-Mile Point.

May 22. The Cooperstown National Bank moved into its new quarters in the Bowen Block from the north side of Main street. The bank purchased the building which it has since occupied.

June 1. The new summer residence of William E. Guy at Leatherstocking Farm was completed at about this time.

June 15. A concrete conduit carrying Willowbrook under Main street was completed by Contractor E. A. Potter and work was commenced on the excavations for the new building for the Arthur H. Crist Co., on the site of the old Central Hotel. The building in later years was known as the Leatherstocking building.

June 26. In the Republican primaries throughout Otsego county the regular organization went down to defeat, at the hands of the section of the party headed by the Hon. Lynn J. Arnold. The Hon. Stephen C. Clark of Cooperstown, candidate for member of Assembly won 57 of the delegates, while the Hon. Charles Smith, the regular organization candidate, had 20. Fitch Gilbert of Gilbertsville, an independent, had 3.

July 1. The new Five-Mile Point Inn, erected for the Five-Mile Point Hotel Company, composed of public spirited local business men, who desired to keep the property from passing into private hands, was completed and opened for business with H. E. Bissell, a former manager of the Hotel Fenimore, in charge. Contractor Fayette Houck of this village was the builder.

July 2. At the Republican County Convention held here the candidates of the Arnold faction of the party were nominated without opposition and the control of the county organization went completely into its hands.

July 4. In a quarrel over a woman to whom both had paid some attention Raymond Gardner, aged 19, was fatally stabbed by Fabiano Palma, aged 30. Palma escaped but was captured by Sheriff Orlo J. Brown and some Oneonta Italians, who assisted him, near Schenevus, and was brought to the county jail. He was indicted on a charge of manslaughter in the first degree but was convicted of second degree manslaughter and sentenced by County Judge A. L. Kellogg to a term of not less than five or more than seven and one-half years in Auburn state prison.

Cooperstown supported a semi-professional base ball team this season with W. D. Howells as captain and manager. The season opened July 3d.

July 12. The Otesaga, the large new hotel erected upon the site of

Holt-Averell on Otsego Lake, which was purchased for that purpose by Messrs. Edward Severin Clark and Stephen C. Clark, was formally opened to the public with Joseph D. Price of New York City as manager. The hotel is still operated here by the original owners and there is no more beautiful or attractive resort in the North. The sporty and exceedingly beautiful 18-hole golf course which has been developed along the Lake shore is one of the chief attractions of the hotel.

July 13-15. The annual convention of the New York State Press association was held at The Otesaga.

July 14. R. E. Bolton, for twenty years engaged in the coal and feed business here, sold his interest in the firm of Bolton and Bronner and retired. The firm was succeeded by Bronner and Wood, the new member being L. N. Wood, formerly connected with the Second National Bank.

July 19. "The Glimmerglass," a daily newspaper published during July and August by the Freeman's Journal made its first appearance.

July 25. The new pipe organ presented to Christ Church by Mrs. Elizabeth Scriven Potter in memory of her husband, the Rt. Rev. Henry C. Potter, was dedicated at the morning service in the presence of a congregation which filled the edifice.

Aug. 14. Barbara Orlando, aged 10 years, a member of an Italian orchestra playing this summer on board the Steamer Mohican fell into the water as the boat was nearing Three-Mile Point under full headway. She was rescued by Arthur Coe, a member of the Otesaga orchestra, who was a passenger and the two were taken ashore by a motor boat.

Aug. 17. Elbert Hubbard, author and publicist, spoke here on the subject, "The March of the Centuries," under the auspices of the ladies of the Universalist church.

Sept. 23. The Hon. Charles E. Hughes, Governor of the State of New York, spoke at the Otsego County Fair, before a large crowd. He was introduced by the Hon. Stephen C. Clark of this village.

Sept. 26. The grandstand, judges' stand, roof garden and a portion of the band stand at the Otsego County Fair grounds were destroyed by fire. The fire started in the upper part of the grandstand. The cause remained a mystery.

The year was marked by notable development in the village as a summer resort and in the building of homes. The Otesaga Hotel and Five-Mile Point Inn were opened and a dozen new dwellings and a fine new business block completed while the large new publishing house of the Arthur H. Crist Co., was nearly complete. During the year 70,000 square feet of cement sidewalk was laid as compared with 50,000 in 1907. Chestnut street was curbed and the east macadamized to be completed the following Spring.

1910—Feb. 21. The Railroad commission of the town of Otsego sold refunding bonds of the town amounting to $14,000 to the First National Bank, the only bidder, for $14,018.20.

April 30. Charles T. Brewer was elected president and Fred L. Quaif vice-president of the Second National Bank to succeed G. Pomeroy Keese and Adriel G. Murphy, respectively, whose deaths occurred a short time previously.

May 1.   The Five-Mile Point Inn opened for the season under the management of L. C. Millard and Son of Oneonta who leased the property for a year.

May 11.   At a special meeting of the Board of Directors of the Otsego County Farmers' Cooperative Insurance Company A. C. Shipman was elected president to succeed Adriel G. Murphy, deceased, and Frank B. Shipman was elected secretary and treasurer, to succeed his father, who had held that office since the organization of the company twenty-four years before.

May 17.   A consignment of 40,000 lake trout fry was placed in Otsego Lake by A. S. Phinney and Game Protector Edward Martin.

June 1.   By this date the Arthur H. Crist Co., publishers of The Otsego Farmer, American Motherhood and Table Talk, and proprietors of a large legal and general printing business moved into its new building which had been in process of construction for several months. The architect was Frank P. Whiting and the builders Griffith Brothers of Utica. The building fronts 57 feet and Main street with a depth of 142 feet and consists of four stories and a basement with an electrically equipped power house in the rear. The building material was Indiana limestone, pressed brick, reinforced concrete and common brick. It is absolutely fire proof. It has recently been purchased by the Second National Bank.

June 7.   The clothing business of Spingler and Gould was sold to Devere Empie and Laverne Wilson of Oneonta who continued the business under the title, Empie and Wilson.

June 15.   The Hotel Fenimore was leased by L. C. Millard and Son of Oneonta who also operated the Five-Mile Point Inn under a lease.

June 24.   A trial in Supreme Court here, which excited more than local attention and which came to a conclusion on this date was that entitled the People against Charles P. Knapp, growing out of the failure of the Outing Publishing company of Deposit which was closely followed by the crash of the Binghamton Trust company and the Knapp Bank at Deposit. The particular charge on which defendant was tried alleged that he received a deposit knowing that the bank was insolvent. He was found guilty by the jury after deliberating all night and was sentenced by Justice Henry B. Coman of Oneida to a term of not more than two or less than one year at Auburn State prison. The trial was held here on a charge of venue granted the defense.

June 28-29.   The twenty-eighth annual convention of the Street Railway association of the State of New York was held at the Otesaga Hotel.

July 8.   Blendon Campbell, the celebrated American artist, who painted the two large paintings at the entrance of the ball room at the Otesaga Hotel, arrived here to superintend the placing of the canvases.

July 8-9-10.   The centennial of Christ Church was celebrated. On one evening the old churchyard where Father Nash lies buried with many of his parishioners of a century before, was illuminated. A centennial picnic was held at Three-Mile Point and on the closing day, Sunday, the rector, the Rev. Ralph Birdsall, delivered a sermon on "Father Nash."

July 13-16. The seventeenth annual convention of the New York State Bankers' association brought over 300 delegates and members of their families to the Otesaga.

Aug. 29. Mrs. Theodore Roosevelt, wife of ex-President Roosevelt, and their two sons, Quentin and Archie Roosevelt, were included in a party entertained at luncheon at the Otesaga by Mrs. Douglas Robinson, Mr. Roosevelt's sister, of Henderson.

Sept. 7. A man who gave his name as George B. Corrigan of Columbus, O., was arrested at Oneonta through the efforts of Sheriff Orlo J. Brown and Special Detective Percy L. Gould for passing lead nickels in Cooperstown. It developed that he had been spending the summer at a hut at the Gazley stone quarry on the Lake where he had made the counterfeit money from solder purchased at a local plumbing shop. He was taken to Utica and arraigned before the United States Commissioner there.

In September Mrs. William Constable sold Glimmerglen on Otsego Lake, for twenty-five years the summer home of the Constable family, to William Truslow Hyde of New York City.

Sept. 21. There was a sensation not on the entertainment program of the Otsego County Fair when a stranger evidently intoxicated imitated a professional high diver and jumped from the top of an 80-foot ladder into a tank of water. He recovered at the county jail.

Sept. 26. The Otsego County Board of Supervisors in special session inspected the newly constructed Cooperstown-Three-Mile Point state road and voted to protest against its acceptance by the state on account of faulty construction. It was alleged that the specifications as to the quality of material were not followed by the contractors.

Sept. 28-29. The annual New York State Conference of the Daughters of the American Revolution brought over 200 members of that organization here.

In October the Fenimore Hotel was purchased by James J. Byard, Jr., who offered it for sale.

Oct. 9. The Rev. Sidney S. Conger, for twelve years pastor of the First Presbyterian church, tendered his resignation.

In November William L. McEwan and Frank B. Shipman were appointed members of the Board of Education of Union Free School district No. 1 to succeed William Festus Morgan and the Rev. Sidney S. Conger, resigned.

Nov. 21. The Board of Supervisors were notified that the state had accepted the Cooperstown-Three-Mile Point state road from the contractors despite its protest.

Dec. 12. The final Teachers' Institute, which had been an annual affair in Cooperstown for years, was held in the High school building during the week. Over 200 teachers were in attendance from the First Commissioner district of Otsego county. The Institutes were abolished by an amendment to the state Education law.

In December John W. Brown, for several years county superintendent of the poor, purchased Carr's Hotel and placed that old and well known property in excellent condition. The hotel was operated under his personal management for several years.

CHAPTER VI

FROM 1911 TO 1915

1911—Jan. 1. The Otsego Republican, established as The Tocsin in 1829 having taken the name, "The Otsego Republican" two years later, was purchased by the Arthur H. Crist Co., and the two combined under the name, "The Ostego Farmer and Otsego Republican."

Jan. 1. Harry J. Wilson of Roscoe, Delaware county, became proprietor of the Hoffman House.

A report from the Federal Census Bureau at Washington placed Cooperstown's population in 1910 at 2,484, and that of the town of Otsego at 4,267.

Feb. 1.   John K. Doane, for ten years secretary of the Cooperstown Y.M.C.A. tendered his resignation to take effect on this date.

The first troop of Boy Scouts was organized in Cooperstown at about this time. The Rev. Frank S. Squyer, pastor of the Baptist church was the Scoutmaster.

March 3. The nomination of George M. Wedderspoon to become Postmaster at Cooperstown was confirmed by the U. S. Senate and he took office, succeeding Albert S. Potts, a short time thereafter.

March 15.   The Cooperstown Y.M.C.A. was changed at this date to the Village Club with James A. Davidson as manager. The new club was opened the middle of May.

March 25.   The Bell and the Independent Telephone systems, both of which had operated in this village for some time, were consolidated and from this date the Bell system only has existed in Cooperstown.

April 6.   A Village Improvement society was organized having for its object "the improvement and ornamentation of the streets, residences and public grounds and Lake front of Cooperstown, by planting and cultivating trees, removing unsightly objects and doing such other acts as shall tend to improve and beautify the village." The society maintained its existence for only a short time.

April 10.   A curfew ordinance was adopted by the Village Trustees requiring that children be kept off the street after 9 o'clock from May 1st to October 1st, and after 8 o'clock for the remainder of the year. It was enforced for a short time.

For the purpose of protecting the water supply the Board of Health of the State of New York presented a set of rules and regulations relating to Otsego Lake which have since been in effect. The responsibility of enforcement rests with the Cooperstown Aqueduct association who make frequent inspections and report to the state board.

April 16.   A beautiful window in memory of Daniel Baker Boden and Mary Ashton Boden, long associated with the history of the church and village, was unveiled in Christ church. The window was the gift of their children.

April 30. The Rev. Edward C. Petrie of Sayre, Pa., became pastor of the First Presbyterian church.

May 5. Through the generosity of Miss Florence V. Sill, a building containing a mortuary, delivery and pathological rooms was added to Thanksgiving Hospital in memory of her brother, the late Dr. Henry. D. Sill. This building was formerly Dr. Sill's office at "The Maples," the Sill home on Chestnut street, which was removed to the hospital grounds and placed on a foundation adjoining the main building west of the Nurses' Home.

June 15. The new country home, Fynmere, built by James Fenimore Cooper of Albany, on his property east of this village, was completed and occupied by the family.

In June the Utica Knitting company, which had operated the mills at Phoenix Mills for some time, closed down the plant.

June 20. The Hickory Grove Inn opened for the summer with Earl N. Hoke as proprietor.

June 26. The twenty-ninth annual convention of the New York State Street Railway association brought 100 delegates and their families to the Otesaga.

J. Arthur Olson, a local mechanic, constructed an aeroplane this summer.

Early in the year there was projected under the leadership of the Rev. Dr. J. Aspinwall McCuaig a movement to establish on the Brooks property on the West side of Otsego Lake—a short distance north of Cooperstown a permanent summer camp of the Boy Scouts of America. The project had the support of the national organization and received large publicity in the press throughout the country. The first encampment opened July 12th and continued for several days with an attendance of about 150 Scouts. General Field Secretary Preston G. Orwig of the Washington headquarters was present, representing the National organization. The Hon. Daniel D. Frisbie, speaker of the New York State Assembly brought the greetings of Governor Dix and Admiral Herbert W. Savory of the British Navy and General W. S. Edgerley, U. S. A., retired, were among the speakers. An interesting feature of the encampment was the visit of a group of artists connected with the Vitagraph company of America for the purpose of taking photographs for moving picture films. The scenario for the picture made at this time was written by Dr. Joseph B. Cooke of Cooperstown. The company included Miss Florence Turner, popular screen star, and James Hallock ("Hal") Ried, playwright. The movement, however well planned, was probably premature as it died before another year.

The Hotel Fenimore was opened for the summer about July 1st by James J. Byard, Jr., proprietor, with C. B. Meredith, manager.

July 23. Pasquale Favole, an Italian employed by E. A. Potter as a foreman of laborers in building the Bissell cottage on Otsego Lake, was drowned in about 8 feet of water in front of the dock from which it is thought he fell as he was looking into the water.

July 29. Road oil was used in Cooperstown for the first time. The application was made from the railroad crossing to Woodside Hall and created considerable consternation among housewives for a time on account of the effect it had on carpets when tracked in by members of the family.

The Junior Order of American Mechanics of Pennsylvania camped near Three-Mile Point for the week of August 6th. They were accompanied by Alexander's famous band.

Aug. 14. The state convention of the United Order of American Mechanics, attended by about seventy-five delegates, was held at the Hotel Fenimore this week.

Hops were still an important crop in this vicinity. Hundreds of pickers arrived the latter part of August for the harvest.

Sept. 1. The law firm of Campbell & Pierson was formed by Samuel J. Campbell and Adrian A. Pierson and commenced business in the Brooks block.

At the close of the season the management of the Otesaga Hotel, J. D. Price and Paul L. Pinkerton, announced a very satisfactory summer's business nearly twice that of the last year.

Sept. 2. The village supported a strong professional base ball club this season winning the pennant in a series of games with Oneonta, Richfield Springs and Morris.

Moving pictures of "The Deerslayer" were made by the Vitagraph company in September. The company reconstructed "The Ark" of James Fenimore Cooper on the Sunken Island and produced a picture very faithful to the text. Bringing a number of famous screen actors and actresses here the village for the first time had the opportunity of witnessing a real moving picture in the making. The picture was shown in hundreds of picture theatres throughout the country and proved a fine piece of publicity.

Sept. 19. R. LeRoy Karrer, aged twenty, bellboy at the Otesaga, was drowned while swimming in Otsego Lake. His home was in Brooklyn.

Dec. 1. The Cory hardware business, one of the oldest mercantile establishments in Cooperstown, was purchased by Ernest Tibbitts and Kenneth W. Root who conducted it under the title, Tibbitts and Root.

The contract for digging and filling the ditch for the sewer from Pioneer street to Susquehanna avenue was awarded in December to E. A. Potter.

Dec. 19. Russel Warren, owner, announced that the properties of the Clinton Mills Power company and the Cooperstown Gas company had been taken over by the interests operating the Colliers hydroelectric development and that the electric supply for this village would be furnished by that plant.

Dec. 25. A new baptistry of carved oak in memory of the late George Pomeroy Keese was dedicated at Christ church. It was presented by the family of the late Mr. Keese, who was elected Vestryman in 1858, and served as Warden from 1905 until his death in 1910. Mr. Keese was for over half a century prominently connected with the business and social life of the village. He was a great grandson of Judge William Cooper and a grand nephew of James Fenimore Cooper.

1912—Jan. 25. Garry Benson, proprietor of the famous hotel and Turkish baths, The Tub, at Albany, became the owner of the Hotel Fenimore and the house which had been closed since early Fall was opened late in May with a Board of Trade banquet.

In March Judge Lynn J. Arnold resigned as a member of the Board of Education and was succeeded by Judge Nathaniel P. Willis.

March 20. The home of Dr. A. J. Butler at the corner of Glen avenue and Grove street was destroyed by fire which is supposed to have started from the furnace. The house which was known as Terrace Cottage was erected by Henry F. Phinney in 1870.

April 14. The fact that Arthur Ryerson of Philadelphia and Ringwood at the head of Otsego Lake was included among those lost in the sinking of the White Star Liner "Titanic," which collided with an iceberg off the coast of New Foundland brought a realizing sense of the world-wide disaster to Cooperstown. The Ryerson family, Mr. and Mrs. Ryerson, their daughters, Suzette and Emily, and their son, John, with Miss Grace Scott Bowen who had acted as tutor to the children, had been touring Europe when they received news of the death in an auto accident April 8th at Philadelphia of another son, Arthur Ryerson, Jr. They sailed on the Titanic the following Wednesday. When the ship hit the iceberg the women and children were placed in lifeboats and were picked up six hours later by another liner and brought safely to land.

May 1. The Five-Mile Point Inn opened for the summer under the management of J. Dana Whipple.

The erection of a number of dwelling houses west of Thanksgiving Hospital led the trustees of the hospital and other property owners to tender to the village the right of way for a street which was accepted. Maple street, (the name already under general use being retained) thus came into official being. A concrete sidewalk was constructed this summer.

May 14. Eugene D. Stocker was appointed Second Deputy State Fire Marshal.

May 15. John R. Kirby purchased the interest of his partner, John A. Briggs, in the coal and feed business which they had conducted as Kirby & Briggs for a few years. W. Scott Root became a partner a short time later and the business was conducted as Kirby and Root.

May 27. The Cooperstown Band which at this time was under the direction of Prof. A. deJ. Allez, gave a concert at the Village Hall.

The Village Improvement society did a good piece of work in constructing a small park on what was formerly an unsightly place at the foot of River street. The Lakeside was filled in and the bank terraced

June 30. George N. Smith was appointed manager of the Village club to succeed James A. Davidson, resigned.

July 1. Coville S. Derrick took possession of the Wagner Greenhouse on Main street which he purchased a short time before.

In June the management of the Cooperstown Country club had the plant growth cleared out of Blackbird Bay, Otsego Lake, and that ground reclaimed by extensive filling to make room for tennis courts.

June 25. The Cooperstown Automobile club was organized. The first officers were: George H. White, president; S. L. Warrin, vice-president; Dr. James Burton, secretary and M. H. Bronner, treasurer.

July 6. A building used by the International Milk Products company for storage and the D. & H. roundhouse were consumed by fire. The first named structure was owned by E. A. Potter. Following this fire it was arranged by the Village Trustees and the International company to have the whistle of the plant blown in case of a fire, as it had become apparent that the bell at the Village Hall was ineffectual as an alarm.

July 22. A new and permanent dock on the Lakefront of Lakewood cemetery, built through the efforts of Mrs. Frank M. Turnbull was completed.

Aug. 11. Alexander's Band of Wilkes-Barre, Pa., and the Junior Order of United American Mechanics camped on the Fair Grounds for a week. They numbered 300 or more and furnished delightful entertainment not only for themselves but for the village as well.

Aug. 14. Governor John A. Dix and party visited Cooperstown and spoke from the porch of the Hotel Fenimore. Later he was entertained at supper in the hotel dining room. Governor Dix, accompanied by Mrs. Dix and Mr. and Mrs. Thomas B. Proctor of Utica were entertained by Mr. and Mrs. John M. Bowers at Lakelands over the week-end September 14th and 15th.

Aug. 22. A new infirmary at the Orphan House of the Holy Saviour, the gift of Deaconess Pell-Clarke, was opened to public inspection for the first time. The building was originated through the efforts of Leslie Pell-Clarke, and Mrs. Pell-Clarke completely renovated and equipped it in his memory.

Aug. 25. The safe at Carr's Hotel, John W. Brown, proprietor, was opened between 1 and 3 a. m., and $640 in cash taken.

Sept. 17. Scott Layten and "Jock" Newkirk, drew to shore in a seine from the bottom of Otsego Lake a part of a human skeleton, which was thought to have been the remains of one of the New Berlin men drowned in the Lake off Five-Mile Point July 24, 1904. The other was recovered in the same accidental manner a short time before.

Sept. 28. Thomas McDonough was burned to death in a dwelling house fire on Lake street. The house was owned by Mrs. Wm. D. Aren and was occupied by Torrence Olendorf and family with whom McDonough boarded.

At this time, the first of October, there were eighteen places in the town of Otsego licensed to sell alcoholic liquor, fifteen of which were in Cooperstown.

Oct. 17. An attempt to sell at auction the Fenimore Knitting Mill property at Phoenix Mills failed on account of the absence of bidders.

It was announced that no bid below $17,500 would be considered and that three lots were reserved. The machinery was sold at private sale at this time.

Oct. 31. Joseph K. Choate, who since 1908 had been manager of the Otsego & Herkimer electric railroad running from Mohawk to Oneonta, severed his connection with that company and went to Morristown, N. J., where he had charge of the Morris County Traction company. He was succeeded by S. Walter Mower of London, Can.

1913.—Jan. 1. Robert L. Davidson, who since 1874 had been an employee of the Clark Estate, retired as manager of the Fenimore Farm of Mr. Edward Severin Clark and was succeeded by Fred Taber, whose term of office as county superintendent of poor had just expired.

Jan. 9. The arc lights heretofore used for lighting the streets of the village were supplanted by incandescents.

Jan. 11. Through the contributions of private citizens, mostly members of the summer colony, a chemical engine was acquired by the Cooperstown Fire department.

Jan. 29. In a ruling handed down by Justice Albert F. Gladding at Binghamton the act of the Otsego County Board of Supervisors in changing the time of town elections bi-annually from the spring to the date of the general election in the fall was upheld.

In February the holders of the second mortgage of the Five-Mile Point Hotel association, who bid in the property at a foreclosure sale earlier in the year, organized themselves into the Cooperstown Realty company. The corporation was capitalized at $8,000 and the directors were M. H. Bronner, Harris L. Cooke, John F. Brady, and Lee B. Cruttenden.

March 11. The Democratic village ticket headed by W. Dean Burditt for mayor, defeated the Republican and Citizens' ticket by a large majority at the annual corporate election. The outgoing board of trustees adopted a resolution fixing the salary of Village President $300 per year.

April 1. Charles S. Stanton succeeded Allen O. Choate as superintendent of the Clinton Mills Power company.

April 16. The firm of Wood Brothers succeeded Bronner & Wood, dealers in flour, feed and coal, when Ralph B. Wood of Rochester purchased the interest of M. H. Bronner and became the partner of L. N. Wood, his brother.

April 17. In Supreme Court here Justice A. L. Kellogg sentenced Kearney Caulkins, Paul McBride and Joseph Heinman, after the first had been convicted and the last two pleaded guilty to an indictment charging assault in the first degree for a murderous attack made upon Eben M. Temple, an aged resident of the village, January 22nd, as he was about to leave his room at the Hoffman House. McBride and Heinman confessed stating that McBride concocted the scheme with the object of robbing Mr. Temple. Caulkins wielded the club and Heinman watched while the other two were attempting to go through his pockets. Caulkins was tried after entering a plea of not guilty and was convicted. He received a sentence of not less than four and one-half or more than nine years at Auburn State prison, McBride not less than four or more than seven at the same prison, and Heinman was sent to the Elmira Reformatory under the rules of that institution.

April 21. At a special meeting the Board of Village Trustees adopted a resolution authorizing the Cooperstown Gas company to give up its franchise upon serving formal notice upon the Board and sixty days' notice to the users. The plant which was owned and operated in connection with the Clinton Mills Power company, which supplied the village with electricity, by the owners of the Colliers power plant, had not been a paying proposition for some time and it was the expressed desire of the owners to have the plant, old, dilapidated and supplied with antiquated equipment, declared a public nuisance and allowed to suspend operations for a period of five years. The Village Board, however, took the course outlined above in the hope that a new and well equipped plant would be built near the village, a new and modern franchise obtained and the gas business placed on a more satisfactory basis. The idea that there was a real need for gas in Cooperstown did not seem well founded, for there has never since been raised a formal request for service of this character. The service was discontinued September 5th, when after a somewhat determined effort on its part to keep the franchise, the company fulfilled its agreement with the Board of Trade and citizens, made by treaty through the Public Service commission. The plant was promptly torn down and dismantled and the company legally dissolved.

May 3. Fred Lettis managed the Five-Mile Point Inn which opened for the season on this date.

Nine cans of piké perch fry were placed in the Lake by the Board of Trade and Cooperstown Fish & Game club late in April.

This summer marked the completion of the development of Pioneer street the last of the building lots on the east side of the street having been sold by Arnold & Cooke, who opened the tract, having been sold in May. New and attractive dwellings sprang up rapidly and the street became one of the most important residential sections in the community.

June 1-5. The centennial of the Cooperstown Methodist Episcopal church was celebrated with appropriate services. In connection with this event the pastor, the Rev. Albert Clarke, published a history of the church in this community which has proved a valuable historical record. Another feature of the occasion was the burning of a mortgage of $1,600 which had been paid as the result of a subscription campaign freeing the property of debt.

June 11-12. The annual meeting of the Otsego Universalist association was held at the church in this village.

The paving of Chestnut street was completed to the corporation line this summer.

June 23-27. The thirtieth annual convention of the American Institute of Electrical Engineers was held at the Otesaga with an attendance of 200.

June 30. The receipts of the Cooperstown post office for the past year totalled $22,635.64, as compared with $20,717.40 for the preceding year.

July 6. The largest catch of Otsego bass from the Lake ever recorded in its history took place. Theodore House and his father near the old stone quarry hauled seine and landed the enormous number of 714 of the fish. On the same day "Jock" Holcomb on the same ground hauled in 446. On July 4th Edward Farquharson and Jack Hibbard made two catches one numbering 430 and one 231. Fred House later in the day brought in a seine containing 197 bass. The number of bass caught this year was greater than ever before—or since. The Lake had been protected for several years against hauling seines and had also been frequently stocked.

July 11-12. The New York State association of American Architects was formed at a meeting held at the Otesaga.

Aug. 2-3. Governor and Mrs. William Sulzer spent the week-end at the Hotel Fenimore.

Aug. 19-20. The twentieth annual convention of the Otsego County Firemen's association met here.

Aug. 21. A syndicate composed of Martin Moakler, James J. Byard, Jr., W. D. Burditt and Jay D. Wilson purchased the real estate of the Fenimore Mills at auction sale at $3,900.

Sept. 8. The Association of Edison Illuminating Companies of America held its annual convention at the Otesaga this week.

In September the Clark Estate purchased the Armine Gazley property at the foot of Nelson Avenue completing the Lakefront owned by them from the Otesaga to Blackbird bay with the exception of the street, and bringing the Country club and golf course within easy reach of the hotel.

Sept. 23. The store of N. W. Cole, Cooperstown's oldest business man, was closed as the result of the foreclosure of a chattel mortgage given to M. M. Willis.

Sept. 28. Following a week's campaign of publicity through the mails, newspapers and by other means "Everybody in Church" day was observed by the Cooperstown church with great success, all the places of worship being well filled with exceptionally large congregations.

Sept. 29. A class of eighty new members of Cooper (Cooperstown) and Milford Tents, K. O. T. M., received the second and third degrees. About 350 members of the Order attended the ceremonies.

Oct. 6. By a vote of 302 to 74 the tax payers of the town of Otsego voted to sell to the Delaware & Hudson company the stock in the C. & S. V. railroad which it owned at $7,500. The C. & S. V. road is known as the Cooperstown branch of the D. & H. In addition to the purchase price the company agreed to immediately discontinue the arbitrary freight charges on hay, lumber, coal, grain and feed, and on or before January 1, 1915, wipe out all other arbitraries, and further to build within two years a new passenger station here of such architecture, size and general character in keeping with the dignity, importance and historic character of the village—all of which were honorably carried out.

Nov. 4. At the general election the excise questions were again submitted in this town which went wet by larger majorities than ever.

In November over 800 relics of Indian times were presented to the museum at the Village Club by Dr. James C. Ferguson of St. Paul, Minn., a former resident.

Dec. 21. The body of a new-born babe was found in the Susquehanna river just below the Main street bridge by some boys throwing
stones in the water.

1914.—Jan. 2. John E. Milburn, an employee at the Hoffman
House, died at Thanksgiving Hospital of burns received when he was
scalded by water from the furnace. He was intoxicated at the time.

Jan. 16. At a joint meeting of the executive committee and officers
of the Otsego County Farm Bureau association, which was organized
early in the year at Oneonta, it was decided to located the headquarters
at Cooperstown and Floyd S. Barlow of New Brunswick, N. J., was
engaged to act as the first agent. The first office of the association was
located in the Davidson block on Main street, now owned by Ray F.
Williams.

Feb. 1. Clermonte G. Tennant, who had spent the greater part of
his time at Albany in connection with his duties as deputy attorney general made an arrangement with Attorney General Carmody whereby he
was able to open an office in Cooperstown for the practice of law although he continued to handle special matters for the state.

Feb. 9. After conducting a trunk and harness business here for
thirty years Joel G. White sold to Walter I. Gardner.

Feb. 10. A slight earthquake shock was felt in the village.

Feb. 13-14. Thirty-two inches of snow fell in eighteen hours exactly equalling the snowfall in the great blizzard of 1888. In the '88
blizzard, however, the snowfall was spread over forty-four hours.

In February announcement was made that the stock of goods of
Herman Reisman, who had been in the clothing business here since 1884,
would be sold and Mr. Reisman retire from active trade.

The ice did not leave the Lake this Spring until April 19th.

April 28. The proposition to establish a fire alarm system in
Cooperstown was defeated at a special taxpayers' election; 68 no, 40 yes.

May 1. Two new squash courts were completed at the Village
Club.

The pavement of Chestnut street from the railroad crossing south
to the Corporation line was completed early in June.

June 5. A band of sharpers buncoed N. C. Clute, an aged resident,
out of the sum of $740 in a flim-flam game. They were connected with
a Wild West Show which exhibited here on the Fair Grounds. The
manager of the show, although claiming no knowledge of the affair,
settled with Mr. Clute at the urgent request of Sheriff Ziba L. Holbrook,
by repaying $525.

June 3-5. The 119th annual convention of the Otsego Baptist association was held in Cooperstown.

June 26. Dr. James Burton after practicing his profession here for
twenty years, left for Pasadena, Calif., accompanied by Mrs. Burton and
daughter, Miss Margaret Burton. Dr. Burton was succeeded here by
Dr. H. L. Cruttenden of Morris to whom he sold his practice.

June 24. The Board of Directors of the Second National Bank
elected F. W. Spraker cashier to succeed George M. Jarvis, deceased.
Lynn T. Pier was made assistant cashier to succeed Mr. Spraker and

Harry H. Willsey teller. Mr. Spraker had been associated with the bank twenty-six years.

July 10. A cloudburst following a thunder storm did considerable damage in the immediate vicinity of Cooperstown. A small brook south of the village became a raging torrent and caused several thousand dollars loss to property on the Keese farm occupied by C. M. Allison, the farms of George Thayer and Peleg Smith.

July 26. Henry Geyer, a chauffeur from Buffalo, was drowned in Otsego Lake near Point Florence, while swimming.

A new bridge over the river on Susquehanna avenue was erected this summer by the Owego Construction company. The expense, $2,-240 was met by the towns of Otsego and Middlefield. F. Ambrose Clark paid $500 for the old bridge.

Trout fishing in Otsego Lake reached its zenith this season. Sixty-nine of the fish weighing 543 pounds were reported by anglers. Of these Alexander S. Phinney, Cooperstown's foremost fisherman, brought in thirty-four weighing 272 pounds.

Aug. 21. The racing stable at Iroquois Farm was burned to the ground.

Sept. 3. . The sum of $1,600 was raised at a lawn fete at Fernleigh, the summer home of Mr. and Mrs. Stephen C. Clark, for the benefit of the American Red Cross.

Sept. 6. The sugar and milk plant of the International Milk Products company was destroyed by fire. The fire was believed to have started from a boiler. The loss was about $7,500.

Sept. 16. After over forty years of active service with the National Express company, thirty-two of which were spent in Cooperstown, Allen Gallup retired as the local agent of the company.

Oct. 7. The first annual field day of the Cooperstown Fire department took place at the Fair Grounds. The department withdrew in 1913 from the county firemen's association and this event was substituted to take place of the participation by the members in the annual tournament.

Oct. 9. William Sulzer, impeached Governor of New York State, spoke before a good sized audience at The Village Hall at an evening meeting.

Oct. 13. Former President Theodore Roosevelt addressed a large crowd at the Village Hall at an afternoon meeting in the interest of the Bull Moose party.

Oct. 16. The loyalty and enthusiasm of Cooperstown women to a worthy cause was demonstrated by their enthusiastic attendance at a public meeting held at the home of Miss Florence V. Sill which resulted in the organization of the Cooperstown War Relief association which had as its purpose relief of suffering in Europe due to the World War and in the United States from unemployment. The officers were: Miss Sill, president; Mrs. H. L. Brazee, secretary, and Mrs. Nathaniel P. Willis, treasurer.

Dec. 10. Deputy Sheriff Scott Layten was severely cut on the right cheek as he was endeavoring to put a prisoner, who had obtained

a half pint of whiskey, in the tramp room of the county jail.   Sixteen
stitches were required to close the wound.

1915.—Jan. 3.   A rood screen, given by James Fenimore Cooper of
Albany and Fynmere in memory of his great grandfather, Judge William
Cooper, the founder of Cooperstown, was dedicated at Christ church.
The dedicatory sermon was preached by the rector, The Rev. Ralph
Birdsall.

Jan. 30.   An airplane constructed at the Francis Wagon Works in
this village was given a successful try-out on the frozen surface of Otsego
Lake.   The builder was a Cooperstown boy, J. Arthur Olson.

The Fenimore Mills property at Phoenix Mills was purchased early
in February of Martin Moakler by Lester I. Dingee of Philadelphia.

Feb. 22.   Samuel L. Warrin, a former member of the executive
board of the Orphan House of the Holy Saviour and the agent of the
Otsego County Society for the Prevention of Cruelty to Children, formally asked the State Board of Charities at Albany to remove Miss Victoria LeMoyne as superintendent.   The matter; which excited considerable local comment, reached a crisis on the day preceding when the
entire staff quit their positions upon return of Miss LeMoyne from a
two-weeks' vacation.   A number of the children also left but all were
located and returned to the home before nightfall.   Miss LeMoyne alleged that the movement was started by Mr. Warrin out of personal an-
tagonism to her.

March 6.   Acting for the First National Bank, holders of a large
part of the first mortgage of $15,000 against the property, Cashier
George H. White bought the Five-Mile Point Inn under proceedings
instituted by the holders of the second mortgage.   Mr. White's offer,
which was $5,000, was the only one received.   The property was form-
erly owned by Cooperstown business men who purchased the land of
Weddersoon & Whipple, when the old hotel, which stood on the
point, burned in 1908.   The sum of $15,000 was paid for the land and
over $20,000 spent in erecting the Inn, which was completed in 1909.
The investment was made by public spirited citizens in order to keep the
popular resort open to the public.   The business, however, proved dis-
appointing and the sale was the culmination of a rather complicated
business affair.   As a result the stockholders and holders of the second
mortgage bonds received no return whatever for the money they invested.   The holders of the first mortgage received about 25 per cent.
The property was purchased of Mr. White a few days later by J. Dana
Whipple.

In March Harry Freeman purchased the control of Herrieff's
Clothes Shop and conducted it thereafter under his personal management as Freeman's Clothes Shop.

March 15.   The Bundy & Cruttenden company was incorporated
and took over the business heretofore conducted under the titles of
Bundy Brothers and Bundy Brothers and Cruttenden.   The capital stock
was $27,000 and the incorporators were Lee B. Cruttenden, Mrs. Adelia
Bundy, Martin H. Bronner, Wilbur M. Bronner and Frank Lettis. Coin-
cident with the consummation of this transaction the Bronner Shoe

Store, conducted by W. M. Bronner, was purchased by Leon H. Ellsworth and M. H. Bronner closed out his furniture business to give his personal attention to the enterprise. Mr. Lettis, who had formerly been engaged in the dry goods business here and more lately of Fort Plain, was another active member of the organization.

April. 2 Twenty-one members of the Senior class of the Cooperstown High school left for a trip to Washington, D. C. Miss Antoinette K. Owens of the Faculty acted as chaperone.

Susquehanna avenue from Elm street to the river bridge was paved this spring.

Work on the state road from Cooperstown to Milford was commenced in April.

April 30. The Freeman's Journal company was reorganized Rowan D. Spraker and Harry H. Willsey were elected directors. The following were the officers: George H. Carley, president; Rowan D. Spraker, vice-president and Harry H. Willsey, secretary and treasurer.

May 10. Governor Charles S. Whitman accepted the resignation of the Hon. Nathaniel P. Willis as judge of the Court of Claims of the State of New York. Judge Willis held the office for only a short time when the prospect of dissolution of the Court under Constitutional revision made it seemingly unwise for him to close his office and discontinue a large law practice.

May 25. The sum of $400 for band concerts the coming summer was voted at a special village election.

June 7. Justice Albert H. Sewell in Supreme Court here granted an order changing the name of the Orphan House of the Holy Saviour to the Susan Fenimore Cooper Foundation, Inc., in honor of one whose work had played a great part in its founding. Later in the month the St. Christina School of Saratoga Springs was moved to Cooperstown and both it and the Foundation jointly conducted under the auspices of the Sisters of the Albany Diocese of the Protestant Episcopal church, in charge of Sisters Hilda and Pamela. The main building on Beaver street was called St. Saviour's House and the St. Christina school was opened in the Byard house on Pioneer street. At the final meeting of the Orphanage board resolutions were adopted expressing appreciation for the accomplishments of Miss Victoria E. LeMoyne as superintendent for a period of four years.

June 14. A resolution prohibiting the sale of Grade C milk in the corporate limits was adopted by the Board of Village Trustees.

June 28. W. Scott Root was elected president of the Cooperstown National bank to succeed the Hon. Andrew R. Smith, deceased. Frank M. Smith, son of the deceased president, was elected a member of the Board of Directors.

July 1. Ray F. Williams and Fred Lettis opened a meat market in the former Davidson block on Main street.

In July Otsego Lake rose eighteen inches in a comparatively short time establishing a new record for high water at this season of the year.

The first Redpath Chautauqua to be held in Cooperstown occurred in July.

July 23. Francis S. Marden, Jr., of New York City, coxswain of the Harvard Freshman crew, was drowned in Otsego Lake while swimming near the Spaulding dock.

Aug. 21. James J. Byard, Jr., of Cooperstown and Ceylon H. Lewis of Syracuse were appointed receivers of the Otsego & Herkimer Electric railroad by Federal Judge Ray of Norwich as a result of a disagreement between the stockholders and bondholders as to the financing of the enterprise. Mr. Byard had active charge of the road and S. Walter Mower continued as manager during the receivership which continued only about a month when the road was turned over to the Equitable Trust company of New York which had acquired all the securities.

Aug. 31. The final meeting of the summer of the local Emergency War Relief organization was held at the home of Mrs. Waldo C. Johnston.

Sept. 7. A large sum of money was raised for the American Red Cross at a benefit entertainment and fair held at the Village Club during the afternoon and evening. Mrs. Stephen C. Clark and Mrs. Isaac Vanderpoel were at the head of the committee in charge of the affair.

A Domestic Science or Homemaking course was established at the Cooperstown High school with the opening of the Fall term.

Sept. 20. George H. Carley, editor of the Freeman's Journal, succeeded George M. Wedderspoon as post master in Cooperstown.

Sept. 22. Vice-president Rowan D. Spraker became General Manager of The Freeman's Journal having purchased shares of stock in the company to equal those of Mr. Carley.

Oct. 3. The Hermitage, one of the most beautiful camps on Otsego Lake, eight miles from Cooperstown, was destroyed by fire. The property was owned by Dr. Devere S. Byard of New York City and was occupied at the time by the family of James J. Byard, Jr., of Cooperstown, who had barely time to escape although the greater part of their personal effects were lost.

The population of the village as shown by the state census was 2,662, a gain of 178 in five years.

In October a collection of sixty-five individual exhibits, the gift of Robert Sterling Clark to the Village Museum, arrived from Paris and was arranged for display. They included many relics and specimens gathered by Mr. Clark on his travels through this country, Europe, Asia and Africa.

Oct. 20. B. Albert Cook, who had acted as manager of the Star Theatre for eighteen months, became its proprietor.

Oct. 28. C. L. Stone of St. Louis, Mo., succeeded S. W. Mower as general manager of the Otsego & Herkimer railway.

Nov. 1. Water meters were installed in all services by the Cooperstown Aqueduct association and thereafter water users paid for the service on the basis of the amount used. Formerly the charge was made on a per-faucet basis.

Frank Stevens and Harrison B. Converse purchased the Pratt Feed Store on Railroad avenue.

CHAPTER VII

FROM 1916 TO 1920

1916.—Jan. 1. William C. Smalley of Mt. Upton leased the Village Hall and commenced the moving picture business in Cooperstown. At the outset he operated four evenings a week.

Feb. 1. Prof. W. H. Martin completed twenty-five years as director of the Alfred Corning Clark gymnasium. For more than a decade following this date, Prof Martin continued in active charge of the gymnasium and when he completed a term of thirty-six years in that position he left a deep impress upon the life of the community where he had ministered to the physical needs of old and young and took an active part in the advancement of all good causes. He died at 85, September 25, 1927, mourned by all.

Feb. 1. Lester Tunnicliff purchased the American Hotel and converted it into Tunnicliff Inn.

Feb. 18. John Totten, janitor of the First National Bank, committed suicide by shooting himself with a revolver while in the furnace room of the bank. He was fifty-three years of age, and out of regular employment.

March 1. Blake Norton, a carpenter of the village, who confessed to having set fire to the Brady Mills in January, 1915, pleaded guilty to an indictment charging arson in the third degree and was sentenced by Justice Rowland L. Davis to a term in Auburn state prison of not less than one year and five months and not more that two years and six months. He told the Court that he was intoxicated at the time and thought he started the fire to warm himself.

March 1. Overlook property on Pine street was purchased of the George B. Woodman estate by George H. White.

March 14. At the annual corporate election, the sum of $25,000 was appropriated for the construction of a new village sewer system.

April 1. Hiram D. Reed, a rural mail carrier, killed a snake in a snowbank, while making his deliveries and brought the reptile to the village.

April 17. Fred Bliss started a motor bus line between Cooperstown and Oneonta.

April 25. Michael McMoon resigned as sexton of the church of Our Lady of the Lake after twenty-one years of faithful service.

In June the contract to construct the new village sewer system was awarded by the Board of Trustees to Thomas W. Chapman and Lynn G. Parshall. Morrell Vrooman of Gloversville was engaged earlier in the year as supervising engineer. The work was commenced immediately and completed promptly.

June 15. The grocery firm of Beattie & Doubleday was dissolved, William Beattie having purchased the interest of his partner, William P. Doubleday.

June 29. Formal dedication of the beautiful new passenger station of the Delaware & Hudson railroad in this village. John K. Tener, president of the National Base Ball League; Harry M. Hempstead, president of the New York National League Club; Col. L. F. Loree, president of the Delaware & Hudson company, and Dr. John H. Finley, commissioner of the Department of Education of the State of New York, were among the prominent guests on this occasion. The principal address was made by Commissioner Finley. The building in every respect fulfilled the promise of the company to construct a station that should be a credit to the village.

July 10. Frank Hale was elected cashier of the First National Bank to take effect August 1.

Under an appropriation by the Village Trustees a series of concerts was given during the summer by the Cooperstown band.

July 15. Pursuant to consent granted by the Public Service Commission, the Otsego & Herkimer company, operating the electric line between Herkimer and Oneonta and connecting by a branch with Cooperstown, assumed the name, Southern New York Power and Railway corporation.

Aug. 1. The Cooperstown unit of the Otsego county Home Bureau was organized. Mrs. David R. Dorn was the first president.

Aug. 5. The Cooperstown Postoffice was moved from the Pioneer street building, now known as the Chamber of Commerce building, to the Story block on Main street, owned by George H. Carley.

Aug. 14. The town clock in the tower of the Village Hall was illuminated by action of the Board of Trustees.

Aug. 23. On account of the prevalence of an epidemic of infantile paralysis about the state it was determined to omit the holding of the Otsego County Fair this year. The date of the opening of the Union and High school was also postponed for several weeks on this account.

Sept. 16. The new G. A. R. monument in memory of the soldiers and sailors who fought in the Civil War, presented by Mr. Edward Severin Clark, and erected on the Court House grounds, was dedicated. The principal address was made by the Hon. George W. Ray of Norwich, Judge of the Federal Court.

Sept. 16. A ten-days' campaign to raise a large endowment fund for the Susan Fenimore Cooper foundation came to an end, the total subscribed at that time being $193,000.

James J. Byard, Jr., was chosen Democratic presidential elector from the thirty-fourth Congressional district in October.

Oct. 3-5. The Eighteenth annual convention of the New York State Historical society was held at the Village Hall. Among the speakers were Dr. Edward Page Mitchell, editor-in-chief of the New York Sun, and the Hon. Willard Bartlett, Chief Judge of the Court of Appeals of the State of New York.

In November the Colliers Light, Heat & Power company extended its electric service to Bowerstown.

Nov. 28. The annual convention of the thirteenth Capitular district of the Grand Chapter of Royal Arch Masons of the State of New

York was held in Cooperstown directed by R. W. Marshall F. Heminway, Grand Lecturer and James H. Gerling, assistant Grand Lecturer.

In December members of the Famous Players, Inc., came to Cooperstown and made moving pictures of the herds of sheep at Iroquois Farm to be used in the production of Dickens' "Great Expectation."

Dec. 10. John D. Larkin of Buffalo purchased the interest of Messrs. Edward Severin Clark, Stephen C. Clark and the Hon. Lynn J. Arnold in the Arthur H. Crist Co., publishing house located here.

Dec. 26. The Board of Village Trustees formally voted to accept the offer of Mr. and Mrs. William T. Hyde to donate the sum of $10,000 toward the cost of paving and improvement of Main street, under certain conditions relating to the manner in which the project should be carried out. This included the removal of wires and poles, erection of boulevard lights, planting of shade trees, etc.

1917.—In January the Clark Estates purchased the Jay Colburn farm, Grasslands. It was incorporated with the Iroquois Farm of Mr. F. Ambrose Clark. The same purchaser also acquired the vacant lot at the corner of Chestnut and Lake streets, formerly owned by L. Averill Carter.

The last week in January the three banks of this village announced that the rate of interest on savings accounts, Christmas clubs and certificates of deposit would be increased from three to four percent, compounded quarterly.

Otsego Hall, the well known summer hotel on Nelson avenue, was purchased of Mr. and Mrs. L. H. Spencer by the Clark Estates.

Feb. 12. Village President E. D. Boden announced that William E. Guy of St. Louis and Cooperstown had generously offered to donate the sum of $2,000 toward paving Nelson avenue. The gift was accepted.

The suit to recover damages in the amount of $5,000 brought by Miss Victoria E. Le Moyne, formerly Matron of the Orphan House of the Holy Saviour, against Samuel L. Warrin, a former member of the Board of Trustees of that institution for alleged slander, was tried at the February term of Supreme Court here before Justice M. H. Kiley and a jury. Miss Le Moyne alleged that Mr. Warrin was responsible for her dismissal as matron. The jury returned a verdict of no cause for action.

THE WORLD WAR STARTS

April 6. News of the President Woodrow Wilson's Proclamation that a state of war existed between Germany and the United States found Cooperstown loyally and unitedly ready to do its "bit" and more in every line of service. At a meeting held at the Village Hall March 22nd in anticipation of the eventuality of war, which by that time seemed certain thirty-nine young men signified their desire to form a local detachment of Company G of Oneonta. On April 8th, Easter Sunday, twenty-seven of these, who were successful in meeting the physical test, were sworn into service. They were Frederick Reynolds, George L. Deakin, John

W. Stiles, Cecil Champlin, Clyde Hayne, Franklin Hayne, Elmer Ellsworth, Robert Crandall, Harry Campbell, Milton Eckler, Robert B.
Lutes, Edward A. Francis, James Paul Francis, Louis Frankewich, Raymond K. Harvey, Harold Doolittle, Ambrose Campbell, Walter Campbell, Paul Sibley, Henry Reed, Henry House, James Douglas Johnson,
Robert Cobbett, Albin Johnson, Frank C. Bliss, George T. Record, Walter Herrick.

April 10. The pent-up feelings of patriotism burst forth on the
evening of this date when a great mass meeting in honor of the above
listed volunteers was held at the Court House, every seat and every inch
of standing room being filled. William Beattie presided and prayer
was offered by the Rev. Edward C. Petrie, pastor of the First Presbyterian church. Addresses were made by the Rev. Ralph Birdsall, Clermonte G. Tennant, the Hon. Nathaniel P. Willis, George H. Carley and
William L. McEwan.

April 18. Another great public demonstration took place on this
date when fully 2,000 people of the village and vicinity gathered at the
D. & H. station to bid farewell to the Volunteers—the first of the long
series of departing manhood groups to leave this station for the training
camps and thence, for a majority, for overseas service. The Volunteers,
however, first went to Oneonta where they were quartered at the Armory of Company G. Raymond Harvey and Ennis Durfee were enrolled before departure of the recruits and left with them for Oneonta.
Before the boys started they were presented with a purse of seventy-
five dollars by local business men; each with a "housewife" containing
scissors, needles, thread, etc., by the Cooperstown Rest club, and Mrs.
George H. White remembered each with a sum of money. Floyd
Brown, H. Lynn Marble and Raymond E. Gage, who also joined the
detachment, were detained here for a time to undergo operations, but
joined them later. Prayer was offered by Bishop J. W. Hamilton of
Washington, D. C., a few patriotic songs were sung, and the whistle of
the International Milk Products company sounded a long blast, the band
played "The Star Spangled Banner", as the train drew away from the
station.

April 5. At the Village Club several women's organizations of
Cooperstown, upon the invitation of the local unit of the National Surgical Dressings committee, which had been quietly carrying on war relief work for some time, met and formed a combined war relief association to become a detachment of the National League for Women's
Service. The organizations represented were the National Surgical
Dressings committee, Otsego Chapter, D. A. R., Cooperstown Suffrage
club and the Ladies' Auxiliary of the Sons of Veterans. A general committee was formed from the various organizations and the following
officers were elected : chairman, Miss Grace Scott Bowen; vice-chairman, Mrs. Richard Davidson; secretary, Mrs. Alexander Ogden Jones;
treasurer, Mrs. H. L. Brazee; chairman Red Cross committee, Miss
Florence V. Sill.

April 9. The taxpayers of the village voted, 262 to 36, to improve
Main street by laying a bitulithic pavement, installing boulevard lights
and planting shade trees. Toward this project Mr. and Mrs. Wm. T.

Hyde had offered to give the sum of $10,000. Village sewer bonds in the sum of $25,000 were sold to Isaac W. Sherrill & Co., Poughkeepsie, at $105.38.

April 11-16. The annual session of the Wyoming Conference was held here with Bishop Joseph W. Berry presiding.

April 21. One of sixty meetings held about the county for the purpose of mobilizing agriculture to the highest efficiency for the War was held in Cooperstown with Pierstown and Whig Corners cooperating. At about this time the Otsego county agricultural committee to cooperate with the Farm Bureau for these ends was appointed. It was composed of Messrs. Stephen C. Clark, George H. White, Floyd S. Barlow, Miss Florence H. Freer, Waldo C. Johnston, Douglas T. Johnston and Frank M. Smith. Harris L. Cooke of this village was selected to act as supervisor of the state military census to be taken in Cooperstown.

April 23. At a meeting of the Otsego County Agricultural society it was voted that no county fair be held this fall.

April 25. The Cooperstown Chapter, American Red Cross, was organized with 171 members and the following officers: Miss Florence V. Sill, president; Miss Helen Patterson, vice-president; Miss Maud L. Merchant, secretary; Mrs. Russel Warren, treasurer; William Beattie, Harris L. Cooke, Ceylon K. Lippitt, Ralph W. Ellsworth and Robert M. Bush, executive committee.

April 27. With resources of $3,500 and a charter membership of 201 the Cooperstown Chamber of Commerce was organized superseding the Board of Trade which had functioned here for some years. The first Board of Directors was Edward D. Boden, H. L. Brazee, Robert M. Bush, John F. Brady, James J. Byard, Jr., Stephen C. Clark, W. W. Hovey, W. T. Hyde, Douglas T. Johnston, Lee Kinne, Edward Martin, E. A. Rounds, Kenneth W. Root, Charles A. Scott, E. A. Stanford, C. L. Stone and N. P. Willis. The first officers were H. L. Brazee, president; C. L. Stone, first vice-president; W. W. Hovey, second vice-president; James J. Byard, Jr., secretary; Robert M. Bush, treasurer.

In May Douglas T. Johnston was appointed Otsego county representative of the New York State Food commission. Miss Bernice F. Mason was named his assistant.

The piece of land known as Fernleigh-Over was donated Cooperstown residents for use for small garden plots during the summer as a food relief project. The land which was plowed and harrowed was divided into plots, 30x40 feet each, and a nominal rental of one dollar each charged.

May 20. Cooperstown Council, No. 1879, Knights of Columbus was instituted at a largely attended meeting at the Village Hall with seventy-five charter members. The major degree was conferred by District Deputy Larkin and his degree team from Rome, N. Y. Other official dignitaries of the order present were Supreme Knight, James A. Flaherty of Philadelphia, State Deputy Finnegan of Brooklyn and Supreme Secretary William J. McGinley of Brooklyn. The first officers of the council were: Grand Knight, Edward I. King; Deputy Grand Knight, John V. Clark; Recorder, John Moakler, Jr.; Financial Secretary, James M. Lynch; Treasurer, Bernard W. Clark; Lecturer, John F. Ledwith; Chancellor, Wm. R. Adams; Advocate, J. Leo Falvey; Warden, Patrick O'Malley; Inside Guard, Matthew McDonough; Outside Guard, James B. Pepper; Trustees, John F. Brady, the Rev. T. J. McLaughlin, Malachi Kraham; Chaplain, the Rev. John C. Carey.

May 28. A $25,000 issue of Cooperstown paving bonds was sold to Sherrill & Co., of New York at $101.40.

July 1. Miss Ellen Wilson retired as village librarian. She had ably filled the office since 1898.

July 16. A whirlwind campaign for the sale of the first issue of Liberty bonds closed after a week's duration. A total of 1,064 subscriptions was taken amount to $420,850.

The fact that Cooperstown's connection with Indian affairs is not purely legendary was conclusively demonstrated in June when the skeleton of an Iroquois warrior was discovered by David R. Dorn and George N. Smith on an Indian site which was developed by Prof. W. K. Morehead and an expedition in May, 1916, just south of the village near the banks of the Susquehanna river. The skeleton was about eighteen inches beneath the surface of the ground. An Iroquois pipe and a steel hunting knife were found on the body. The only other object in the grave was an English gun flint. The find was placed in the village museum.

As a local addition to the intensive food campaign which was waged throughout the country in connection with the war, Mrs. F. Ambrose Clark established a complete community kitchen in the building adjoining the Alfred Corning Clark gymnasium which was provided through the generous act of Mr. Edward Severin Clark. All housewives of the community were invited to use the equipment for canning their fruits and vegetables. The kitchen was largely used and much surplus food preserved. Many modern canning ideas brought here by experts became the general practice in the community as a result of this project.

July 16. The members of Cooperstown detachment of Company G who had been on leave of absence at their homes here for a short time, having received orders to mobilize with the company at Oneonta, returned to the Armory there and were sworn into the Federal service.

The selective draft having been passed by Congress, Otsego county was divided into two districts, the first with headquarters at Oneonta, and the second with headquarters at Cooperstown. The Board in charge of the Cooperstown district was composed of Russel Warren, chairman, of Cooperstown, George T. Brockway of Richfield Springs, clerk, and Dr. H. V. Frink of Richfield Springs, physician. The rooms of the Board were located in the Grand Jury room of the Court House. The first quota from this district numbering sixty-five, was drawn the latter part of July. All counties were given credit for enlistments up to June 30th, thus materially reducing the quotas in both local districts. From this time on detachments from this district were constantly leaving for the mobilization camps as they were selected by the Boards and their physical condition passed under the rules of the draft.

The First Regiment of the New York National Guard of which Company G containing a large detachment of Cooperstown volunteers was a unit left September 25th for the camp at VanCortlandt Park, New York City, where it had been stationed since the middle of August, en route for the training camp at Spartansburgh, South Carolina. They were located in that place Oct. 1st.

Besides those mentioned already the Cooperstown detachment included the following who enlisted before the company left Oneonta: Leon Eckler, Burt Martin, Henry Martin, Clifford Ferris, Ennis Durfee, Leo Leach, Ralph Gage, Truman Smith, Albert Seeber, Lawrence Callahan, Frank Every.

Among the others from Cooperstown who had volunteered for service in the Army or Navy up to about this time were Sgt. John H. Clarke, Captain Joseph B. Cooke, Raymond Gage, Floyd Brown, Wilbur Wilson, Thomas Gilliland, Edson Cookingham, Major Robert S. Clark, Major Stephen C. Clark, Dr. Floyd J. Atwell, Robert D. Caney, Fred Stilson, Orazio Durso, George Scrum, Charles Gustafson, S. Beach Cooke, James Fenimore Cooper, Jr., Henry S. Cooper, Stephen J. Johnson, William E. Guy, Jr., David Wade Guy, Wm. Festus Morgan, Jr., William Quaif, Bowne Davidson, Lt. Donald P. Davidson, Ford Wedderspoon, Paul Grey, Robert S. Arnold, Alfred Cobbett, Dr. Arthur H. Martin, Joel Foster Bowers, George Brown, Ralph Hyde, Carlyle M. Keyes, Anthony McKim, R. Campbell Smith, Jr., Lemaire Zabriskie, Miss Florence Wardwell, Miss Hilda Larrabee. The above list contains names of several who were not residents of Cooperstown but who were members of well known Cooperstown families or members of the Cooperstown summer colony.

According to the records of the Edgewater Weather bureau, kept by Miss Florence Keese, the heat of the first part of the week of July 28th was the most excessive in the history of the village, the temperature ranging from 90 to 92 degrees. On the night of July 31st it did not fall below 80 degrees F.

Under newly enacted regulations relating to the sale of liquor the local excise board in August decided upon the following places in the town of Otsego where liquor might be sold: Carr's Hotel, Tunnicliff Inn, Hoffman House, Pioneer Hotel, Five-Mile Point Inn, Pratt's restaurant, the Arbor, in Cooperstown, and Matteson's Hotel at Oaksville. Under this provision five licenses in this village and three outside were denied.

Aug. 1. Ralph S. Baker of Perry, N. Y., assumed the position of secretary of the Chamber of Commerce. He was the first paid secretary ever employed by that organization.

Sept. 7. At a special village election the taxpayers voted 120 to 75, not to oppose the application of the Southern New York Railway corporation to abandon its franchise on Main street between Chestnut and Pioneer and on Pioneer to the Lake front, as the result of a considerable sentiment favoring the removal of the tracks from Main street which was being paved and improved. In this the railway company concurred. No tracks were ever built on Pioneer street.

Sept. 14. A new fire alarm code was adopted by the Fire department.

Oct. 1. The three local drug stores decided not to renew their
storekeepers' licenses but to take out druggists' licenses under which
alcohol could be sold for medical and industrial uses, and wines and
liquors upon a physician's prescription only.

In October the Otsego and Delaware Telephone company moved its
headquarters and switchboard from Main street to the Steere building,
formerly the residence of R. Heber White on Pioneer street, near Main.

In the campaign for the Second Liberty loan the sum of $510,000
was subscribed through the three Cooperstown banks.

Oct. 27. The flag pole erected at the "Four Corners," at the corner
of Main and Pioneer streets through the courtesy of W. C. Stokes, W.
C. Flanders, F. Ambrose Clark, James Fenimore Cooper, W. T. Hyde,
Stephen C. Clark and Alexander S. Phinney, was dedicated. The address of the occasion was made by Mr. Cooper. The first flag was presented by Miss Florence Virginia Sill.

Nov. 6. Following a campaign of several months' duration vigor-
ously conducted by the "drys," the town of Otsego gave negative majorities on the license question at the general election as follows: Saloons,
289; storekeepers', 275; hotels, 187. Pharmacists' licenses were granted
by a majority of 69. At the same election the town voted against woman
suffrage by a majority of 27. The proposition was carried in the ·state,
however.

This Fall a new 12-inch sewer was laid from the International Milk
Products company plant along Grove street and including Beaver and
Delaware streets. The company paid one half of the cost which amount-
ed to about $6,000.

In November the pinch of the war as regards rations began to be
felt in the village with housewives closely rationed on sugar and flour
which were doled out in lots of a few pounds, when it could be obtained
at all.

The new Main street pavement, with shade trees and boulevard
lights, was completed in December.

Dec. 7. Vito Candello, convicted of attempted murder in the
second degree, in County Court here, was sentenced by Judge A. L.
Kellogg to a term of not more than sixteen years and six months and not
less than ten years at Auburn state prison. Candello was indicted for
attempting to murder Francisco Spano, a fellow workman at the home
of W. T. Hyde, July 11th.

1918.—The year opened with the village deeply immersed in war
work and all loyal citizens devoting their energies to backing up at
home the boys at the front. In addition to the rationing of food in effect
in the preceding year January was not past until the order of the National Fuel Administration brought four so-called "lightless" nights per
week, when the use of all illumination exclusive of dwellings was reduced to a minimum and all places of business, industries, etc., except
those engaged in the sale of food, drugs, etc., were closed one day a
week—Mondays generally speaking. The county was organized for

the sale of War Saving Stamps—Baby Bonds—with George H. White of Cooperstown, chairman. The Hon. Adrian A. Pierson of this village was the chairman for the town of Otsego. A goodly sum of money was raised in this manner. Drives for the support of the work of the Y.M.C.A., Knights of Columbus and other organizations among the soldiers were common and well supported. In January George H. Carley in charge of the first local Y.M.C.A. campaign reported over $1,000 raised here for that organization.

Jan. 21. After several months of investigation the Cooperstown Chamber of Commerce purchased of Otsego Lodge, No. 138, F. & A. M., its three-story stone building on Pioneer street at $4,000. The building was made a community headquarters with offices for the Otsego County Farm and Home Bureaus, 4-H Clubs on the second floor, while on the first floor was opened a general committee room for all organizations, rest room, officers for the County S. P. C. C., and Chamber of Commerce offices.

In February J. Dana Whipple sold the Five-Mile Point Inn and thirty acres of land to Bruce L. Beals of Scranton, Pa., who established a summer residence there.

Feb. 16. The Cooperstown Savings and Loan association, which was incorporated and chartered early in the year opened an office in the Chamber of Commerce Building. The association was formed as one of the first projects of the Chamber of Commerce during the first year of its existence. The first officers were: President, M. E. Lippitt; vice-president, R. W. Ellsworth; secretary, Ralph S. Baker; treasurer, B. Frank Murdock; auditors, Frank B. Shipman and Fred P. Fuller; appraisers, James J. Byard, Jr., W. P. K. Fuller and Charles A. Scott; reappraisement, John F. Brady, Melvin C. Bundy; attorney, James J. Byard, Jr.; executive committee, M. E. Lippitt, Ralph W. Ellsworth, Ralph S. Baker and B. F. Murdock, Jr. These held office until the first annual meeting.

Feb. 25. Louis G. Freiss of New York City purchased the grounds of the Otsego County Agricultural society in this village at $12,000. The only other bid was made by Charles T. Brewer for the Second National Bank, the holders of the mortgage. The property, which includes about twenty-six acres of land and adequate buildings in excellent repair, had been held by the society since about 1870. For many years it was a successful enterprise but for some time preceding the sale the annual Fairs had failed to pay so that a balance of some $3,000 was wiped out and a debt gradually accumulated, augmented by fire loss, which finally brought the grounds under the hammer. Arthur H. Crist was elected president of the society in 1916 and a movement to place it on a sound financial basis was well under way but came to nothing when an epidemic in the county of infantile paralysis prevented the holding of a Fair that Fall. No Fair was held in 1917 on account of the exigencies of the World War.

In March it was reported that there was one automobile for each fifteen people in Otsego county.

The Cooperstown postoffice to March 2nd had reported sales of $1,379 in War Saving stamps and $4,123 in Thrift Stamps.

March 11. At the Village election the propositions to expend $400 for band concerts and $200 for support of the Fire department were carried.

Harris L. Cooke, local fuel administrator, in March promulgated instructions from the national body, laying down rules under which coal might be obtained. Dealers were allowed to deliver only two-thirds of the amount ordered over six tons until all similar orders had been filled, and consumers were required to fill out a blank showing amount used the preceding year and the amount required for the following year, the amounts ordered from other dealers, etc.

Another indication of the stringency of war conditions is the following extract from a statement published in March by the local dry goods dealers: "War time conditions in the mercantile field have become serious. Goods are scarce and hard to get. Prices are constantly changing and every merchant who successfully meets the conditions with justice to all his customers, must practice economy in every department of his business. A committee of local dry goods merchants has recently met and agreed on certain reforms in discounts, and, cancelled the sending of all piece goods, except floor coverings, to customers' homes."

April 3. Military drill began at the High school grounds of all boys of the ages of 16, 17, and 18 years, in accordance with the universal military training law. First Lieutenant Henry G. McLaury of Company G., 10th Infantry, New York Guard, was in command.

April 9. Harris L. Cooke, Chairman of the towns of Otsego, Middlefield and Hartwick, for the third Liberty Loan, announced that the quota for the district was $324,700. The campaign was in progress for three weeks and the sum of $446,150 was raised, Cooperstown subscribing $415,150 of that amount.

In April James Fenimore Cooper made a gift of a $1,000 Liberty Bond to the First Presbyterian church in memory of his grandmother, Mrs. Catherine Fuller Barrows, and his mother, Mrs. Mary Barrows Cooper. Another gift of $200 to be used in redecorating the Chapel was made at about the same time by Mrs. Hannah Pickens, as a memorial to her son, Guy M. Pickens.

April 30. According to its first annual report the Cooperstown Chapter, American Red Cross, during the year shipped 110 cases of war supplies over seas including 40,611 articles. Among these were: compresses, 12,075; rolled bandages, 4,121; triangular bandages, 3,763; abdominal bandages, 1,768; T bandages, 1,006; gauze wipes and sponges, 4,319; absorbent and irrigation pads, 2,115; hospital shirts, 1,625, and other articles too numerous "to mention."

May 4. The petition of David H. Willsey, president of the village, to compel the assessors to assess the property of the village in accordance with article 6 of the Tax Law was granted by the State Tax commission. Under this ruling village property, formerly assessed at about 35 per cent of its true value, has since been assessed at its full value. The action was taken because by a provision of the village charter the trustees are bound not to levy a tax of more than ten dollars per thousand upon the assessed valuation of the property. The expenses of the village had increased by this date to such a point that it became impossible to pay the bills which the taxpayers had authorized and keep within this ratio. The simple expedient of increasing the assessments to their full value was resorted to to relieve the situation.

May 15. At a meeting held at the Clark Estate offices it was announced that the Otsego County Fair Grounds, which were sold at auction earlier in the year, were bought by Mr. Edward Severin Clark and that the Fair would be continued as soon as the War was over.

May 18. A local drive for the American Red Cross was opened with a parade including more than 1,000 members of the Cooperstown chapter, other women's organizations, school children, business men, floats, the Cooperstown band and Hartwick Fife and Drum Corps, followed by field day sports and exercises. The week's events also included a ball and cabaret. The total sum contributed was $11,535.89, the quota being $5,000.

May 25. The current was turned on the new boulevard lights on Main street for the first time.

June 9. The pump house of the Cooperstown Aqueduct association was badly damaged by fire.

June 12. Sugar, by order of the food commission, was sold in the village in amounts not exceeding two pounds to an individual—when there was any to sell.

June 15. The large new stone barn at the Fenimore Farm of Mr. Edward Severin Clark was opened with a dinner to 150 employees who had a part in its construction. The barn has stanchions for eighty head of cattle and is modern in every particular. Frank P. Whiting of New York City was the architect.

In June the Government accepted the offer of Mr. Edward Severin Clark to place the new Mary Imogene Bassett Hospital, in process of erection here, at its disposal for use as a hospital for convalescent aviators. The work was rushed to completion. The Alfred Corning Clark gymnasium, the Village Club and the golf links were thrown open to the aviators, the majority of whom were officers, and everything possible was done the make their stay here enjoyable.

June 22-23. The State Conference of Chamber of Commerce Secretaries was held here with nearly thirty cities represented.

June 30. Edward D. Lindsay was elected cashier of the Cooperstown National Bank succeeding Robert M. Bush, who resigned after filling that position for a period of eleven years.

July 1. Pathfinder's Lodge, the camp established by Miss Valerie Deuscher at "The Dugway" on the east side of Otsego Lake, opened for its first season.

In July the poles and wires of the Southern New York Power company were removed from Main street.

During the summer, F. Ambrose Clark introduced an innovation at the Iroquois Farm by the replacement on account of the war of five men employed at the dairy house by five young women from New York and Brooklyn. Two of the "dairy maids" looked after the herd of forty prize cows, cleaned the stables, and managed the milking machines; two others attended to the separating of the milk, the bottling and butter making while the fifth had charge of the milk route.

July 4. Independence Day was celebrated by a program of athletic events, a parade and addresses by Governor Charles S. Whitman and Justice Abraham L. Kellogg of the Supreme Court with a street dance in the evening. Thousands attended the event.

July 11. The Cooperstown platoon of Co. G, New York Guard, formed here to be a part of the company replacing for home duty the National Guard, now overseas, had its first drill in uniform.

On account of the difficulty experienced by the Clark Estates by reason of war conditions in securing labor, many men of the village turned out and assisted in work toward the completion of the Mary Imogene Bassett Hospital which had been turned over to the Government for use as a convalescent hospital for aviators.

Aug. 7. Ernest Thompson Seton, the noted naturalist, author and lecturer, presided at a Grand Council at Pathfinder's Lodge on Otsego Lake.

Through voluntary labor contributed by Contractor David H. Willsey and his force of carpenters as well as by several other interested citizens two new bath houses were erected at Three-Mile Point for the use of bathers.

Aug. 16. The sum of nearly $300 for the improvement of Three-Mile Point was raised at a Street Fair held under the auspices of the Chamber of Commerce.

Aug. 22. John Kendrick Bangs, the American author, was the speaker at a lawn fete at Brookwood Point, the summer home of Mrs. F. dePuyster Townsend which netted the sum of $300 for the relief of devastated parts of France.

Aug. 23. The International Milk Products company, with plants at Cooperstown, Schenectady, Middleville, Gouverneur and New York City was taken over by the Nestle Food company.

Sept. 19. At a special election the voters of the town of Otsego gave large majorities, roughly 5 to 1, in favor of no license on all four propositions.

Miss Ella R. Falvey, superintendent of Thanksgiving Hospital for seven years, left the last week in September for her home at Camden, N. Y. She was succeeded by Miss Marletta S. Newell, who had been the assistant superintendent for some time.

In October and November, Cooperstown was in the grip of the terrible epidemic of influenza which swept the country. Churches, schools and theatres were closed and all public gatherings prohibited by order of the Board of Health. Hardly a home or an individual escaped the ravages of the disease and there were several deaths. A diet conducted by the local Red Cross Chapter, supplied many homes where all members were ill without the possibility of securing help or nurses and brought relief of a valued nature.

The local campaign for the Fourth Liberty Loan closed in October. Cooperstown, with a quota of $570,200 subscribed $615,900 in this campaign. Harris L. Cooke was the chairman of the Cooperstown organization.

In October the Geiger-Crist company was organized in connection with the Arthur H. Crist company, of this village and brought the business and mechanical equipment of Today's Housewife from Canton, O., where it had heretofore been published by H. M. Geiger, to Cooperstown.

Nov. 7. The rule prohibiting public gatherings on account of the influenza epidemic was lifted by the Board of Health.

THE WAR ENDS

Nov. 11. News of the signing of the Armistice by Germany reached Cooperstown at 3:10 a. m., just twenty-five minutes after it had been officially sent out from Washington. At exactly 4 o'clock the whistle of the Nestle plant was sounded and the great news was passed like wild fire to the awakened populace, and from then on until a late hour at night the village celebrated with all the abandon with which it had entered into every branch of war service. The church bells rang, tin pans, tin horns, tin wash tubs and every other sort of noise-making article was pressed into service, and pandemonium broke loose. The morning was chiefly occupied by the citizens in parading the streets and serenading leading citizens who joyfully responded to invitations to express their sentiments on the victory of the Allies. Impromptu parading continued until 2 in the afternoon, when school having been dismissed, a formal parade started from the High school building led by the children and proceeded to Main street where short exercises were held at the Liberty Pole at the Four Corners. All business places and manufacturing plants were closed for the day and everybody devoted themselves to the expression of personal jubilation. But there was a still greater parade in the evening. Promptly at 7 o'clock the line formed at the Village Hall with H. R. Skirving as marshal and led by the Cooperstown Platoon of Company G it made its way up and down Main street again and again extending the whole length of the business section while red fire burned along the curbing. At the close the crowd proceeded to the Court House opposite which on the Byard lot at the corner of Main and Pine streets a monster bonfire was lit and an effigy of the Kaiser, termed "the beast of Berlin," was burned, while the crowd led by the band joined in singing patriotic songs and thus in Cooperstown ended "Der Tag" on which the German war lords had been counting for so many years.

In the references to the opening of the war many of the volunteers who early enlisted in the service were mentioned. A more complete list will be found at the end of this history.

The Cooperstown boys who at the outset of the war volunteered for service with Company G remained in France in the vicinity of Amiens after the signing of the Armistice until a few days previous to Thanksgiving when they were transported to the Embarkation Area near Le Mans and the most of them returned during the first three months of the year 1919.

Company G was drafted into Federal service August 5, 1917, and was transferred to the famous 107th Regiment October 10, 1917. It was in training at Camp Wadsworth, Spartanburg, S. C., for seven months and left America May 10, 1918, embarking from Newport News. Two of the vessels which carried the boys overseas were the Antigne and the Susquehanna.

Landing at Brest, May 24, 1918, they were brigaded partly with the British Army which included the Australians under Sir General Ronaldson, and were engaged on the British sector in skirmishes, battles, engagements, and expeditions on the East Popernighe Line, Dickiebusch sector; Hindenburg line, Lasalle river, Jonc De mer and St. Maurice river.

The record of heroism and accomplishment of the 107th Regiment is one that will ever live in the history of the World War. As a specific illustration of the high place which the regiment held in the minds of the commanders the following letter is published from among many as a fitting commentary to go down in the annals of our village:

"Now that the American Second Corps is leaving the British Zone, I wish once more to thank you all, officers, non-commissioned officers and men under your command, on behalf both of myself and all ranks of the British Armies in France and Flanders, for the very gallant and efficient service you have rendered during the period of your operations with the Fourth British Army.

"On the 29th of September you took part with distinction in the great and critical attack which shattered the enemy's resistance in the Hindenburg line and opened the road to final victory. The deeds of the 27th and 30th American Divisions, who on that day took Bellicourt and Nauroy and so gallantly sustained the desperate struggle for Bony, will rank with the highest achievements of this war. They will always be remembered by the British regiments that fought beside you.

"Since that date, through three weeks of almost continuous fighting, you advanced from one success to another, overcoming all resistance, beating off numerous counter attacks and capturing several thousand prisoners and many guns. The names of Brancourt, Premont, Busigny, Vaux Andigny, St. Souplet and Mazinghein testify to the dash and energy of your attack.

"I rejoice at the success which has attended your efforts and I am proud to have had you under my command.

"(Signed)   D. HAIG, Field Marshal."

Dec. 9. At the annual meeting of the Otsego County Agricultural society Mr. Edward Severin Clark was elected president and it was announced that the annual Fair, suspended for two seasons, would be resumed in the Fall of 1919.

Dec. 16. Ralph S. Baker, for a year and a half the paid secretary of the Chamber of Commerce, tendered his resignation to take effect January 1st.

1919.—Jan. 1. The law firm of Cooke & Basinger was formed by Harris L. Cooke and Harold T. Basinger succeeding the firm of Arnold & Cooke, Judge Lynn J. Arnold having retired from the partnership.

Cooperstown's last livery business conducted by L. M. Barnum for many years passed early in the year when he disposed of his horses and equipment at public auction at the Hartson stables. This property was purchased by J. Harry Cook, who moved Cook's Auto & Supply company there and opened a garage and machine shop. Thus the motor car supplanted the horse as a commercial enterprise as it had already begun to in private and business use. In ten years from this date, where Cooperstown formerly boasted three livery stables, it came to support a half dozen or more large and thoroughly equipped garages and machine shops with many gas and service stations.

Jan. 1. Justin Lange resumed the proprietorship of Carr's Hotel, which for a number of years had been conducted by John W. Brown, who retired from the Hotel business at this time.

Jan. 13. Edward A. Stanford became secretary of the Cooperstown Chamber of Commerce.

The first of the year Mrs. Della Thompson Lutes, who came to Cooperstown eleven years preceding, to become Editor of American Motherhood, was appointed editor of Today's Housewife, a position which she held with distinction as long as the magazine was published here.

By the first of February there were fifty aviators located at the Mary Imogene Bassett Hospital, being operated by the U. S. Government through the generosity of the owners, as a recreation and convalescent institution. The aviators were cordially received in local social circles.

Feb. 17. Frank C. Carpenter became owner of a third interest in the Freeman's Journal company, the remaining portion being owned by George H. Carley and Rowan D. Spraker. The reorganized firm purchased the Hartson block on Pioneer street at this time to which the business was moved at a later date from the Ironclad building on Main street. Mr. Carpenter owned a half interest in the John Wilcox company at Milford, publisher of the Milford Tidings and doing a large mail-order business in school novelties, which was taken over by the purchase of the remaining interest from the widow of the late Mr. Wilcox.

Feb. 17. A new era dawned in village politics when a union ticket was named by the two party caucuses for the annual charter election, March 11th. It was the unanimous opinion of both caucuses that a political fight annually in the selection of village officers was unwise and contrary to the best interests of the community. A mutual understanding was established which, with the exception of one year, has been carried out down to date under which the offices are alternated between the two parties, one caucus nominating half the candidates and the other the remainder, each endorsing the other's selections Thus the party entities are maintained without subjecting candidates to the annoyance of conducting a political campaign.

March 20. The Freeman's Journal company, Inc., was sold to Augustus Paul Cooke, who had only recently returned to Cooperstown after an absence of seven years in the Southwest. The principal stockholders of the company before the sale were George H. Carley, Rowan D. Spraker and Frank C. Carpenter who also owned the John Wilcox company at Milford This business they continued.

March 30. Daylight saving was observed in Cooperstown this summer the clocks being set one hour ahead on this date.

April 1. Albert Simonson became the village ice dealer having purchased the business of George B. Horton.

Early in April William T. Hyde, owner of Glimmerglen Farms turned over his summer home, "Glimmerglen," on Otsego Lake to the Military Relief department of the American Red Cross to be used as a hostess house for the patients at the U. S. Aviation hospital here.

The use of the Hyde house caused the removal of this phase of the war relief work from the home of Mrs. F. dePuyster Townsend at Brookwood Point where it had been located since January.

On April 1st Adrian A. Pierson, district attorney of Otsego county, announced the dissolution of the law firm of Campbell & Pierson owing to the decision of his partner, J. Samuel Campbell to remain indefinitely in the new position with the government administrative bureau of the Canal Zone at Panama, which he had recently taken up. The firm was in existence for ten years.

April 26-28. Fifty members of the State College Y.M.C.A. Secretaries' association gathered here in annual convention.

In the latter part of April the Rev. Father Miles Lowell Yates accepted the call to become rector permanently of Christ church. Father Yates came to Cooperstown in the summer of 1918 to assist the Rev. Ralph Birdsall during his illness and continued the work of the church after the Rev. Mr. Birdsall's death.

May 3. Miss Mildred L. McEwan, aged 22, daughter of William L. McEwan of this village, and Lt. Smith Clark, aged 22, of San Diego, Calif., a patient at the aviation hospital here, were drowned in Otsego Lake when the canoe from which they were watching an airplane, capsized. The accident occurred north of Kingfisher Tower. The body of Miss McEwan was recovered after a five-days' search about fifty feet from the shore and in 75 feet of water; that of Lt. Clark twenty-four hours earlier in about 100 feet of water, twenty yards from shore.

May 9. Cooperstown subscribed the sum of $450,200 for the Victory Loan, conducted by the Government. The quota was $419,300. George H. Carley was the local chairman.

May 12. The three National banks of Cooperstown had combined deposits of four and a half million dollars. Based on the population of the banking district this showed an average per capita wealth of $1,000.

May 20. The last of the aviators at the Rest and Recreation Hospital quartered at various places in town awaiting the completion of the Mary Imogene Bassett Hospital were moved to the new building by this date. The patients at this time numbered ninety.

May 23. Horace Seegar, aged thirty years, shot and killed himself in a secluded spot on Hannah's Hill. He was believed demented.

June 2. The Phinney lot, located in the heart of the village between Main street and Susquehanna avenue, was leased for a period of two years by the Playgrounds committee of the Chamber of Commerce, and thus Cooperstown first came into possession of historic Doubleday Field where according to the decision rendered in 1908 by the National Base Ball commission, Abner Doubleday, later Major-General Doubleday, laid out the first base ball diamond and invented the national game.

In July, Edgewater, the stately home of the Keese family for nearly three-quarters of a century, was purchased by Arthur M. Field of Asheville, N. C., possession being given April 1, 1920. Construction of the house was commenced in 1804 by Isaac Cooper, a brother of James Fenimore Cooper, and one of the most promising young lawyers of his day. Three years were spent before the house was completed. The

Cooper family occupied it only a short time, their residence having been cut short by the death of Mr. Cooper. It was used as a girls' seminary for several years and in about the year 1840 it was purchased by Theodore Keese. In about 1849 when his son, G. Pomeroy Keese was married to Caroline A. Foote, the young bridegroom and his bride moved to Edgewater and lived there in happy married life for more than sixty years. Fifty years after their wedding reception, there was held on the same lawn, their golden wedding celebration. Mr. Field has since completely restored and improved the property.

July 20. After having been closed for two months for improvements during which time services were held in the chapel, the Presbyterian church was opened. The interior of the auditorium was completely redecorated in amber shades, pilasters and an arch in the predominating colors of the woodwork set off the organ transcept from the rest of the church, and two beautiful doors of Gothic design, the gift of Mrs. Sands Shumway and family in memory of Lansing T. Shumway, were placed between the church and the vestibule.

July 28. Lieutenant George Schofield, a patient in the U. S. Aviation hospital here, swam from the Springfield landing to the Otesaga dock in approximately six hours. He was accompanied by another aviation officer in a row boat.

Aug. 12. The Glimmerglass, the summer daily newspaper, was sold by the Freeman's Journal company, to the John Wilcox company the daily, in fact, reverting to the same publishers who began it in 1909.

Aug. 13. The annual convention of the New York State Sheep Breeders' association brought more than 300 delegates to Cooperstown.

Sept. 1. The Otsego County Fair, omitted for a time on account of the war and other reasons, was resumed through the generosity of Mr. Edward Severin Clark, who purchased the grounds and led in the reorganization of the society.

An ice famine early in September of two days' duration was relieved when A. Simonson, the local dealer, secured a supply of ice from Norwich.

Sept. 23. The contract for the Three-Mile Point-Springfield Center-Warren state road construction was let by the State Highway department to the Dale Engineering company at Utica at $328,811.

According to the will of Mrs. Jasper Schrom, offered for probate in the Surrogate's Court, in September the sum of $2,000 was bequeathed to Miss Nellie Clinton of Marcy Hall, the income to be used for the purpose of caring for her pet cats.

Sept. 29. Waldo C. Johnston, agent of the Clark Estates and a former captain in the air service, and Lieutenant Sheridan flew in a giant war plane from New York City to Cooperstown in ninety minutes.

Oct. 20. William C. Smalley, who for some time had operated the Village Theatre, a motion picture house, purchased Carr's Hotel from Justin Lange. Mr. Lange first bought the property from the Carr

Estate in 1904, operated it for seven years, and then sold it to John W. Brown who sold it back to Mr. Lange January 1st of this year.

Oct. 21. The U. S. Aviation hospital, in operation in Cooperstown for nearly a year, was officially closed, with the departure of Col. Nelson A. Gapen and his staff and Master Hospital Sergeant Martin and his staff of enlisted men. During the time the hospital was located here more than 500 officer patients were treated, the highest number at one time being 112. Major Francis H. Poole, Major A. E. Ludwick and Col. Gapen were in command successively.

Nov. 4. The town of Otsego again voted dry on all propositions at the general election.

Nov. 6. The local post of the American Legion, later Clark F. Simmons Post, No. 579, was organized. The first officers were: President, Dr. F. J. Atwell; first vice-president, William P. Little; second vice-president, Stephen C. Clark; third vice-president, Mrs. Alma J. Barnes; secretary, Frederick L. Reynolds; treasurer, Alfred R. Cobbett.

1920.—Early in the year Melvin C. Bundy purchased the Hotchkiss Farm of 360 acres, a mile and a half west of the village, and took immediate possession.

An important business transaction was consummated in January when Charles A. Scott took over the interest of Mrs. H. A. C. Church in the long established drug firm of Church & Scott. Following this action the business was incorporated with the name remaining unchanged. The directors were Charles A. Scott, Ernest M. Clapsaddle and S. P. Scott with Mr. Scott, president and treasurer, Mr. Clapsaddle, vice-president, and S. P. Scott, secretary. The business was founded by Henry C. Church, later became Shumway & Church and later still, Church & Lamb. Mr. Scott had been connected with the business for twenty-five years and Mr. Clapsaddle for twenty-three years. The firm of Church & Scott was formed in 1899, and had continued without change for a longer period than any other firm then doing business on Main street.

In January the Court of Appeals sustained the will of the late William C. Rhinelander of New York City under which the Susan Fenimore Cooper Foundation received a legacy of $8,000 and had a contingent interest to the extent of $12,000, in a trust fund created thereby.

Supreme Court Justice Michael H. Kiley in January decided a legal controversy which arose between W. Scott Root and Dr. John B. Conkling over the matter of sewer rights, in favor of Dr. Conkling. The houses of the litigants adjoined on Nelson avenue and Mr. Root sought to establish his right to sewer across Dr. Conkling's property.

Jan. 18. A blizzard which raged for three days came to an end. At one time while it was in progress the temperature dropped to twenty-five degrees below zero. Drifts on the Southern New York line between Mohawk and Richfield Springs were higher than the cars.

Jan. 30. G. Reed Sill purchased the half interest in the business of Taylor and Ellsworth, dry goods merchants, which had been held by Mrs. Ralph W. Ellsworth since the death of her brother, the late Arthur

J. Taylor, and the new firm became known as Ellsworth & Sill. The business was founded by Mr. Taylor in 1898 in what was then known at the Tyley store in the Basinger block and Mr. Ellsworth became connected therewith in 1904. In December of that year the firm of Taylor and Ellsworth was formed.

Feb. 1. L. A. Pratt took possession of the Pioneer Hotel and it became Hotel Pratt. Many notable improvements were made in the property.

In February it was announced that the receipts of the Cooperstown postoffice having jumped from over $20,000 to over $80,000 a year since Today's Housewife, a magazine published by the Geiger-Crist company, later the Cooperstown Press, there was every reason to believe that the office would be classified in the first class.

Cooperstown was entirely isolated from February 15th to 17th by a great storm which raged for two days unabated. All travel by steam, electricity, motor car or horsedrawn vehicles was prevented by the great drifts. Schools were closed and church services omitted. Business was at a standstill. It was the worst storm the village had experienced since March 1, 1914. The snow stood over four feet deep on the level.

Feb. 22. At a meeting held at the Court House which was called by the local post of the American Legion, twenty-three certificates of gratitude from the French government to the next of kin of the men who lost their lives in the World War were presented with fitting ceremonial. The recipients were Frank M. Bliss, Mrs. Mary F. Hopkins, Frank Herrick, Mrs. Emma Hecox, Mrs. Elva Kilts, Mrs. Nora Strong, Mrs. Odella Johnson, Mrs. Charles Coleman, Mrs. Minnie Genter, Mrs. Mina Turner, Mrs. Edward Odell, Riley Miller, Mrs. Julia Manzer, Abe Winn, Mrs. Lillian R. Armstrong, Mrs. William Cobbett, James E. Stiles, Daniel Linney, Mrs. Effie Kaemerling, Fenimore Peet, Martin Ward, James C. Hayne, Mrs. L. J. Reed. Not all the above were residents of Cooperstown but were included in the territory covered by the Post. Dr. F. J. Atwell, Post commander, presided and addresses were made by Judge Nathaniel P. Willis and Clermonte G. Tennant.

March 9. At the corporation election this year there were two tickets in the field representing the Republican and Democratic parties. The Republicans favored fusion but the Democrats declined to continue the plan. The result of the election showed the voters strongly desirous of eliminating politics from village elections as every candidate on the Democratic ticket was defeated with the exception of one constable. Proposals to appropriate $15,000 to pave Elm street and $5,000 for the purchase of the Phinney lot, where Doubleday Field is now located, were defeated at this election.

March 15-16. Another great blizzard more paralyzing to traffic than the storm of February closed the northern end of the Southern New York line, from Richfield Springs to Mohawk, for more than a week and caused the line serious loss.

April 2. At a meeting of the Board of Directors of the First National Bank George H. White was elected president to succeed Judge Lynn J. Arnold.

Cooperstown observed Daylight Saving Time this summer, the clocks having been set ahead early in April.

The Cooperstown Platoon, New York Guard, of which George H. Carley was commander, continued its activities for some time following the war and used rooms in the Murdock block on Main street as an armory which was suitably fitted up at the expense of the state.

In April, William C. Smalley, who a short time preceding purchased the property, closed the portion of Carr's Hotel formerly used as the bar and reading room. J. Harry Cook conducted the main portion of the hotel which he owned, as a rooming house.

In May the U. S. Senate confirmed the reappointment of George H. Carley as postmaster for a second term of four years dating from January 6.

The name "Templeton Lodge" was resumed by the hotel on Nelson avenue replacing "Otsego Hall" which had been in use for several years.

June 1. M. F. Augur, proprietor of Augur's Corner Bookstore, purchased and took possession of the block at the southeast corner of Main and Pioneer streets in which the business is located.

June 5. The Freeman's Journal, which had been conducted for fourteen months by Augustus Paul Cooke as editor and proprietor, reverted to the former owners.

June 23. The annual summer meetings of the Associated Dailies of New York State, the New York State Press association and the Susquehanna Valley Press association were held contemporaneously in Cooperstown, a three-day session opening on this date. The meetings were held at the Court House and a shore dinner was served at Three-Mile Point following a trip around the Lake on the Steamer Mohican.

July 9. Operation of the Southern New York Railway which was tied up by a strike existing for five days was resumed under an agreement reached through the intercession of the Cooperstown Chamber of Commerce which provided for the arbitration of the question of wages, the employees having accepted the principle known as the "open shop."

The census of 1920 showed the population of Cooperstown as 2,725 an increase of 241 in ten years.

The State of New York spent about $5,000 for repairs to the Cooperstown Armory this summer.

The Southern New York Railway improved its roadbed on Chestnut street this year by making important repairs including a new concrete pavement between the tracks, new base and new rails. The work was in progress several months. At one time the condition of Chestnut street became practically impassible and the Chamber of Commerce took the matter to the Public Service commission.

During the summer the Cooperstown Chamber of Commerce conducted a subscription campaign to raise funds for the purchase of Doubleday Field an option for which had been secured in 1919. The committee in charge was Dr. E. L. Pitcher, George H. Carley, L. J. Gross, Dr. H. L. Cruttenden and M. F. Augur. This committee succeeded in raising a goodly sum and especial efforts made individually by Dr. Pitcher, who took a most active interest in the matter for a long period, brought in subscriptions from all over the country.

The greater part of the construction of the concrete state highway between Three-Mile Point and Springfield Center was completed this year. The Dale construction company of Utica did the work.

In September the Geiger-Crist company purchased a site on Nelson avenue and commenced the erection of a model home and testing house for Today's Housewife. The house, for which the material was furnished by the Aladdin company, was completed, furnished and thoroughly equipped in due time and was operated until the publishing house was closed here. It was then purchased by Bruce L. Hall, who occupies it as a dwelling at present.

Sept. 6. President John A. Heydler of the National Base Ball League was in Cooperstown and umpired an inning of a base ball game between Cooperstown and Milford teams in formal opening of Doubleday Field. He was accompanied by Umpire McCormick of the National League who officiated during the balance of the contest. The movement to establish at this field a national memorial to the founder of the game, General Abner Doubleday, for whom the field was named, was instituted. This movement has taken several forms to date but has as yet failed of consummation. The subscription fund raised by the Chamber of Commerce on this date amounted to $3,019, to which was added $450 as the result of a Street Fair and gate receipts to the opening game. This amount was later increased somewhat and the field was purchased at $5,000. The balance was voted a few years later by the taxpayers of the village which took the title.

Sept. 28. Cooperstown Post No. 579, American Legion, purchased Parshall's restaurant, operated for years by Mr. and Mrs. Frank G. Parshall here, and opened as a public restaurant with Legion club rooms on the second floor. The business was located in the DeLong block at the corner of Chestnut and Main streets.

Oct. 6. The Knox school for girls opened at the Otesaga Hotel with an enrollment of 162 students and a faculty of 38. The school was established at Briarcliff Manor by the late Mary Alice Knox. On the death of Miss Knox in 1911, Mrs. E. Russell Houghton took it over. After the destruction by fire of the Briarcliff buildings in 1912, Mrs. Houghton incorporated the school and moved it to Tarrytown-on-the-Hudson where the school had a steady development until it outgrew its attractive buildings. The magnificent building operated as the Otesaga Hotel in summer provided a splendid location for the school.

Oct. 15. Judge Nathan L. Miller, later Governor Miller, addressed a Republican political rally at the Court House.

A piece of coast defense artillery alloted to the village by the War department arrived in October and was placed in front of the Court House facing Pine street.

Nov. 1. The new restaurant and club of the American Legion Post was opened. The Post issued common and preferred stock to finance the enterprise, the common being taken by the members, while the preferred was sold to the local public which liberally supported the project.

Nov. 15. At a mass meeting of members of the Dairymen's League held at the Court House it was voted to buy or build a large milk plant in Cooperstown to serve its members in this territory.

Nov. 16. The new Masonic Lodge rooms on the third floor of the block at the corner of Main and Pioneer streets which were purchased by Otsego Lodge, No. 138, F. & A. M., from the Bunyan Estate, were used for the first time at a communication when the second degree was conferred before a large number of the brethren. For beauty of furnishings and decorations the Lodge rooms equalled any in this part of the state. In the preceding March the Lodge issued bonds in the sum of $25,000 with which to pay for the property and make the improvements following a favorable vote by the membership.

Nov. 20. The grocery business conducted in Main street for many years, first by G. M. Grant & Co., later by R. Heber White under the same title, then by William Beattie and W. P. Doubleday, and for 10 years by Mr. Beattie as sole proprietor, was closed.

Dec. 14. The office building at Glimmerglen, the home of Mr. and Mrs. William T. Hyde of this village, was wrecked when an acetylene gas plant exploded. Two employees sleeping in the rooms on the second floor were stunned. The loss was estimated at $5,000.

In December the Leatherstocking corporation, a holding company operating the Otesaga, Templeton Lodge, Golf course, Leatherstocking garage and other properties of the Clark Estates was incorporated.

CHAPTER VIII

FROM 1921 TO 1925

1921.—During the week of January 15th M. E. Lippitt and Eugene Becker purchased of Mrs. Flora Mallory of Cooperstown and Mrs. George Dewing of Ilion the property on the west side of Otsego Lake known as the Hickory Grove Farm including the Hickory Grove Inn and 1,600 feet of Lake front, and started the Hickory Grove development.

Jan. 26. The Chamber of Commerce took over the Hotel Fenimore from Garret J. Benson of Albany at $32,000. The majority of the purchase price was guaranteed by William T. Hyde cooperating with the local business men. Following this action the Natty Bumppo Hotel company was formed and papers filed with the Secretary of State at Albany. The capitalization was fixed at $50,000 of 500 shares which were sold locally.

Feb. 18. The local campaign for the support of the relief of starving children of Europe in charge of Herbert Hoover came to an end with a total contribution of $4,959.84 as compared with a quota of $2,500. Harris L. Cooke was the chairman.

March 30. Fire totally destroyed the tenant house on the Uncas Farm of August A. Busch at Three-Mile Point with an estimated loss of $12,000.

May 19. The Cooperstown Platoon of Company G, 10th Infantry, was disbanded in accordance with a General Order from the Adjutant General and the thirty-one members honorably discharged.

The pavement of Elm street from Susquehanna avenue to Pioneer street and of Pioneer from Elm to the top of Phinney Hill was completed this summer. Wm. E. Guy of Cooperstown and St. Louis contributed $500 toward the latter project.

June 15. The New Fenimore Hotel opened under the management of H. L. Kimball as a year-round hotel.

Au Petit Chamonix, a new coffee house on Lake street, was opened in June under the management of Dr. Marguerite S. Cockett, Miss Louise Rennie and the Misses Helen and Elizabeth Patterson.

June 18-25. The American Golf Association of Advertising Interests held its annual tournament on the Cooperstown links. The association has met in Cooperstown for this event annually since that time with the exception of one year.

July 1. Work started on the new theatre erected by William C. Smalley on the site where stood the wing of the old Carr's Hotel.

Aug. 1. The concrete state road from Three-Mile Point to Springfield Center was completed by the Dale Engineering company of Utica. A celebration of the opening of the new road was held by the people of Cooperstown by a visit to Richfield Springs on the evening of the

12th of August in which many participated. A motor cavalcade formed at the Fenimore sounding tin horns and other implements of noise and proceeded to Richfield Springs over the new road. The people of Richfield Springs returned the visit a short time later.

A Masonic Fair held at Smalley's Otsego Lake pavilion proved a decided success and netted the order a profit of $3,681.22.

Sept. 10. The Cooperstown base ball team which provided entertainment for lovers of the national game during the summer played its final game. From the standpoint of the number of games won the season was an outstanding success but from the financial standpoint it was a failure as the books showed a large deficit.

Sept. 12. At a special meeting of the Natty Bumppo company it was voted to increase the capital stock from $50,000 to $100,000, and the property was turned over to the company by William T. Hyde, who financed the project.

Sept. 25. The Dairymen's League Cooperative association, Inc., announced the purchase of the plants of the Nestle's Food company in Otsego county including the large station and factory in this village. The plant was opened under the new ownership October 22nd.

Oct. 30. The stockholders of the Arthur H. Crist Co., Inc., voted to change the name of the publishing concern to the Cooperstown Press, Inc. On the same day the name of the Geiger-Crist Co. was changed to Today's Housewife, Inc.

During the Fall a campaign carried on by the Cooperstown Chamber of Commerce to secure members of the Savings & Loan association met with decided support, nearly 1,000 members being enrolled. Ceylon K. Lippitt was chairman of the committee.

1922.—Jan. 2. William C. Smalley's new Cooperstown Theatre having a seating capacity of 800 and modern in its entire equipment, was opened to the public.

The work of consolidating the plants of the Freeman's Journal company and the John Wilcox company in their new location at No. 38 Pioneer street, formerly C. R. Hartson's cafe, was completed the first week in January. It was the fourth home the Freeman's Journal had occupied in 114 years.

Jan. 11. The Cooperstown Woman's club was organized at a meeting held at the Hotel Fenimore with 53 charter members. The first officers were: President, Mrs. Alexander S. Phinney; Vice-president, Mrs. Nathaniel P. Willis; Recording Secretary, Mrs. Harris L. Cooke; Corresponding Secretary, Mrs. Harry L. Cruttenden; Treasurer, Mrs. Clermonte G. Tennant; Directors, Mrs. William T. Hyde, Mrs. Edward D. Boden, Mrs. H. L. Kimball and Mrs. W. I. Smith.

In February the general offices of the Southern New York Railway which had been located here for several years, were moved to Oneonta by General Manager C. E. Graves.

Right Eminent Commander George C. Hanford of the Grand Commandery Knights Templar of the State of New York in January granted a dispensation for a new Commandery in Cooperstown which became known as Otsego Commandery, No. 76. The first officers named in the dispensation were: Eminent Commander, M. E. Lippitt; Generalissimo, Berton G. Johnson, Captain General, George H. Carley.

The music and sporting goods business conducted on Main street by Squire D. Brooks was purchased by Owen G. Clark in February. Mr. Clark greatly improved the property and added a thoroughly modern and sanitary soda and confectionery department.

An Oneonta Theatre was added by William C. Smalley to his already growing chain which now included Cooperstown, Worcester, Oneonta and Stamford.

Feb. 24. Edward D. Boden purchased the business of the Slote Art Store on Main street. The business was conducted as Boden's Stationery and Art Store.

In March Moses E. Lippitt purchased the interests of Frank B. Shipman, William C. Smalley and James J. Byard, Jr., in the Otsego Lake Transit company.

March 10. Stock and fixtures, uninsured, to the value of $1,500 in the store of Samuel Sapienza on Main street were destroyed by fire. Through the instrumentality of Mrs. Waldo C. Johnston, the Cooperstown Woman's club and others, a benefit cabaret was held for Mr. Sapienza which netted over $600.

March 15. The first survey for the proposed Cooperstown-Schuyler Lake highway was commenced. The contract for this road was not let until 1929.

Early in April a new farm implement store was opened by the A. H. Murdock Implement company in the building on Railroad avenue formerly occupied by the Francis Wagon Works.

Late in March Lester J. Clark, for many years a valuable employee of the McEwan Hardware company, became a member of the firm.

This year about $11,000 was spent in street improvement including the pavement of Elm street and the resurfacing of Main between Chestnut and Railroad avenue.

Through the efforts of the Otsego County S. P. C. A. the Legislature of the state passed and the Governor signed a bill enabling the Village Trustees to prohibit the use of steel traps within the corporation limits.

April 1. A fine new office building and workshop of Derrick, the Florist, connected with the Main street greenhouses, were opened.

May 3. Typifying the spirit of America toward the boys of the World War who today occupy unknown graves the members of Cooperstown Post, No. 579, American Legion voted to change the name to Clark F. Simmons Post in honor of Clark F. Simmons, who was the only Cooperstown member of the A. E. F. who made the supreme sacrifice and whose body was not recovered.

May 19. Bruce L. Hall purchased the interest of his partner,

Harry M. Parker, in the business conducted under the title, Kirby & Root, and the name was changed to Bruce L. Hall, Inc.

June 3. The Mary Imogene Bassett Hospital was opened to the public. The first officers were Edward Severin Clark, President, Samuel L. Warrin, Vice-President, Waldo C. Johnston, Secretary and Treasurer. The Chief of Staff was Dr. Mary Imogene Bassett. The hospital was erected by Mr. Edward Severin Clark, and comprises a main structure with two large wings, pathological laboratory, isolation ward, nurses home, keepers' quarters and power house. The construction is entirely of fieldstone and it has a capacity of about 90 beds. The patients were transferred from the Thanksgiving Hospital on June 30th.

June 14. John D. Rockefeller, John D. Rockefeller, Jr., and three sons and William Rockefeller were members of a party of 12 who spent the night at the Hotel Fenimore.

In June a middle academic school was established at the Susan Fenimore Cooper Foundation.

In July Edmund Walker of New York City purchased the controlling interest in the Cooperstown Press, Inc., from the Clark Estates.

July 14. The Little Chamonix Theatre on Lake street was opened. Many delightful plays were presented by talented local actors while the theatre was conducted.

Aug. 1. The Hon. Nathaniel P. Willis, a wellknown attorney of this village, became counsel for the Delaware & Hudson company.

Aug. 2. The Hon. Adrian A. Pierson was elected a member of the Board of Education in a hotly contested election of district No. 1 in which he received 258 votes to 248 for his opponent, Edward Martin.

Aug. 16. The Cooperstown Woman's club opened club rooms in the King building at No. 52 Pioneer street. The new club consisted of a large reception room, modern kitchen, cloak room and lavatory.

During the week ending August 26th the National Archery Tournament was held at the polo grounds on the Iroquois Farm of Mr. F. Ambrose Clark bringing there many notable figures in this form of sport from all parts of the country.

Owing to extensive repairs in progress at the First Baptist church including new interior decorations and new floor coverings, services were held for a short time in September in Smalley's Theatre. The Rev. C. E. Brown, who became pastor of the church September 1st, preached his introductory sermon in the theatre.

Sept. 12. Otsego Commandery, No. 76, Knights Templar, was formally instituted by Right Eminent Sir George Hanford of Syracuse, Past Grand Commander of the State of New York.

Sept. 25. Dr Royal S. Copeland, Health Commissioner of the State of New York and later U. S. Senator from this state, addressed 300 farmers of Otsego county at a meeting held at the Village Hall in the interest of a better understanding between the consumer and producer of milk.

Oct. 1. William C. Lewis of New York City became president and general manager of the Cooperstown Press.

During this Fall the sum of $10,000 was expended by the Natty Bumppo Hotel corporation, operating the New Fenimore, in improving the property. A new laundry was installed in the basement, many of the baths were rebuilt and changes were made in the elevator power and heating systems.

Nov. 1. Mrs. Della Thompson Lutes, for fifteen years a resident of Cooperstown, where she acted as editor-in-chief of American Motherhood and Today's Housewife, became editor of Modern Priscilla, the well known woman's magazine of Boston, and moved to that city.

Nov. 26. Hugh Walpole, the English novelist, spoke before a large audience at the Knox School on the subject. "Books and Friendship."

The year closed with coal conservation an emphatic necessity on account of the closing down of the anthracite mines in Pennsylvania by reason of a general strike.

1923.—Jan. 1. A fire which caused a loss of $10,000 to the stock of the J. C. Jones Variety store, was through the earnest efforts of the firemen confined to the basement of the Russell block where the store was located. The loss was covered by insurance.

At the opening of the year George H. Carley retired from the presidency of The Freeman's Journal company, having disposed of his holdings to other stockholders. Mr. Carley was connected with the Journal as part or sole proprietor for twenty years filling the editorial chair with ability for much of that time. After his appointment as postmaster in 1915, however, his active participation ceased and he served as a stockholder and as president of the company.

Jan. 15. H. L. Brazee sold an interest in the Rexall Drug store of which he had been the sole proprietor for some years, to Harry O. Withey of this village and the business was continued as Brazee & Withey.

Feb. 14. The opening of a new village laundry to be conducted in connection with the New Fenimore hotel was announced.

Feb. 22. The world famous Flonzaley String Quartet gave a concert in the Liberal Arts course at the Knox school.

Feb. 26. Floyd S. Barlow resigned as manager of the Otsego County Farm Bureau association and early in March Harlo P. Beals of Wayland, Steuben county, was chosen as his successor. Mr. Barlow was the first manager of the Bureau in this county and conducted its affairs for nine years with the exception of one year when he was manager of the Otsego County Improvement association which he was instrumental in founding. He was possessed of marked ability as an organizer and although the Improvement association was short lived he led in the formation of several county Breeders' clubs, in the eradication of tuberculosis in cattle and did important work in the establishment of the county-aid system of highways, which have prospered to the present date. He was an enthusiastic advocate of reforestation for poor farmland in the county and in this connection projected the Otsego County Forestry Company which was not successful financially although the movement has developed in a marked manner in other ways.

March 12. At the annual charter election the taxpayers voted 150 to 38, an appropriation of $1,275 to be expended for the purpose of taking over from the Chamber of Commerce of Doubleday Field, formerly known as "the Phinney lot." The sum represented the amount of the mortgage against the property.

March 14. W. E. "Pussyfoot" Johnson, the nationally and internationally known prohibition advocate addressed a large congregation at the First Presbyterian Church.

April 26. Elizabeth Morey, six-year-old daughter of Mr. and Mrs. Walter E. Morey of Oneonta was killed in an accident at the Grasslands corner, south of the village. The tragedy occurred a few hours after the car in which she was riding turned turtle. Her mother, grandmother and great grandmother were injured in the crash, which resulted when the driver turned too sharply to avoid colliding with a car coming down the Toddsville hill.

May 1. A terrible tragedy occurred near Cobleskill in which David Graham, aged twenty-one, son of Mr. and Mrs. William F. Graham of Cooperstown lost his life when the car which he was driving in company with Ernest R. Lippitt skidded on a sharp turn and after striking a tree and a stump at the roadside finally turned turtle. Mr. Lippitt was seriously though not permanently injured.

May 7. A complimentary dinner in honor of Justice Abraham L. Kellogg of the Supreme Court was given at the Hotel Fenimore by the Otsego County Bar association which had only recently been organized. The Hon. Charles C. Flaesch of Unadilla acted as toastmaster and the speakers included the Hon. Nathaniel P. Willis, Congressman John D. Clarke, of this district, Congressman Lewis Henry of Elmira, Justice Henry V. Borst of Amsterdam, Judge A. J. McNaught of Delaware county, Judge W. M. Kent of Tompkins county, Judge James P. Hill of Chenango county, Judge Joseph D. Senn of Madison county, the Hon. James T. Rogers of Binghamton and Clermonte G. Tennant of Cooperstown. Members and invited guests to the number of 150 were present. On the following day a fine oil portrait of Justice Kellogg was unveiled in the court chamber at the Court House in this village with appropriate ceremonies.

May 22. A group of distinguished women including Mrs. Franklin D. Roosevelt, wife of the former Assistant Secretary of the Navy, later elected Governor of the State, Mrs. Alfred E. Smith, wife of Governor Smith, and Mrs. Daniel O'Day, vice-chairman of the Democratic State committee, was entertained at dinner by Mrs. William T. Hyde followed by a reception at the New Fenimore.

May 25. Marcy Hall, the beautiful stone home of the Misses Nellie, Fannie and Abigail Clinton, was badly damaged by fire which originated in the fireplace. The house was built by Elias Root of Root & Beadle, brewers. In 1880 it was bought by Erastus F. Beadle, the famous publisher of Beadle's dime novels, who improved the property considerably. The name was given the house by Melvin C. Bundy, who purchased the property of Laverne Ingalls in 1905, in memory of Newton L. Marcy, the father of Mrs. Bundy.

June 24. On this date the historic elm tree at the corner of Main and Fair streets fell to the ground, during a heavy storm. The tree stood directly in front of the old Cooper home. Many of the older residents were reminded of the occasion when the late John Worthington ascended in a balloon at the Otsego County Fair grounds and landed in this tree.

June 28. Dr. F. J. Monaghan, Commissioner of Health of New York City addressed a meeting of the Otsego County Dairymen's League at the Village Hall.

The Ethical Culture Society of New York City opened a summer school-camp on Hyde Bay, Otsego Lake, this summer. The Dower House was leased as headquarters The camp proved a success from the outset.

July 1. Rear Admiral Newton A. McCully, U. S. N., arrived at Camp Fenimore on Otsego Lake to spend a few days. At the close of the war Admiral McCully brought several children of Russian refugees to this country and conducted their education. For two summers they were at Camp Fenimore.

July 9. The application of the New York State Gas & Electric company for a perpetual franchise in Cooperstown was refused by action of the Board of Village Trustees.

July 11. The business men of Cooperstown to the number of 150 or more attended a farewell dinner given at the New Fenimore Hotel in honor of Attorney James J. Byard, Jr., on the eve of his departure for Oneonta. The principal speaker was the Hon. Roland L. Davis, Justice of the Appellate Division of the Supreme Court.

July 13. Otsego Lake took its inexorible toll once more when Harry Faraday, eight-year-old son of Mrs. Elsa J. Faraday of Brooklyn was drowned in about eight feet of water near Camp Hist eight miles from Cooperstown. It is thought that the lad was playing in a motor boat anchored near shore and fell into the water.

July 19. For the second time the taxpayers of the village by a vote of 87 to 10 authorized the purchase of Doubleday Field. The special election was made necessary to provide for a legal technicality which arose when the village authorities prepared to exercise the authority granted at the previous election.

Aug. 10. The memory of the late President Warren G. Harding, whose death occurred on August 2nd, was honored with appropriate observances by the village. At noon all business ceased. At 3 o'clock all citizens' activities were halted for five minutes and people stood reverently in silence and prayer. At 4 o'clock the memorial services were held at the Court House. President Frank Hale of the Chamber of Commerce. presided and the eulogy was delivered by the Hon. Nathaniel P. Willis.

Aug. 11. The new Mohican garage building just completed on Chestnut street by Harry Fowler and J. William Thayer was opened for business. The garage was 120 by 60 feet in dimensions and thoroughly appointed for motor car service in every particular.

Aug. 24. "Mother Goose Fantasy," an elaborate operetta directed personally by Arthur Nevin was presented by the girls of Pathfinder's Lodge at the Otesaga before a large audience.

Sept. 5. The property on the east side of Otsego Lake, formerly known as "The Dugway," and more recently occupied by Pathfinder's

Lodge, Inc., organized here by Miss Valerie Deuscher, was sold to the stock company which operates the Camp by James J. Byard, Jr.

The fine new house of Mr. Robert Sterling Clark at Bowerstown was completed in September.

Sept. 29. By virtue of an order in Supreme Court granted by Justice A. L. Kellogg Doubleday Field was formally transferred to the Village of Cooperstown to be used as a base ball park and public playground. The greater part of the original purchase price of $5,000 was raised by the Cooperstown Chamber of Commerce under the leadership of Dr. E. L. Pitcher.

Oct. 2. The large barn on the Iroquois Farm of Mr. F. Ambrose Clark was totally destroyed by fire. With the structure nearly 100 tons of hay and thousands of bushels of oats and other grains were lost. The loss was estimated at about $200,000.

Oct. 15. Several fires preceding this date led the Village Trustees to take action to replace the old and worn-out fire engine with a modern pumper and it was voted to purchase a La France engine. Sentiment favoring the selection of a pumper of another make crystallized in the presentation of a petition asking that a Special Election be called at which the taxpayers might express their choice but on October 12th this petition was denied. The village was to be equipped with two pumpers, however, for on December 1st Mr. Edward Severin Clark announced that he had purchased an Ahrens-Fox pumper which would be donated to the village.

Oct. 27. Prof. Stephen Leacock of Mc Gill University, the well-known humorist, spoke at the Knox school in the Liberal Arts Course.

Oct. 31. The Cooperstown Press, Inc., the large publishing house employing upwards of 200 people, closed its doors, when the Irving Bank-Columbia Trust Co. of New York City, as trustee under the first and refunding mortgage to secure an issue of $250,000 face value of bonds, took possession of the property. The cause for the failure was ascribed to a lack of working capital necessary to care for a rapid expansion in business.

Nov. 16. Irving Bachellor, one of America's leading men of letters, spoke at the Knox school, before a large audience.

1924—Jan. 14. The Cooperstown Rotary Club, organized the latter part of the preceding December, was formally presented with its charter by District Governor Edwin R. Weeks of Binghamton, the ceremonies being in charge of the Oneonta club. The ceremonies were held at the New Fenimore Hotel. The first Board of Directors of the new club were: Harris L. Cooke, Frank B. Shipman, M. E. Lippitt, W. M. Bronner, Hubbard L. Brazee, the Rev. C. E. Brown, and the first officers were: President, the Rev. C. E. Brown; first vice-president, Harris L. Cooke; second vice-president, Frank B. Shipman; secretary, George H. Carley; treasurer, Hubbard L. Brazee; sergeant-at-arms, W. M. Bronner.

Jan. 12. The Cooperstown Fire department was reorganized at a meeting held at the Village Hall in order to meet the new conditions brought about by the substitution of new motor pumpers for the old fire engine. The International Hose company was assigned to the LaFrance pumper and its name changed to Pumper Company, No. 1, while the Iroquois company was assigned to the Ahrens-Fox pumper and became Pumper Company No. 2. The members of the Clark Hose company who desired joined one of the above. The Mechanics' Hook & Ladder company was retained to have charge of the hook and ladder truck.

Jan. 17. The tax payers of the Town of Otsego by a margin of 55 to 7 voted to appropriate the sum of $10,000 to construct a bridge over the Susquehanna river on Main street in this village. The bridge joins the towns of Middlefield and Otsego and the proposal called for each to bear half of the expense. On the same date the tax payers of Middlefield defeated the appropriation by a vote of 20 to 43.

Feb. 13. A fine portrait of the late County Judge James W. Barnum of Cherry Valley was hung on the walls of the Supreme Court Chamber at the Court House in this village. Judge Barnum occupied the bench from 1896 to 1908.

Feb. 16. The bells of the churches were tolled and the flags of the village lowered to half mast while the earthly remains of President Woodrow Wilson were laid at rest in the Cathedral of Saints Peter and Paul in Washington, D. C.

Feb. 29. The sum of $286.70 was realized from an entertainment for the benefit of Russian refugee children in Servia held in the gymnasium of the Knox school under the auspices of the Cooperstown Woman's club.

March 7. The Hon. Peter G. Ten Eyck of Albany, president of the Chamber of Commerce in that city and of the New York State Automobile association, and vice-president of the New York State Farm Bureau Federation, was the principal speaker at a joint dinner of the Cooperstown Chamber of Commerce and the Cooperstown Automobile club at the New Fenimore Hotel.

March 19. At a joint meeting of the Town Boards of Middlefield and Otsego it was voted to expend the sum of $12,000 to erect a concrete and steel bridge on Main street over the Susquehanna river in this village.

March 28. The building and plant of the Cooperstown Press. Inc., which a short time before went into bankruptcy, was sold at mortgage foreclosure brought by the Irving Bank-Columbia Trust company of New York City to Mr. Waldo C. Johnston for the Leatherstocking corporation at $140,000. The sole bid was made by Mr. Johnston.

In May the pavement of Fair street from the Mary Imogene Bassett Hospital to the Park was completed. A new grandstand was erected by the village on Doubleday Field this spring.

June 1. Berton G. Johnson assumed the duties of local postmaster to succeed George H. Carley under appointment by President Coolidge.

June 2. The Cooperstown Fish & Game club placed 70,000 young muskalunge in Otsego Lake.

June 11-12. The annual meeting of the Otsego Baptist association opened in the Baptist church in this village.

Early in July two real estate transactions involving property at the foot of Fair street were announced. James J. Byard, Jr., of Oneonta purchased of B. G. Johnson the Lake front property occupied by the Otsego Lake Transit company. This property was located on the west side of Fair street. Following this sale, M. E. Lippitt, president of the Transit company purchased of Mrs. A. M. Kerr, of Elizabeth, N. J., the cottage at the corner of Lake and Fair with lands extending to the Lake front on the east side of the street and the company's ticket office and business headquarters were moved to that location.

July 5. The Otsego County Children's Health camp located on Glimmerglen Farm No. 2 through the generosity of William T. Hyde opened under the auspices of the County Tuberculosis and Public Health association. Here a number of undernourished children were cared for during the summer with very beneficial results.

July 8. According to the report of the trustees of Lakewood cemetery made at the annual meeting the permanent endowment fund had reached the sum of $40,000.

July 19. The new Main street bridge over the Susquehanna river built jointly by the towns of Middlefield and Otsego was opened to the public. The contractors for the concrete work were E. A. Potter and Arthur Stevens. The steel work was provided by the United Construction company of Albany. The cost of the sidewalks over the bridge was borne by the village. Crossing at this point had been closed to traffic since September, 1923.

In July the election of the Rev. Dr. Charles R. Myers of Mt. Carmel, Pa., as president of Hartwick Seminary was announced. The placing of Dr. Myers at the head of this time-honored Lutheran school, located a short distance south of the village, brought to an end a brief period of unrest in its affairs which arose over a disagreement earlier in the year between the principal, Prof. J. H. Dudde and the students and at one time threatened to result in the closing of the school. Dr. Myers not only brought to the Seminary a new era of prosperity but made a marked impress upon the village of Cooperstown for his breadth of vision and keen intellectuality. He was frequently called upon to speak at local affairs of a civic nature and in the local churches where he was heard with edification.

Aug. 9. The annual outing of the Veterans' association of the Delaware & Hudson company was held in Cooperstown and brought over 800 members and their friends and families here.

Aug. 16. The annual Otsego County picnic under the auspices of the Otsego County Farm and Home Bureaus brought a crowd of between 4,000 and 5,000 people to the Fair Grounds. The speaker of the day was the Hon. Louis G. Michael, foreign agricultural economist of the U. S. Department of Agriculture.

Trout fishing in Otsego Lake was reported as exceptionally good this summer. On August 17th the Hon. Frank M. Smith of Springfield Center caught one which weighed 17½ pounds.

Aug. 27. Students of the Cooperstown High school won three places out of the first five and six out of the first ten in the list of students of the county eligible for university scholarships based on the records of their High school course. The six were: Grace L. Wood, Clyde A. Reynolds, Mary J. McRorie, Mary A. Martin, Anna E. Cunningham and Mildred Gallup.

Sept. 22. The Otsego-Schoharie Boy Scout council secured from George Hyde Clarke a site at Hyde Bay on Otsego Lake upon which to establish a summer camp.

Oct. 2. Attention not only in Cooperstown but through this part of the state was attracted to the rapid development of the moving picture business by William C. Smalley, proprietor of Smalley's Cooperstown Theatre, and the Smalley Theatre Chain. On this date Mr. Smalley opened his fourteenth picture house located at Hamilton, Madison county.

Early in October Street Commissioner Michael MacMoon and his force finished the paving of Church street. This completed the pavement of the block enclosed by Beaver, Fair, Church, Pioneer, Elm and Susquehanna streets.

Oct. 8. The patriotic decorative system installed on Main street by the Chamber of Commerce was seen for the first time at a Street Fair held for the purpose of raising funds for a program of Winter sports. The project netted $300.

Nov. 17. Damages in the sum of $500 to Thera M. Noble and $1,100 to William A. and Lucy A. Noble of Oneonta were awarded in Supreme Court by the jury which heard the evidence in the suit brought against Walter L. Murdock of that city to recover damages for fraud it being alleged by plaintiffs that they were led to retain stock which they owned in the bankrupt Miller-Strong Drug company of which he was an agent through misrepresentations. The case was of exceptional interest in Cooperstown by reason of the fact that considerable stock in the defunct company had been sold here.

Dec. 7. An open meeting of Leatherstocking Council, No. 1879, Knights of Columbus, held at Smalley's Theatre was attended by a large audience which had the opportunity of hearing several distinguished officers of the organization including Supreme Knight Joseph A. Flaherty of Philadelphia, Supreme Secretary William J. McGinley of Brooklyn, State Deputy Daniel A. Tobin and Edward F. McSweeney of Boston, secretary of the historical commission of the order.

Dec. 15. Extensive plans for winter sports under the auspices of the Chamber of Commerce were announced by the Winter Sports Committee. These included the erection of a toboggan slide on Fair street north of Main, the organization of hockey teams, the flooding of Doubleday Field for skating and a community hike to Fly Creek on New Year's Day followed by a community dance at the Village Club in the evening.

Elaborate decoration of Main street with vari-colored electric lights and evergreen trees was carried out by the Chamber of Commerce during the holidays.

Dec. 23. The Cooperstown Rotary club entertained seventy-five needy children of the county at dinner at the New Fenimore Hotel followed by a Christmas party with a Christmas tree and gifts for all at Smalley's Cooperstown Theatre.

Dec. 30. The Freeman's Journal Christmas Fund for Otsego County's Twenty Neediest cases, which was established in 1921, was closed with a total subscription of $558.20. The Fund is administered in Cooperstown with the Otsego County Child Welfare society. In 1921 the total amount subscribed was $200; in 1922, $458; in 1923, $490.30.

1925.—Jan. 1. A Linn tractor equipped with a snow plow was purchased by the town of Otsego and used to good advantage in winter in keeping the highways open for traffic.

Jan. 24. An eclipse of the sun, ninety per cent total was viewed with interest by the entire village. Many went to Mt. Vision where the totality was complete.

Jan. 29. The worst blizzard since 1914 was experienced in Cooperstown. Some fourteen inches of snow fell in one night superimposed on some two feet already on the ground. Traffic on the highways leading to the village was badly tied up for two or three days.

Feb. 10. The Flonzaley string quartet appeared in another concert at the Knox school.

Feb. 15. The plant of the Dairymen's League in Cooperstown was leased by the Borden Farm Products company handling the pooled milk of the League from this date. The product has since this date been shipped to New York City in fluid form, the manufacture of milk products at this plant which was carried on on a large scale by the League, having been abandoned.

Feb. 28. An earthquake shock of about a minute's duration of sufficient intensity to cause pictures on the wall to shake and dishes to rattle was experienced here.

March 5. The Cooperstown Bar Association gave a testimonial dinner at the New Fenimore Hotel in honor of County Judge Adrian A. Pierson at the opening of his term of office. During the evening he was presented with a fine ebony gavel by his friends of the bar.

April 30. Pursuant to announcement made in 1924 the Mary Imogene Bassett Hospital was closed and the patients transferred to the Thanksgiving Hospital which was completely renovated and restored through the generosity of Mr. Edward Severin Clark and for a time the old hospital served again as in former years as a medical center.

May 27. Hubbard L. Brazee was elected President of the Second National Bank and Wilson E. McGown a director to succeed Charles T. Brewer, deceased. Mr. Brazee was elected a director of the bank in 1909 and had served continuously in that capacity since.

May 28. As the result of the burning out of a generator set at the power house during an electric storm the 60-cycle current was eliminated from the service supplied the village by the New York State Gas & Electric corporation causing considerable hardship and loss to local business for a period of three weeks while a new set was being built.

June 8-9. The annual mid-summer meeting of the New York State Automobile association was held in Cooperstown. The event brought 250 members and their wives to the New Fenimore Hotel where official headquarters were established and where the annual banquet was held. The business sessions were held at the Village Hall. Among the speakers were Col. Frederick Stewart Greene, head of the department of Public Works, the Hon. Mark Graves, state tax commissioner and Major John A. Warner, superintendent of State Police.

June 15-16. The New York State Association of Electrical Dealers and Contractors held its annual meeting at the New Fenimore Hotel. About sixty delegates were present and the gathering closed with a clam bake at Three-Mile Point.

June 30. Lester G. Bursey of Chelsea, Mass., who had been appointed director of physical education at the Cooperstown High school and coach of its athletic teams, arrived in Cooperstown to have charge of the Cooperstown Playgrounds which were conducted here for the first summer through the cooperation of several local bodies.

July 5. George Ditzel, aged 19 of Newark, N. J., instructor in manual training at Camp Fenimore, drowned while swimming in Otsego Lake as the result of a heart attack. The tragedy occurred near the camp.

Aug. 11-12. A street fair held under the auspices of the Chamber of Commerce netted the sum of $1,184.75.

Sept. 1. The milk shipping plant of the N. Van Son company located here was taken over by the Fort Schuyler Farms, Inc., of Utica, of which W. W. Hovey, formerly a resident of this village was president.

Sept. 15. Kenneth W. Root purchased the interest of his partner, Ernest A. Tibbitts, in the hardware business which they had conducted since 1911 and continued it under his own name as sole proprietor.

Sept. 7-8. The annual meeting of the executives of the 28th district, Rotary International was held at the New Fenimore.

Sept. 8. The Hon. Owen D. Young of New York and VanHornesville, chairman of the Board of Directors of the General Electric company of Schenectady, was the speaker at the annual dinner of the Otsego-Schoharie Bankers' association at the Otesaga.

Oct. 15. Herbert L. Kimball resigned as manager of the New Fenimore and he was succeeded by W. H. Craig of Sharon Springs.

Nov. 16-17. The 125th anniversary of the founding of the First Presbyterian church in Cooperstown was observed with appropriate services. The church is the oldest in the village. The historical address was delivered by the Rev. Dr. E. C. Petrie, the pastor. Among the other speakers were the Rev. Dr. Robert I. McBride of Elizabeth, N. J. and the Rev. Dr. Newell Woolsey Wells of Brooklyn, both former pastors.

Nov. 17. Returns from the state census published about this date gave Cooperstown a population of 2,752, a gain of 27 in five years.

Nov. 18. The mysterious disappearance of Miss Alice Corbett of Utica, daughter of Mr. and Mrs. James Corbett, well known summer residents of this community, from her room at Smith College, Northampton, Mass., stirred the village. No solution has ever been arrived at in this case which seems to have gone down in history as one of the unsolved problems of the time.

Nov. 30. The sum of $500 was appropriated by the Chamber of Commerce for a Winter Sports program to be carried out the coming season.

Dec. 28. Announcement was made at about this time of the formation of the Bavarian Hop Farms, Inc. The company, of which Martin Moakler of this village, and Hugo V. Loewi of New Jersey were the promoters, took over 1,000 acres of farm land in the town of Middlefield to be devoted to hop culture.

CHAPTER IX

FROM 1926 TO 1929

1926.—Jan. 12. A total of $6,012,102 insurance in effect was shown by the annual report of the Otsego County Farmers' Cooperative Fire Insurance company given at its annual meeting, while the assets of the Cooperstown Savings & Loan association according to the annual report published at about this time for the year ending December 31, 1925, were over $37,000.

Feb. 5. A concern known as the Safeway Transportation company, organized during the preceding year to operate motor busses between Albany and Cooperstown and Richfield Springs was denied a certificate of convenience and necessity by the Public Service commission.

Early in February Martin Moakler of this village purchased the Hoffman House, the large hotel on Main street more lately known as the New Park Hotel, and in its early days as the Ballard House.

During the winter a well sustained and successful kindergarten was conducted by the Cooperstown Woman's club at its club house on Pioneer street. Mrs. Rutledge B. Manchester was the instructor.

Feb. 17. Mr. and Mrs. James Fenimore Cooper of Cooperstown and Albany announced a gift of $50,000 to provide the largest undergraduate scholarship at Yale University. Under the terms of the gift preference is given to students from Cooperstown and Albany. The scholarship was given in memory of their son, Capt. James Fenimore Cooper, Jr., a B. A. student at Yale in the class of 1913, who died at Camp Dix, N. J., of pneumonia February 17, 1918, after an illness of only nine days.

Feb. 19. The commodious and modern new building housing the business of Cook's Auto & Supply company, located on the site of the old Carr's Hotel, which had been in process of construction for some time was completed and opened to the public.

Feb. 20. Herman Egner of Morris Plains, N. J., purchased the Hoffman House.

Feb. 22. Washington's Birthday was marked by the end of the coal famine in Cooperstown, which this village suffered in common with the rest of the country, by reason of a strike of the miners in the Pennsylvania coal fields. On this date five carloads of coal came to town and was carefully distributed by the local dealers. It was the first anthracite coal received here since October, 1925. Despite the lack of coal there was no suffering and a vast amount of knowledge was gained by local residents as to the use of coal substitutes such as soft coal, coke and wood. Of course there were many who were well supplied with anthracite which had been purchased the preceding Spring.

March 9. At the annual village election the sum of $3,000 was voted, 128 to 68, to purchase the Mitchell lot adjoining Doubleday Field to be used ultimately as a free parking for cars. Lately the parking spaces on Main street had become entirely inadequate to meet the demand so that motorists driving to the village for trade were often compelled to drive some distance to locate a spot in which to leave their cars.

March 14. The Cooperstown Choral society, organized by a large number of the music lovers of the village under the leadership of Prof. A. deJ. Allez, presented the oratorio "The Messiah" by Handel at Smalley's Theatre, before a crowded house. The offering for the benefit of Thanksgiving Hospital amounted to $315.

March 16. A special election of Union Free School district, No. 1, of the Town of Otsego, the proposal to appropriate the sum of $50,000 to build and equip a new gymnasium for the High school was defeated by a vote of 189 to 339.

May 1. A sensation of no little extent was caused by the performance of a wedding ceremony on the stage of Smalley's Theatre in this village. The bride was Miss Florence Niles and the groom Edward LeMay, both of Richfield Springs. The ceremony was performed by the Rev. Arthur Landmesser, pastor of the Methodist church at Hartwick. The bride was the recipient of a number of valuable gifts sent by the local business men.

May 12-14. The Spring meeting of the New York State Federation of Women's clubs brought 200 prominent club women to Cooperstown. The event opened with a luncheon given by Mrs. William T. Hyde at her summer home, Glimmerglen. At the annual banquet at the Hotel Fenimore on the evening of the 13th the principal speaker was Mrs. Florence E. S. Knapp, Secretary of State, who was later convicted of embezzlement of state census funds and served a term in prison.

May 14. Paul Edward Gray, aged 23 years, was drowned in Otsego Lake. The fatality occurred in about eighty feet of water near Pathfinder's Lodge. He had been fishing from a row boat and was seen by his uncle, George Holcomb to plunge into the water. Although Mr. Holcomb went to the spot at once it was four hours before the body was recovered with grappling hooks.

July 1. Following the completion of extensive repairs and improvements, Herman Egner, the new proprietor opened the Hoffman House under the name, the New Park Hotel.

July 4. Camp Deerslayer, the district Boy Scout camp established the preceding year at Hyde Bay on Otsego Lake, opened for the season.

July 12. The annual convention of the New York State Retail Jewelers' association opened at the Otesaga with a large number of members in attendance.

July 17. Camp Minnetoska, established by the Girl Scouts of Otsego county, opened on the Kiley property on the west side of the Lake. Like the Boy Scout Camp Deerslayer, it came to be a permanent institution, although its location was eventually changed. The moving spirit in the formation of this camp was Miss Mary H. Pickard, a member of the High school faculty, and for several years captain of Fenimore Troop.

July 22. A teriffic windstorm, called by some a "twister" and by others a "cyclone," swept in a narrow path through a path of limited extent in this locality uprooting hundreds of trees but fortunately causing no loss of life or serious injury. A most unusual and amazing phenomenon for this place was the raising of a water-spout on Otsego Lake estimated at forty feet in height which traveled across the water from just above Five-Mile Point to Pegg's Point on the east side where it was broken up. During the progress of the storm which lasted only half an hour the temperature dropped sixteen degrees.

Aug. 15. Application of the tuberculin test to the cattle of the township was completed and it was reported that reactions were shown in 620 out of 2,500 cattle tested.

Aug. 20. Henry Farquharson, an 84-year-old citizen of this village, was killed when struck by a motor car near Duanesburgh, as he was crossing the road.

Sept. 4. The stockholders of the Natty Bumppo Hotel company, owners of the Fenimore Hotel, at a meeting held on this date approved the sale of the hotel property to Mr. Edward Severin Clark.

Sept. 8. The Clark Estates, through Mr Waldo C. Johnston, formally offered Cherry Tree Point on Otsego Lake to the Otschodela Boy Scout council to be used as a summer camp, and it was decided to change the location of the camp from Hyde Bay to the new site.

During the summer a campaign to raise the sum of $10,000 by popular subscription to meet the expected deficit for the operation of Thanksgiving Hospital was carried on. On September 28th it was announced that the campaign had reached the desired goal the total of $10,028 having been subscribed. A considerable amount in additional contributions was received during the subsequent weeks.

Oct. 25. James Doran, a member of Boy Scout Troop 12, was invested with the rank of Eagle Scout, the first to be awarded in the village, at a Court of Honor held in the Methodist church. The winning of this award was significant of the general high standing attained by the local troop which for years has been under the leadership of Scoutmaster C. B. Johnson.

Nov. 1. Fire, which was thought to have had its origin in a defective chimmey running from a fireplace, destroyed the main building of the Susan Fenimore Cooper Foundation on Beaver street. There were eighty children in the building at the time and they left the building in an orderly and quiet manner upon the sounding of the fire alarm. The Foundation was temporarily located at Templeton Lodge. The burned building was dedicated September 22, 1883.

Nov. 6. Hugh Walpole, the English author, addressed a large assemblage in the assembly hall at the Knox School.

Nov. 14. The Sunday School of the First Presbyterian church

celebrated its 100th anniversary by the presentation of a pageant written for the occasion by the Rev. Dr. E. C. Petrie, the pastor. The pageant depicted the formation of the first Sunday School in Cooperstown and the importance of Christian education.

Nov. 16   The Cooperstown Chapter, American Red Cross, raised and forwarded the sum of $411 for the relief of sufferers in a great Florida flood disaster.

Nov. 28.   The Bundy & Cruttenden company which had done business here in the retail field for many years was reorganized when Wilbur M. Bronner purchased the interest of Frank Lettis and was elected president and treasurer.

Dec. 2.   At a meeting of the members of the Mary Imogene Bassett Hospital a new Board of Directors was elected and at a subsequent meeting of the Board, Dr. James Greenough of New York City was elected president and Dr. Henry S. F. Cooper, vice-president. It was announced at this time that it was planned to reopen the hospital early in 1927 under the management of Dr. Greenough.

1927—Jan. 1.   Judge Nathaniel P. Willis, a prominent attorney of Cooperstown, was appointed counsel for the Delaware & Hudson company and from this time until his death at the age of 56, August 27th of this year, was engaged at the general offices of the company at Albany although he maintained his residence in this village.

Jan. 7.   Troop 12, Boy Scouts of America, located here was declared the winner of an efficiency test in which all the troops of the Otschodela council, covering the counties of Otsego and Schoharie participated. The Cooperstown troop defeated Troop 23 of Oneonta by one point.

Jan. 29.   Percy Grainger, the Australian pianist, gave a highly appreciated concert at the Knox school.

Feb. 8.   County Judge Adrian A. Pierson of this village was appointed Master of the First Veil of the Grand Chapter, Royal Arch Masons of the State of New York.

March 22.   The Mary Imogene Bassett Hospital which had been closed for a few years was reopened as a general hospital under the management of Dr. James Greenough with Dr. George M. Mackenzie, formerly of the Presbyterian Hospital in New York City, at the head of the medical staff.

April 10.   Gov. Alfred E. Smith signed a bill legalizing a referendum to be held here on the question of the proposal to close and exchange the portion of Nelson avenue extending from the Lakeshore a distance of 235 feet with the Leatherstocking Corporation for the property from Main street between the building then known as the Leatherstocking building (now the Second National Bank) and the building of the Cooperstown National Bank. At the referendum held on June 7th, by a vote of 211 to 105, the taxpayers of the village approved the exchange and the village came into possession of the present entrance to the playgrounds and base ball park.

April 22.   Dr. E. L. Pitcher, for thirty years engaged in the practice of dentistry here, transferred his office to Albany, where he located in South Hawk street. He was succeeded here by Dr. W. H. Mc-Donald, who had been in his employ for some time, and Dr. LeRoy L. Pitcher, his son who recently graduated from the Harvard School of Dentistry.

April 26. The general contract for the erection of a new building to replace the main structure of the Susan Fenimore Cooper Foundation which was destroyed by fire November 1, 1926, was let by the Board of Trustees to C. M. McLean & Son of Binghamton.

April 28. The capacity of the large dining room of the Hotel Fenimore was taxed to the limit at a testimonial dinner given by the people of Cooperstown in honor of Mr. Edward Severin Clark upon the completion of extensive repairs and improvements and the reopening of that hotel.

May 10. Chairman Frank Hale of the Cooperstown Chapter, American Red Cross, announced that a total of $12,000 had been forwarded to headquarters for the fund being raised throughout the nation for the relief of sufferers in the great floods in the Mississippi Valley which had recently caused untold destruction to life and property. The original local quota was $425.

May 18. Miss Flora Grace Winslow, a nurse at the Mary Imogene Bassett Hospital, committed suicide by drinking poison at her room at the Nurses' Home. Her home was at Hinman Hollow.

June 1. The pavement of Lake street between Chestnut and Pioneer was completed. The improvement of this street served to divert much through traffic from Chestnut street and relieve congestion at its crossing with Main.

June 10. George W. Lang after twenty-seven years in the shoe business here, sold out to Paul A. Clark and retired from active life.

July 1. New pavements on Walnut and Court streets were completed.

July 8. Harry Allen, a resident of Springfield Center, was crushed to death under a ton of stone which fell upon him in the excavation under the old building of the Susan Fenimore Cooper Foundation, which was being removed to make way for the new structure. The victim of the tragedy was employed as a laborer by C. M. McLean & Son, contractors.

July 17. Miss Jane E. Green of Fultonville, a student at the New York State College for Teachers at Albany, who had just arrived with a family with whom she was employed for the summer, was drowned in Otsego Lake off Eldred Point.

July 30. The transfer of the personal and real property of the Thanksgiving Hospital to the Walling Home for Aged People under terms proposed on July 15th was completed when Justice A. L. Kellogg granted a Supreme Court order approving the sale of the property under the terms proposed earlier in the year by the hospital board and unanimously accepted. Under the terms of the offer the nominal sum of $5,000 was paid for the property and the Home was given the income from $50,000 of the hospital endowment for five years with the possibility that this fund might become permanently its own. The income from a fund of $15,000 was also set aside for the care of inmates of the Home who might become patients at the Mary Imogene Bassett Hospital. This institution was first projected at Oneonta with the purpose of locating it in that city, but this generous proposal provided superior quarters to those available there.

Aug. 1. The lease of Cherry Tree Point on Otsego Lake to be used as a site for Camp Deerslayer was formally presented to the Otschodela Council, Boy Scouts of America, by Scoutmaster C. B. Johnson of Troop 12 on behalf of Mr. Stephen C. Clark.

Aug. 25. Between 1,000 and 1,200 Masons of the Otsego-Schoharie district attended the annual picnic of that order at the Lake front.

In September Will S. Basinger completed a very absorbing series of reminiscences of village life and incidents which were published in The Freeman's Journal and created widespread interest.

Sept. 3. The season of the Otsego Lake base ball club closed. The communities of Cooperstown and Springfield Center early in the year joined hands and formed an association for the purpose of placing a professional team in the field. The club became a member of the Mohawk Valley League and was successful in winning the pennant. Of a total of 63 games played 44 resulted in victory. Donald H. ("Tuts") McBride of Utica, former Hamilton College coach, was the captain and manager.

Oct. 8. A terrible tragedy occurred on the highway in the town of Springfield near West Village in which Mrs. John W. Brown and Mrs. L. Marks, both well-known residents of Cooperstown, lost their lives. Mrs. Brown and Mrs. Marks had started that morning in the Brown car with Mrs. Marks' daughter, Miss Dorothy Marks, as driver, to go to Albany. About halfway down an incline in the highway the car skidded on the slippery road and turned at right angles the rear end hitting a bread truck and the front a Ford. The Brown car was not overturned but both Mrs. Brown and Mrs. Marks were thrown out. Mrs. Marks struck the pavement upon her head, and died within fifteen minutes. Mrs. Brown received injuries from which she died at the Mary Imogene Bassett Hospital the next day. Miss Marks was painfully hurt also but recovered from the effects of the crash.

Oct. 20. The last $500 Village Hall bond was retired. The bonds were issued in 1887 for a total amount of $20,000.

Nov. 3. Mrs. Waldo C. Johnston of this village completed a transcontinental flight from New Brunswick, N. J., to Los Angeles, Calif., as a passenger in a U. S. air mail plane. The trip occupied from Tuesday afternoon until 5:30 p. m. Pacific Coast Time, Thursday. Mrs. Johnston has the distinction of being the first woman to fly across the continent in a mail airplane.

Nov. 21. The Otsego County Home for Aged People was opened with a family of ten occupying the building formerly known as Thanksgiving Hospital which had been completely restored and redecorated by interested friends. Mrs. John B. Conkling was appointed superintendent.

Dec. 19. The Otsego County Board of Supervisors voted to establish a county laboratory at the Mary Imogene Bassett Hospital with a branch at Oneonta and appropriated the sum of $3,000 for that purpose.

1928.—Jan. 9. A proposal to exchange Three-Mile Point, owned and operated by the village as a public bathing beach and picnic ground, for the Five-Mile Point property including the Five-Mile Point Inn, was vetoed by the Board of Village Trustees as contrary to law and undesirable. When Samuel M. Shaw, the veteran ex-editor of The Freeman's Journal, and George Brooks, a prominent local attorney, in 1899 through the far-seeing interest in the welfare of the community brought about the purchase of Three-Mile Point at a moderate price from William Cooper, a descendant of Judge Cooper, who left the property by will to his children, their enterprise and wisdom was widely heralded and the movement had the solid backing of the community. Through this transaction Mr. Cooper enabled the village to acquire a playground and Lakeside resort the denial of which to their forefathers had nearly caused a riot and it is evident that the feeling still exists that it should be retained forever for this purpose as the action of the Board of Trustees seemed to find almost unanimous popular favor. There was the further consideration, moreover, that a special act of the Legislature would have been required to enable the village to own property outside the three-mile limit. The exchange would have enabled August A. Busch, owner of Uncas Lodge, west of the Point, to have added the valuable property to his holdings and unquestionably would have been desirable from his standpoint.

Jan. 11. Hubbard L. Brazee retired from the drug business in which he had been interested for twenty-six years, in order to devote his entire time to the affairs of the Second National Bank of which he was president. His interest in the drug business was purchased by his partner, Harry O. Withey.

Jan. 23. George Barrere, the world's greatest flute virtuoso, and the Ensemble of which he was the leader, gave a concert at the Knox school.

Jan. 27. A newly formed organization, The Cooperstown Players, having for its purpose the presentation of home talent dramatic performances on the local stage, made its initial public appearance at Smalley's Theatre in a Gala Entertainment. The organization not only purposed through its activities to cultivate a more general interest in the drama but to devote as large a portion of the proceeds of its productions as possible to worthy causes of a public nature. The work of the members included not only that of acting in various roles when selected for the casts but in producing all the details demanded for the complete performance, such as scenery, stage settings, lighting, properties, etc., and all members were expected to cooperate in any manner for which they might be called upon. No solicitation is made for the sale of tickets but the plays are given on a strictly professional basis so far as the support of the public is concerned. Dr. Joseph B. Cooke was the first managing director and the first complete performance was given on the evenings of the 1st and 2nd of March when "Love Among the Lions" was given in a very successful manner.

March 7. Dr. Charles R. Myers, principal of Hartwick Seminary, was elected president of Hartwick College at a meeting of the Board of Trustees held at Albany.

Eagle street, Estli avenue and Main from the river bridge to Estli avenue were paved this summer as the result of action taken March 15th by the Board of Village Trustees.

March 26. Robert Winter, the six-year-old son of Mrs. William Cleary, died at the Mary Imogene Bassett Hospital from injuries he received when hit on Main street by a motor car driven by Seward A. Pierson.

April 16. The Board of Directors of the Cooperstown Chamber of Commerce voted to participate in the celebration in the summer of 1929 of the Sesqui-Centennial of the local features of the Sullivan-Clinton campaign of 1779 in connection with similar celebrations to be held throughout the state. The account of the famous dam built by General James Clinton at the outlet of Otsego Lake and of the vital importance of this operation to the general campaign appears in the earlier pages of this volume. That Cooperstown was the logical point for one of the celebrations was early recognized by the State Historian, Alexander C. Flick, and the department of Archives and History under whose auspices the celebrations were planned and the sum of $2,000 from $70,000 appropriated by the Legislature was allocated for the local celebration.

April 28. At a special election of the qualified voters of school district No. 1 of the Town of Otsego a bond issue in the sum of $150,-000 was authorized for the purpose of making extensive additions to the Cooperstown Union and High school building. For some time many of the grades had been overcrowded and early in the year part time instruction was forced by the conditions in one grade. The requirement of the State Department of Education that a gymnasium be included in the plans to replace the cramped and poorly adapted room in the basement used for this purpose was also taken into account in preparing the plans which were thoroughly explained to the public in all their details. The vote on the proposition was: yes, 367; no, 128.

May 2. Retirement from retail business was announced by the firm of Bundy and Cruttenden, Inc. This business was established in 1876 by E. S. Bundy and M C. Bundy and Lee B. Cruttenden became associated with it in 1894. The business was incorporated in 1915 with Mr. Cruttenden as president. Upon his death in February, 1926, his son, Dr. H. L. Cruttenden, and daughters, Mrs. Russel Warren and Mrs. Wilbur M. Bronner became directors with Wilbur M. Bronner as president and treasurer. It was decided to close the retail department of the store which handled dry goods and furniture in order to enable the officers to devote their entire attention to the manufacturing of dresses and wearing apparel for girls' schools, a branch of the enterprise which had assumed very substantial proportions.

May 3. The Hon. Frank P. Graves, Commissioner of Education and President of the University of the State of New York, Mrs. Graves,

Ray P. Snyder, Commissioner of Rural Education and Charles L. Mosher, chief of the Attendance Division of the State Department of Education, attended the annual convention of the Eastern Association of District Superintendents at the Hotel Fenimore.

May 17. Miss Madge Heath of London, England, captain of the Westminster district of the Girl Guides, participated in and spoke at a Court of Award held by the Fenimore and Leatherstocking Girl Scout Troops at the High school assembly hall.

May 29. The new building of the Susan Fenimore Cooper Foundation on Beaver street replacing the building destroyed by fire November 1, 1926, was completed and the children took up their home there having moved on this date from Templeton Lodge where they had been housed since the fire.

Early in June announcement was made of the lease of Five-Mile Point Inn to the Sherwood Interstate clubs. At the same time it was stated that the foreclosure proceedings instituted by Herbert Reynolds and the First National Bank of Scranton, Pa., against Ellen E. Beals, et al., had been discontinued. The Sherwood Interstate clubs in which parties from Chattanooga, Tenn., were principally interested, proposed to develop the Inn as a club house and secured options on a large amount of property in that locality. The Inn was operated as a hotel, however, during the summer of 1928, but nothing ever came of the club idea.

June 14-16. The annual summer meeting of the Association of Y.M.C.A. Physical Directors of the State of New York was held at the Hotel Fenimore.

July 3. The Remington-Rand band of Ilion, a famous musical organization connected with the Remington Typewriter company, gave a concert at the Otesaga hotel.

July 7. William Beattie, a former resident of Cooperstown, but who for several years had been located in New York City, assumed his duties as director of the Alfred Corning Clark gymnasium.

During the summer Mrs. Alfred E. Smith, wife of Governor Smith who was later Democratic candidate for the office of President of the United States, was a luncheon guest on several occasions at the Otesaga and visited some of the local antique shops.

Aug. 1. The Public Service Commission of the State of New York handed down an order directing the Delaware & Hudson company to continue the operation of the afternoon passenger train on the Cooperstown branch, which left the village station at 3:20 o'clock and returning, arrived at 7:20. The commission suggested that the company find some way to meet the afternoon demand for service and still achieve its expressed desire to reduce expenses. The order came as the result of a formal protest entered by the Cooperstown Chamber of Commerce through its attorney, Orange L. VanHorne with Harris L. Cooke of counsel against the removal of the train proposed by the company under a new schedule soon to go into effect. A public hearing was held by the Commission at Albany, June 29th, at which time President R. D. Spraker of the Chamber of Commerce and a large delegation of witnesses from this and other villages along the branch submitted evidence showing that the discontinuance of the train would work a serious hardship generally as connections from Cooperstown with the eastern terminal, Albany, and the western terminal, Binghamton, of the Susquehanna division, would be completely lost.

Aug. 13. In consideration of the signing of a ten-year contract for street lighting in the village by the Board of Trustees, the New York State Gas & Electric corporation agreed to rebuild its entire system in the village placing the property in first class condition. This agreement was fulfilled early in the year 1929.

Four cases of infantile paralysis were diagnosed at the Mary Imogene Bassett Hospital following one death from that cause and led to the prohibition of all public gatherings including church services and the postponement of a number of events which had been planned. These restrictions were removed by the local health authorities, August 20th.

Aug. 31. Hundreds of people, not only residents of Cooperstown but from all parts of Otsego county, attended a very elaborate entertainment styled a Venetian Fete on the grounds of Fernleigh mansion generously donated for the purpose by Mr. and Mrs. Stephen C. Clark. The proceeds which amounted to $6,091 went to the Clara Welch Thanksgiving Home.

During the summer the communities of Cooperstown and Springfield Center again enjoyed professional base ball being represented by a fast "Otsego Lake" club which for the second time won the championship of the Mohawk Valley League and a large percentage of its games. George Detore, a Colgate College star, was the captain and manager. George H. Maus, a prominent manufacturer of Amsterdam, whose summer home is on Otsego Lake, was the president of the association for the seasons of 1927 and 1928.

Septe. 25. The Cooperstown School for Boys between the ages of seven and fifteen years was opened for its first year by Chauncey Haven Beasley, headmaster, in the old Burch house which was completely restored by Mr. Edward Severin Clark who had become its owner a short time previously. Suitable additions were erected to provide study rooms, etc., and the school was adequately equipped and furnished.

Oct. 7. The tailor shop of John Schneider was entered during the night and clothing belonging to many residents of the village, which had been left there for repairs and cleaning, was stolen. The value of the goods taken was placed at between $400 and $500. The robbery remained a mystery for several months but was cleared up the following February when the crime was traced to a gang of Oneonta thugs who were implicated in several other burglaries about the county. Some of the loot was regained and the perpetrators punished.

Oct. 11. During the Presidential campaign an interesting debate on the political issues was attended by a crowd which packed the Supreme Court Chamber at the Court House. Mrs. Douglas Robinson, sister of the late President Theodore Roosevelt, presented the case of the Republicans and Miss Mary V. Hun of Albany and Cooperstown, that of the Democrats.

Oct. 22. The Hon. Owen D. Young of New York City and Van Hornesville, chairman of the Board of Directors of the General Electric company of Schenectady, spoke from the porch of the Hotel Fenimore before a large crowd on the occasion of the celebration of the completion of the new Summit Lake (Mud Lake) road between Springfield Four Corners and Van Hornesville. This four-mile piece of concrete highway formed the last link in the improvement of the Otsquaga Trail between Fort Plain and Cooperstown which was a part of the proposed U. S. Route 80 between Indian Lake, N. Y., and Miami, Fla. The celebration was conducted jointly by Cooperstown and Fort Plain, the opening meeting being held at Smalley's Fort Plain Theatre. The caravan then started on its way back to Cooperstown with stops for addresses and music by the Fort Plain and Van Hornesville bands at Hallsville, Starkville, VanHornesville and Springfield Center. At Van Hornesville President Richard E. Sykes of St. Lawrence University spoke as did Mr. Young. Rolling into Cooperstown 150 strong the motor line parked and the party made its way to the Hotel Fenimore where the celebration was brought to a climax, with a pageant showing the progress of locomotion from the primitive trail finding of the Indians to the luxurious motor car of the present day, and the address of Mr. Young followed by a dinner served in the main dining room. Mr. Young in his remarks told of four significant visits which he had made to Cooperstown. The first time he did not come, he said. He went to Three-Mile Point for a Sunday School picnic having been promised a ride on the Steamer Natty Bumppo to Cooperstown, "but when the boat pulled in there were many ahead of me and I could not get on." The second time was when he accompanied his father here with a load of hops. "The third visit," he said, "was the most important one I have ever made anywhere in my life. The story is an old one but perhaps it is so old that the children here don't know it." And then he went on to give the account of how he received his inspiration to study law on a visit as a youth to the Court House in Cooperstown in 1887. "When we arrived the Court was in session and the Court House was crowded. It seemed very cool and shady in the court room. I thought to myself, 'Do men get a living this way?' The cool of the court room and the appeal of the books and witty exchanges of ideas made me determined that if law meant a neat, cool court room; books which I loved, certainly then I thought, 'This is the life for me!' From that time on I never swerved from my desire to study law." The fourth important visit, he said, was on the occasion upon which he was speaking, the celebration of the consummation of the hope which had been his and of many others for twenty years. Orange L. Van Horne, a prominent local attorney, a native of Van Hornesville and a member of the family for which that village was named, acted as toastmaster at the dinner. The address of welcome was delivered by the Rev. Dr. Edward C. Petrie, pastor of the First Presbyterian church, and addresses were made by many visiting village officials and heads of civic organizations, etc.

Nov. 21. The large new block erected by Contractor George L.

Turner on the site of the old Carr's Hotel on Main street to house the business of Cook's Auto & Supply company as opened with a Gala Entertainment. Louis Dean, WGY radio announcer, acted as master· of ceremonies, and Dan Meyerhoff's 10-piece WGY orchestra furnished music for dancing. The building which formed a very attractive addition to Main street, provided spacious and thoroughly equipped quarters for the display of new cars, garage storage, machine shop, parts and accessories and the business offices.

Nov. 28. Announcement was made by the Second National Bank of the purchase of the front half of the Leatherstocking building to be transformed into a commodious new home. Later the entire building and power house was purchased by the bank.

Nov. 26. A star mail route was established between Oneonta and Cooperstown.

1929.—The first half of the last year of the present decade is now history. Favored beyond the lot of most communities of its size in the state we are a prosperous and happy people. As a summer resort our progress has, perhaps, been most marked. The background afforded by the illustrious Cooper, the romance of the Clinton campaign just celebrated, the fame of Abner Doubleday, inventor of base ball, and of Erastus Beadle, publisher of the dime novels of other days add an allurement and charm unique to the varied natural beauty of the Leatherstocking Land in the heart of which Cooperstown lies. Fine hotels, beautiful churches, public and private schools of outstanding excellence, a magnificent hospital, paved streets, pure water from an unlimited supply all conspire to make this a perfect site for homes.

The prophecy of James Fenimore Cooper that someday the Lake would be surrounded with summer places has literally come true so that today unimproved property is very difficult to obtain.

Jan. 15. The Freeman's Journal company purchased of Elizabeth Taylor Smith of Binghamton The Taylor block at the North West corner of Main and Pioneer streets taking possession Feb. 1. The block is occupied on the ground floor by Lippitt Brothers, jewelers, and David R. Dorn, druggist, and on the second floor by Dr. W. H. McDonald, dentist, and F. D. Coleman, photographer. The third floor is vacant. As Mr. Dorn has announced that he expects to give up his lease and retire the Journal company and the John Wilcox company plan to utilize the space thus made available to accommodate the expansion of their large and growing businesses.

Jan. 28. A force of workmen in the employ of Contractor George L. Turner commenced the work of wrecking the large frame building on Chestnut street, opposite the High school building to make place for a new sales and service station for the Burr-Chevrolet Co., R. L. Burr of Binghamton, president, which purchased the site of James J. Byard, Jr., of Oneonta. The passing of the old building, known as Sunnyside, removed one of the old landmarks erected by William M. Clinton shortly after the Civil War. The house was first used as a residence and later as an Episcopal boarding school known as Bede Hall. Later it was purchased by David H. Gregory and was used as a summer home by the family for years.

Feb. 16. On this date Cashier Frank Hale completed forty years of service as an employee and officer of the First National Bank. This evening Mr. Hale was the guest of honor at a dinner given by the Board of Directors and banking force and their families at the Hotel Fenimore and presented with a fine loving cup.

March 13. Speaking before the members of the Cooperstown Rotary club and a large number of invited guests including the directors of the Chamber of Commerce, members of the Board of Village Trustees, and other prominent citizens, Dr. A. C. Flick of Albany, state historian, described the significance of the Sullivan-Clinton campaign of the Revolutionary War, and laid the foundation for the celebration of the local phases of that campaign in Cooperstown the present summer.

April 14. The Girl Scout Captain in this section to receive the Harmon award for 1929 was Miss Mary H. Pickard, captain of the Fenimore Troop of this village. The award consisted of a scholarship in any of the Girl Scout schools for leadership training.

In May workmen commenced demolishing the Alfred Corning Clark gymnasium which had served the needs of the village physically for nearly forty years to make way for a fine new gymnasium containing increased space and facilities, including a new swimming pool. The building was planned by Architect Frank P. Whiting of New York City and will be of the Georgian style of architecture constructed of local stone preserving the colonial feeling of the stone buildings in this part of the country. It will be 140 feet in length on the Park side, where the main entrance will be located, and 44 feet on Main street.

The new additions to the Cooperstown Union and High school building were completed during the Spring and portions brought into use. They comprise two new wings, one at the north and one at the south end of the original building, harmoniously designed by the architects, Kinne & Frank, of Utica, to form an attractive appearance. The new north wing is devoted principally to a fine gymnasium with modern locker rooms, shower baths, etc. The gymnasium proper is of sufficient size to provide for a regulation basket ball court and has a seating capacity in the bleachers and gallery of 600 people. There is also a music room on the second floor of this wing, and a teachers' consultation room. Three new class rooms are provided on each floor of the south wing. The building is heated with hot water and there is a separate hot water system for the showers. An intercommunicating telephone system and a new fire alarm system with eight stations with hose and apparatus add convenience and protection. The entire structure is supplied with modern equipment and furnishings giving Cooperstown a building unsurpassed anywhere. The building was constructed under the personal inspection of George M. Root, a well known local contractor. The builders were C. M. McLean & Son of Binghamton, the painting by B. Frank Beadle of Cooperstown, the electric installation by the Johnson Electric company of Utica and the heating and plumbing by Hammeline & Co., of Utica. The members of the Board of Education under whose initiative the project was carried through from its beginning to a successful termination are Frank B. Shipman, president; M. E. Lippitt, secretary, and Judge Adrian A. Pierson. Prof. M. J. Multer is the efficient and successful principal. Under their direction the school has attained a high place in educational circles of the state and the village is to be congratulated that its building now measures up to that standard.

May 31. J. Dana Whipple purchased the Five-Mile Point Inn property sold at mortgage foreclosure by Referee Adrian A. Pierson. His bid was for $44,250. This was the third time that Mr. Whipple had owned the hotel. The sale was made as the result of mortgage foreclosure proceedings brought by J. Dana Whipple, Frederick L. Quaif and Wilna H. Wilcox, plaintiffs, against Ellen W. Beals, Bruce L. Beals, Second National Bank of Cooperstown, First National Bank of Scranton, Pa., J. Herbert Reynolds, Ford Wedderspoon, Sherwood Interstate Clubs, Inc., Grace Fravor, Annie Fravor and Horace H. Beals, defendants, a judgment having been entered April 15, 1929. At a shortly later date the property was purchased of Mr. Whipple by Mr. Edward Severin Clark.

June 8. A new furniture store was opened by Mr. and Mrs. Chester W. Ingalls in the block at No. 124 Main street which they had purchased a short time before.

June 13. The annual convention of the Physical Education directors of the Y.M.C.A in New York state was held at the Hotel Fenimore with a large attendance.

June 15. The Hickory Grove Farm, located at Six-Mile Point on Otsego Lake, including about 260 acres of farm land, the Hickory Grove Inn and gas stand, and Camp Glimmerglass on the Lake front was sold by Eugene Becker and M. E. Lippitt to Emil Stockhausen of Albany. From the Hickory Grove development as laid out by Messrs. Lippitt and Becker, there have been sold no less than forty-eight lots and new cottages have been erected by the following: A. M. Kerr of Elizabeth, N. J.; George H. Carley of Cooperstown, R. W. Ellsworth of Cooperstown and L. S. Ellsworth of Carlisle, Pa., Charles P. Forshew of Scranton, Pa., George N. Smith and M. F. Augur of Cooperstown, J. Harry Cook of Cooperstown (2), Charles A. Greenidge of Crestline, N. Y., Carl E. Steere of Oneonta, Emil Stockhausen of Albany, J. Irving Hewlitt of Jefferson, N. Y., Owen G. Clark of Cooperstown and Dr. Arthur H. Martin of New York City, C. S. Derrick of Cooperstown, S. C. Derrick of Cooperstown, Clyde S. Becker of Cooperstown, Wm. W. Edwards of Gloversville, Bruce L. Hall of Cooperstown, Harry H. Willsey of Earlville, David H. Willsey of Cooperstown, Frank B. Cooke of Albany, Richard A. Coates of New York City, and Dr. F. J. Atwell of Cooperstown. The development also included camps Natoma and Hickory Grove which were erected before the original plans were made.

Early in June Frank E. Brooke of New York City was appointed superintendent of the Mary Imogene Bassett Hospital.

Street Commissioner Michael MacMoon already has completed this summer the new pavement on Pioneer street from Elm to Beaver. Grading has commenced for the pavement of the Lakewood cemetery road which is being started at the cemetery and will meet the pavement at the foot of the hill which was laid some time ago. These projects, together with the new pavement on River street fro mthe end of last year's construction at the Mary Imogene Bassett Hospital to Main, constitute a most valuable highway program for the year 1929.

June 21. The State Highway Bureau at Albany let the contract for the construction of a new macadam highway from Cooperstown to Schuyler Lake to Shellman, Inc., of Derby, N. Y., the lowest bidders. Work is now in progress on this new road which will be an improvement sincerely desired in Cooperstown for years.

June 26. A proposal to establish a Cooperstown Fellowship to provide assistance to graduates of the Cooperstown High school seeking a higher education was made by Dr. G. Benjamin White, '96, director of the division of biologic laboratories of the Department of Public Health of Massachusetts, and a member of the faculty of Harvard University, at the annual dinner and reunion of the High School Alumni association at the Hotel Fenimore. A committee of which Miss Grace Scott Bowen is chairman was appointed and active steps are already well under way to attain the end desired. At the same gathering, Dr. J. Lynn Barnard, '86, director of social studies for teachers at Ursinus College, Collegeville, Pa., in an adddress, proposed the inclusion of a student guidance program in the High school curriculum and the incoming president, Melvin C. Bundy was instructed to appoint a committee to take leadership in this matter.

June 29. The new garage and service station erected by the Burr-Chevrolet company on Chestnut street near the corner of Elm was opened to the public with a fine display of cars. The building is 100x50 feet in dimensions and fire proof, built entirely of cinder blocks and brick.

July 1. The first annual Field Day of the Otsego County Dairy Improvement association brought members and their families to the number of 2,000 here from all parts of the county. A large program was carried out including the sale at auction of a number of purebred bulls consigned to the sale by leading breeders.

Workmen in the employ of Hopkins & Dentz, New York architects and contractors commenced the week of July 7th, extensive repairs and improvements for the purpose of preserving the "Old Stone House" formerly known as Pomeroy place, at the corner of Main and River streets. The property is now owned by Miss K. L. Mather of Cleveland, O. This house occupies a foremost place among the reminders of the past. Built by Judge William Cooper in 1804 as a wedding gift to his only daughter who married George Pomeroy of Northampton, Mass., grandson of General Seth Pomeroy, who fought at Bunker Hill, the house has always been regarded as a model of plain and substantial architecture. The interesting gable tells the story of the house in stone. "G. A. P. C." are the intermingled initials of the bride and bridegroom, George Pomeroy and Ann Cooper, with the date, 1804. The spread eagle above is not quite as distinct in outline but still visible. After nearly fifty years of occupancy the house changed owners and soon afterwards came into possession of the Bowers family, with whom it remained nearly as long. Pomeroy Place with its century and a quarter of years is the American representative of Berry-Pomeroy Castle, Devonshire, England, built by Sir Ralph de Pomeroy who came over with William the Conqueror and from whom the Pomerory in this country are direct descendants.

July 11-12. The annual summer meeting of the New York Press association was held in Cooperstown with headquarters at the Otesaga. The newspaper men were the guests while here of the publishers of the local newspapers with whom the Cooperstown Chamber of Commerce and the hotel cooperated in a very substantial manner. An elaborate program of entertainment was carried out which included a motor trip to points of interest about the village and tea for the ladies at the home of Mrs. Frank C. Carpenter, served by Mrs. Carpenter and Mrs. Rowan D. Spraker assisted by the wives of the local publishers. This was followed by a trip around Otsego Lake on board the steamer Mohican for all and the next day the entire convention formed a motor caravan for a scenic trip to the newly restored Howe Caverns near Cobleskill with luncheon at the Hickory Grove Inn as guests of the local hosts. At Howe Caverns the visitors were shown the natural underground wonder as guests of the management. At the annual dinner at the Otesaga on the evening of the 11th the speakers were the Hon. Frank J. Loesch, a prominent member of the Cooperstown summer colony, president of the Chicago Crime Commission and a member of President Hoover's commission to investigate crime in the United States; and Dr. Edward Amherst Ott of Ithaca, noted publicist and orator. Among the distinguished guests presented to the gathering by President Fay C. Parsons of Cortland, who acted as toastmaster, was Mrs. Charlotte P. Browning of Chicago and Cooperstown, daughter of Col. John H. Prentiss, founder of the Freeman's Journal nearly 122 years ago. Mrs. Browning received a great ovation of applause as she arose in response to the greeting. Many in the company remembered with appreciation the entertainment she provided when the association met here in 1920. "Mrs. Browning is now ninety-two years of age and it is the hope that she may have many more years to enjoy life among us," said the toastmaster and in this sentiment all heartily joined.

As this book reaches the press, interest in Cooperstown is rapidly centering in the celebration, August 9th and 10th, of the Sesqui-Centennial of the Sullivan-Clinton campaign of the Revolution. Hundreds of individuals and many committees and sub-committees are actively at work in bringing to perfection their participation in the elaborate observance which will be one of the outstanding events of the summer not only in Cooperstown but throughout the state. The town of Otsego and the Village of Cooperstown each have appropriated $500, and there is available from state funds appropriated by the legislature for this purpose, $2,000. In addition the finance committee has met with an enthusiastic response from the citizens of the village with the result that the project appears well financed. Following is a complete list of the committees in charge of the observance:

Executive Committee—B. G. Johnson, Chr., Stephen C. Clark, R. W. Ellsworth, M. E Lippitt, R D. Spraker, George H. White, Frank B. Shipman, Treas. Ernestine T Geddes, Sec'y.

Finance—George H. White, Chr., H. L. Brazee, B. G. Johnson, Russel Warren, Waldo C. Johnston, Wilson E. McGown, Martin Moakler, William C. Smalley, R. W. Ellsworth, W. W. Stokes, Wm Festus Morgan.

Program and Printing—Frank C. Carpenter, Chr., Prof. M. J. Multer, Ernestine T. Geddes.

Parade and Float—A. J. Peevers, Chr., Geo N. Smith, George H. Carley, Fred Hunt, Mrs. John Raubacher, Harris L. Cooke, Mrs. W. M. Bronner, Mrs. Leon H. Ellsworth, Mrs. D. R. Dorn, George Shelley, Mrs. H. Guy Roberts, John Wedderspoon, Miss Naomi C. Burch, C. B Johnson, R. H. Barringer, George Cooper

Pageant Site—Bruce L. Hall, Chr., Harlo P. Beals, A. J. Peevers, Alton G Dunn.

Pageant—Beach Cooke, Chr., Miss Valerie Deuscher, E. L Fisher, Mrs. C K. Lippitt, Mrs. Adrian A. Pierson, Mrs. Arthur C. Fox, J. C. Halvey, Mrs. Wm. Beattie, J. Harry Cook, Miss Bernice Tyler, Miss Agnes Michaels, Miss Marjorie Wicks, Mrs. F. Hamilton McGown, Mrs. L. E. Walrath, Mrs. C. A. Braider, Walter Frankl, Douglas Bailey, Miss Sylvia Lanning.

Publicity—W. R. Littell, Chr., Harlo P. Beals, John B. McManus, Mrs. H. L. Kimball, Lawrence Doran.

Fireworks—Leon H. Ellsworth, Chr., Ralph H. Stafford, Dr. F. J. Atwell, Fletcher A. Blanchard, Harry C. Fowler, Dr. H. L. Cruttenden.

Music—Prof. A. deJ. Allez, Chr., Edward Severin Clark, H. R. Armitage, Alfred R Cobbett, Howard N. Michaels, John Schneider.

Regatta Committee—Lester G. Bursey, Chr., Wm. Beattie, R H. Rogers, Waldo C. Johnston, Jr., Ernest R. Lippitt.

Monument Committee—Stephen C. Clark, Ziba L. Holbrook, B. G. Johnson.

Dedication Committee—Judge A. A. Pierson, Orange L. Van Horne, Clermonte G. Tennant, Rev. Dr Edward C. Petrie.

Decoration—G. Reed Sill, Chr., M. F. Augur, Harry Freeman.

July 22. An eight-oared rowing shell was brought from Syracuse University and placed on Otsego Lake as an addition to the facilities of the Alfred Corning Clark gymnasium.

In July Chief George W. Cooper announced the establishment of a new schedule governing the attendance at fires outside the corporate limits of the pumpers of the Cooperstown Fire department, under which pumpers are scheduled to serve alternately for periods of two months each. In this manner the presence of one pumper in the village at all times will be assured and all cause for misunderstanding between the members of the various companies eliminated.

. July 30. Announcement of the resignation of Harlo P. Beals as agent of the Otsego County Farm Bureau to take effect September 1st was made at a meeting of the Board of Directors held at the Farm Bureau office in this village. Mr. Beals tendered his resignation on July 16th to accept a position with the Grange League Federation. When he took up the work in April, 1923, he found the association in straightened financial condition, with a debt of $6,500 and interest at a low ebb. In six years under his management the debt has been cleared and the finances placed upon a sound basis, the membership increased to 1,136 which ranks third in the state and a fine working organization effected which is accomplishing valuable things for the farming interests of the county.

ROLL OF HONOR

Service Men of The World War From The Town of Otsego.

Salvatore Alotto, Pietro Alotto, John Howard Ameden, Earl Kenneth Anderson, Harry Andrews*, Stanley Andrews, Ensign Robert R. Arnold, Lieut. L. John Arnold, Lieut. Floyd J. Atwell, Sergt. Arthur D. Ayres.

George Arthur Basinger, Frank C. (Corp.) Bliss*, Howard A. Bliss, Joseph M. Brady, Charles D. Briggs, Frank Eugene Butler.

Ambrose Campbell, Harry Campbell, Walter Campbell, Robert Caney, Clarence Carr, De Vaughn E. Carr, Cecil A. (Corp.) Champlin, Morris Augustus Chase, Samuel Harrison Chency, Alfred Hyde Clark*, John H. Clark, Paul Anthony Clark, Ralph Clark, Col. Robert Sterling Clark, Lt. Col. Stephen C. Clark, Joseph Coleman*, Thomas William Coleman, Augustus Paul Cooke, Stephen Beach Cooke, Maj. Joseph B. Cooke, George Coon, Chester W Cooper, Capt. James Fenimore Cooper, Jr.*, Capt. Henry S. Fenimore Cooper, Paul Fenimore Cooper, Lieut. Linn Fenimore Cooper, Robert B. Cobbett*, Alfred R. Cobbett, Robert Crandall, Edward A. Cronauer.

2nd Lieut. Andrew C. Davidson, Sergt. Bowne W. Davidson, Lieut. Donald R. Davidson, Navy Medical Corps, George L. Deakin, Lieut. Vinton A. Dearing*, Raymond Coville Derrick, Arthur Clayton Dow, Fred Dulin, Arizio Durso.

Emil Eschman, Kendric Everett Eaton, Leon Eckler*, Harry Eckler, Milton M. Eckler, Elmer Ellsworth, J. Neil Esmay, Frank C. Every.

Ben Rencler Faulkner, Clifford C. Ferris, Ralph Edward Finch, Paul Flanagan, Lieut. Francis C. Foote, Maj. Morris Cooper Foote, Austin Lee Francis, Edward A. Francis, James P. (Corp.) Francis, Louis Frankewich.

Ralph J. Gage, Raymond Gage, Clarence J. Gardner, Horace Garland, Eugene Garland, Newton E. D. Gilmore, Lawrence Myers Graves, Charles Gray, Harry Gray, Paul Gray, Orville A. Grover, Hyde S. Gruby, Roland Baker Gruby, George W. Gruby, Charles Gustafson, David Wade G. Guy.

James Joseph Haggerty, Harry Harvey, Raymond K. Harvey, Sergt. Raymond Harvey, Thomas G. Harvey, Clyde L. Hayne, James F. Hayne*, Thomas G. Henry, Walter Herrick*, James Edward Herring, Phillip Hoke, John Hopkins, Charles Hopkins*, Lynn House, Henry D. (Corp.) House, Guilford Howard.

Lieut. G. Bowne Jarvis, Albin E. (Corp.) Johnson, Capt. Douglas T. Johnton, 2nd Lieut. Morgan S. Johnston, Capt. Waldo C. Johnston, Stephen Johnson*, Franklin Nichols Johnson, James D. Johnson, Nelson E. Jones, Lawrence Judd.

Sniffin J. Kelly, James Bernard Kiley, Charles Henry Knapp, Byron T. Kniskern, Wesley Knowlton, Ernest C. Kramer.

Norman Largett, Robert E. Lee, Laverne Alonzo Light, William Little, Clifford Lee Loudon, Robert B. (Sgt.) Lutes, Joseph James Lynch.

Louis Mallory*, Clifford Mallory, Horace Lynn Marble, Silas Marsh, Capt. Arthur H. Martin, Bert B. Martin, Henry Martin, Lawrence M. Maxson, Alfred Miller, Alfred Miller, J. Howard Mitchell, John Moakler, Raymond B. More, William Festus Morgan, Harry Mulkins, William John Mumford, Stanley W. Murdock, James McCulloch, Firman McDonald, Joseph E. McDonough, Paul J. McDonough, Charles McGraw*, Lawrence M. McGinley, Joseph J. McGinley.

Ills Narcresson, Horace James Newell.

Wesley J. O'Connor, Joseph O'Malley, Bernard J. O'Toole, George Ollds, Earl Osborne.

Solomon Albert Peet, Philip F. Philbin, Edward S. C. Phillips, Lorren E. Pierce.

Harry Dan Rathbun, Oliver N. Rathbun, William A. Rathbun, George T. Record*, Henry Reed*, Frederick L. Reynolds, Lynn James Reynolds, Nick Rizzo, Clarence Robertson, Arthur P. (Lieut.) Root, Lieut. Donald S. Root, Ensign Douglas Root, Lewis W. Ross*, William Ross, Dewey Rowley.

Earl St. John, Ernest Seeger, D. Paul Sibley, Carl Simons, J. D. Simmons, Clark Field Simmons*, Thomas Benjamin Skuse, Leon Willard Smith, Martin

Smith, R. C. Stager, Clarence Stevens, John W. Stiles*, Fred Stillson, Mortimer Stimers, William Alfred Stocking, Ralph Spraker.

——— Talbot, Hess W. Talbot, Carl R. Temple, James William Thayer, Capt. F. De P. Townsend, Carey C. Tubbs, William Rufus Tuller.

Everett K. Van Deusen, James C. Van Deusen.

Charles L. Walrath, Louis Walrath, Richard Warren, Ford Wedderspoon, Albert John Wedderspoon, Rufus Whipple, Clark C. Whitney, Wilbur Wilson, Harry Winn*, Gerald Frederick Withey, Harold D. Withey, Floyd Wiltse, Alleyn Wood, August I. Wurtzler.

Louis Oswald Yarde, Herman F. Yotz, Jerome D. Young.

Lieut. C. Lemaire Zabriskie.

* Died in service.

Army Nurses Corps.

Ida L. Allez, Marion Augur.
Mrs. Alma J. Barnes.
Ruth S. Cook.
Grace Garland.
Stella Hodge.
Elizabeth Johnston.
Irene Moak, Mary Meeneghan.
Maud Walters.

INDEX

www.ingramcontent.com/pod-product-compliance
Lightning Source LLC
Chambersburg PA
CBHW030918090426
42737CB00007B/241